THE FOUNDERS

The Balkan wars, the Rwanda genocide, and the crimes against humanity in Cambodia and Sierra Leone spurred the creation of international criminal tribunals to bring the perpetrators of unimaginable atrocities to justice. When Richard J. Goldstone, David M. Crane, Luis Moreno Ocampo and Robert Petit received the call, they each set out on a unique quest to build an international criminal tribunal and launch its first prosecutions. Never before have the founding international prosecutors told the behind-the-scenes stories of their historic journey. With no blueprint and little precedent, each was a path-breaker. This book contains the first-hand accounts of the challenges they faced, the obstacles they overcame, and the successes they achieved in obtaining justice for millions of victims.

David M. Crane was the first American to be named the chief prosecutor of an international war crimes tribunal since Justice Robert Jackson at Nuremberg in 1945. He is one of the most recognizable international criminal lawyers in the world, renowned as the person who brought to justice the most powerful warlord in Africa, President Charles Taylor of Liberia. Crane remains the only person to have indicted a sitting head of state for war crimes and crimes against humanity in the modern era. Crane is now leading the international effort to hold President Assad of Syria and his henchmen accountable.

Leila N. Sadat is the James Carr Professor of International Criminal Law at Washington University Law and Director of the Harris World Law Institute. Since 2012 she has served as Special Adviser on Crimes Against Humanity to the ICC Prosecutor, and in 2008 launched the *Crimes Against Humanity Initiative* to address the scourge of global atrocity crimes and draft a treaty on their punishment and prevention. Sadat recently received an Honorary Doctorate from Northwestern University and the Arthur Holly Compton Distinguished Faculty Award at Washington University. She is incoming President of the International Law Association (American Branch) and a member of the US Council on Foreign Relations.

Michael P. Scharf is Dean of Case Western Reserve University School of Law. Scharf is the author of eighteen books, including three that have won national book-of-the-year honors. During the George H. W. Bush and Clinton administrations, he served as Attorney-Adviser for UN Affairs in the Office of the Legal Adviser of the US Department of State. He is the co-founder of the Nobel Peace Prize–nominated Public International Law and Policy Group.

The Founders

FOUR PIONEERING INDIVIDUALS WHO LAUNCHED THE FIRST MODERN-ERA INTERNATIONAL CRIMINAL TRIBUNALS

Edited by

DAVID M. CRANE
Syracuse University

LEILA N. SADAT
Washington University in St Louis

MICHAEL P. SCHARF
Case Western Reserve University

CAMBRIDGE
UNIVERSITY PRESS

University Printing House, Cambridge CB2 8BS, United Kingdom

One Liberty Plaza, 20th Floor, New York, NY 10006, USA

477 Williamstown Road, Port Melbourne, VIC 3207, Australia

314–321, 3rd Floor, Plot 3, Splendor Forum, Jasola District Centre, New Delhi – 110025, India

79 Anson Road, #06–04/06, Singapore 079906

Cambridge University Press is part of the University of Cambridge.

It furthers the University's mission by disseminating knowledge in the pursuit of education, learning, and research at the highest international levels of excellence.

www.cambridge.org
Information on this title: www.cambridge.org/9781108424165
DOI: 10.1017/9781108539852

First published 2018
Reprinted 2018

Printed in the United States of America by Sheridan Books, Inc.

A catalogue record for this publication is available from the British Library.

Library of Congress Cataloging-in-Publication Data
NAMES: Crane, David M., editor. | Sadat, Leila Nadya, editor. | Scharf, Michael P., 1963–, editor.
TITLE: The founders : four pioneering individuals who launched the first modern-era international criminal tribunals / edited by David M. Crane, Leila Sadat, Michael P. Scharf.
DESCRIPTION: New York : Cambridge University Press, 2018.
IDENTIFIERS: LCCN 2017060044 | ISBN 9781108424165 (hardback)
SUBJECTS: LCSH: International criminal courts – History. | Prosecution (International law) – History. | Goldstone, Richard | Petit, Robert, (Lawyer) | Moreno Ocampo, Luis Gabriel | Crane, David M.
CLASSIFICATION: LCC KZ7230 .F68 2018 | DDC 345/.01–dc23
LC record available at https://lccn.loc.gov/2017060044

ISBN 978-1-108-42416-5 Hardback
ISBN 978-1-108-43951-0 Paperback

This book is dedicated to
our colleagues at Nuremberg,
from whence it came

Contents

Contributors

Kofi Atta Annan is a Ghanaian diplomat who served as the seventh Secretary General of the United Nations from January 1997 to December 2006. Annan and the UN were the co-recipients of the 2001 Nobel Peace Prize. He is the founder and chairman of the Kofi Annan Foundation, as well as chairman of The Elders, an international organization founded by Nelson Mandela.

Hans Corell joined the Swedish Ministry of Justice in 1972 and was a member of the Swedish Delegation to the United Nations from 1985 to 1993. From 1994 to 2004, he served as Under-Secretary General for Legal Affairs and the Legal Counsel of the United Nations. In his years of service at the UN, Corell was involved in the establishment of both the ad hoc criminal tribunals and the International Criminal Court. Since his retirement from public service, he has become involved in the work of the International Bar Association; the International Center for Ethics, Justice and Public Life at Brandeis University; and the Hague Institute for the Internalization of Law. He has also been Chairman of the Board of Trustees of the Raoul Wallenberg Institute of Human Rights and Humanitarian Law at Lund University, Sweden (2006–2012). Corell's long and distinguished career in diplomacy, international justice, and foreign affairs has seen him honored with the William J. Butler Human Rights Medal, the Frederick K. Cox International Humanitarian Award for Advancing Global Justice, and the World Order Under Law Award.

David M. Crane was appointed a professor of practice at Syracuse University College of Law in the summer of 2006, after serving from 2002 to 2005 as the founding chief prosecutor of the Special Court for Sierra Leone. He was appointed to that position by the Secretary General of the United Nations, Kofi Annan, on April 19, 2002, with the rank of Undersecretary General. Crane's mandate was to prosecute those who bear the greatest responsibility for war crimes, crimes against humanity, and other serious violations of international human rights committed during the civil war in Sierra Leone in the 1990's. Among those he indicted for those horrific crimes was the president of Liberia, Charles Taylor, the first sitting African head of state in history to be held accountable for war crimes. David Crane was the first American since Justice Robert H. Jackson at Nuremberg, in 1945, to be the Chief Prosecutor of an international war crimes tribunal. The Special Court for Sierra Leone was nominated for the Nobel Peace Prize in 2010. Prior to serving as chief prosecutor, David Crane served over 30 years in the federal government of the United States. The positions he held during his three decades of public service include Senior Inspector General of the Department of Defense, Assistant General Counsel of the Defense Intelligence Agency, and Waldemar A. Solf Professor of International Law at the United States Army Judge Advocate General's School. Professor Crane was on the leadership council of the American Bar Association's International Law Section and served as the Chairman of the Section's Blue Ribbon Panel on the International Criminal Court's 2010 Review Session. He is also a Fellow of the American Bar Association. In 2006, he founded Impunity Watch (www.impunitywatch.net), a law review and public service blog. In 2011, he founded the Syrian Accountability Project, one of the first NGOs to work on the atrocities in Syria. Professor Crane holds a Juris Doctor degree from Syracuse University, a Masters of Arts Degree in African Studies and a Bachelor of General Studies in History, summa cum laude, from Ohio University. For his service to humanity, Case Western Reserve University in Ohio awarded him an honorary Doctor of Laws degree in May 2008, as did Ohio University in April 2017.

Richard J. Goldstone is a former justice of the Constitutional Court of South Africa and has served as a member and chairperson of a number of UN committees and commissions and NGO advisory boards. From 1994 to 1996 he served as the chief prosecutor for the United Nations International Criminal Tribunals for the Former Yugoslavia and Rwanda, and since 2004, he has been a visiting professor of law at a number of prestigious universities. Justice Goldstone has been awarded many awards for his work in the field of international criminal law and justice, including the International Human Rights Award of the American Bar Association and honorary doctorate degrees from universities in South Africa, North America, Europe, and Israel.

Luis Moreno Ocampo Following his successful legal career in Argentina, where he served as the deputy prosecutor in the "Junta trial" in 1985, Luis Moreno Ocampo became the first prosecutor of the International Criminal Court in June of 2003, a role he held until his tenure ended in 2012. In his role as chief prosecutor, Moreno Ocampo conducted investigations in seven different countries and brought charges against some of the worst violators of international law known in modern times. Moreno Ocampo has also served as a visiting professor at Stanford University and Harvard University, as a member of a number of advisory boards, and as chairman of the World Bank Expert Panel on the Padma Bridge Project. He is currently a senior fellow at the Jackson Institute for Global Affairs at Yale University.

Robert Petit has extensive experience as an international criminal prosecutor, having worked as a legal advisor for the Office of the Prosecutor at the International Criminal Tribunal for Rwanda, a regional legal advisor to the United Nations Mission in Kosovo, a prosecutor for the Serious Crimes Unit as part of the United Nations Mission of Assistance to East Timor, and as a senior trial attorney in the Special Court for Sierra Leone. From 2006 to 2009 Petit served as the international co-prosecutor of the Extraordinary Chambers of the Courts of Cambodia, where he was responsible for prosecuting those responsible for violations of international law that occurred in that country in the 1970s. Petit has written extensively on international law and human rights laws, and in 2009, he received the Frederick K. Cox International Humanitarian Award for Advancing Global Justice from Case Western School of Law.

Leila N. Sadat is an internationally renowned human rights expert known for her expertise in public international law, international criminal law and foreign affairs. The James Carr Professor of International Criminal Law at Washington University School of Law, and Director of the Whitney R. Harris World Law Institute since 2007, she is a dedicated teacher and award-winning scholar who has published more than 100 books and articles in leading journals, academic presses, and media outlets throughout the world. In December 2012, International Criminal Court Prosecutor Fatou Bensouda appointed her as Special Adviser on Crimes Against Humanity. In 2008, she launched the Crimes Against Humanity Initiative, an international effort to study the problem of crimes against humanity and draft a global treaty addressing their punishment and prevention. The draft treaty is now available in eight languages and is currently being debated by the UN International Law Commission and governments around the world. From 2001 to 2003 Sadat served on the US Commission for International Religious Freedom. Bilingual in English and French, Sadat has lectured or taught at academic institutions throughout the world, and holds or has held leadership positions in many professional associations and learned societies. Prior to joining the faculty at Washington University, she practiced international commercial law in Paris, France.

William Schabas holds positions at a number of universities across the globe. He was the director of the Irish Centre for Human Rights at the National University of Ireland, Galway, and an invited visiting scholar at the Paris School of International Affairs (*Sciences Politiques*). Schabas has published extensively in the fields of international law and international human rights law, and his writings have been translated into Russian, German, Spanish, Portuguese, Chinese, Japanese, Arabic, Persian, Turkish, Nepali, and Albanian. As a result of his contributions to the field of international criminal law, Schabas has been awarded the Vespasian V. Pella Medal for International Criminal Justice of the Association internationale de droit pénal and the Gold Medal in the Social Sciences of the Royal Irish Academy, as well as honorary doctorate degrees from several universities.

Michael P. Scharf is the Dean of Case Western Reserve University School of Law and the Joseph C. Hostetler – BakerHostetler Professor of Law. Scharf is the author of eighteen books, including *Balkan Justice*, which was nominated for a Pulitzer Prize in Letters in 1997; *The International Criminal Tribunal for Rwanda*, which was awarded the American Society of International Law's Certificate of Merit for outstanding book in 1999; *Peace with Justice*, which won the International Association of Penal Law's book of the year award for 2003, *Enemy of the State*, which won the International Association of Penal Law's book of the year award for 2009; *Shaping Foreign Policy in Times of Crisis* (Cambridge University Press, 2010); and *Customary International Law in Times of Fundamental Change* (Cambridge University Press, 2013). During the elder Bush and Clinton administrations, Scharf served in the Office of the Legal Adviser of the US Department of State, where he held the positions of Attorney-Adviser for Law Enforcement and Intelligence, Attorney-Adviser for United Nations Affairs, and delegate to the United Nations Human Rights Commission. In February 2005, Scharf and the Public International Law and Policy Group, an NGO he cofounded and directs, were nominated for the Nobel Peace Prize by six governments and the prosecutor of an international criminal tribunal for the work they have done to help in the prosecution of major war criminals, such as Slobodan Milošević, Charles Taylor, and Saddam Hussein. During a sabbatical in 2008, Scharf served as Special Assistant to the Chief Prosecutor of the Cambodia Genocide Tribunal. A graduate of Duke University School of Law (Order of the Coif and High Honors), and judicial clerk to Judge Gerald Bard Tjoflat on the Eleventh Circuit Federal Court of Appeals, Scharf is an internationally recognized expert who has testified before the Senate Foreign Relations Committee and the House Armed Services Committee and has appeared frequently in the national news media. He is also host of the radio program, "Talking Foreign Policy," produced by Cleveland's NPR Station and syndicated in Florida, Texas, North Carolina, and Maine. In 2013, Scharf offered the first ever international law MOOC, via Coursera, which has enrolled 120,500 students from 137 countries to date. In 2016, he was ranked as one of the top 20 most-cited authors in the field of international law.

David J. Scheffer holds an endowed professorship and is Director of the Center for International Human Rights at Northwestern School of Law. He currently serves as the UN Secretary General's Special Expert on United Nations Assistance to the Khmer Rouge Trials. Scheffer was the US Ambassador at Large for War Crimes Issues from 1997 to 2001, and he led the US delegation at the UN talks to establish the International Criminal Court. He was also closely involved with the establishment of the earlier ad hoc tribunals. He has published many works on international legal and political issues, and his book *All the Missing Souls: A Personal History of the War Crimes Tribunals* received the 2012 Book of the Year Award from the American National Section of the International Association of Penal Law.

Foreword

> The common sense of mankind demands that law shall not stop with the punishment of petty crimes by little people. It must also reach men who possess themselves of great power.
>
> US Chief Prosecutor Robert H. Jackson, in his opening statement before the International Military Tribunal at Nuremberg in 1945

Throughout history, men of great power have destroyed their own people. Yet it is only recently that mankind has stepped forward and sought to hold those responsible for atrocity accountable. In the past, there was little of this, and the beast of impunity nibbled around the edges of civilization. A commentator once said that the history of mankind is the history of war and the history of war is the history of mankind: an apt point to make.

In the twentieth century, tens of millions of human beings were destroyed at the hands of their own governments. Yet history and circumstance pointed to a possible better place. In the midst of this bloody century there were four bright and shining years that augured well for the future. From 1945 to 1949, the United Nations was formed, the Nuremberg Principles adopted, and key human rights instruments, such as the Universal Declaration of Human Rights, the Genocide Convention, and the Geneva Conventions, were passed. In this short time, the cornerstone of the modern international criminal law paradigm was laid down.

Yet the shadow of the Cold War almost washed away this new hope for humanity. The geopolitical dynamic that split the world almost in half saw both sides look away from human rights abuses and atrocities in order to maintain a political check against the other. This was the true age of the dictator, as strongmen used the standoff between the West and the Soviet bloc to their advantage to seek, establish, and maintain absolute power. When the Iron Curtain rusted and finally fell, mankind paused and considered new ways of holding those who violated international law accountable. Could this be the beginning of the end of conflict, a true democratic world peace supervised by a renewed United Nations?

This apparent new world order quickly slid into a new world disorder. The Balkans, the Great Lakes region in East Africa, West Africa, and Cambodia demanded attention and action. The international community could not simply look away as it had for the past several decades. Could the world establish accountability mechanisms for current events?

During the 1990s, the United Nations stepped in to do just that. Bold action was needed to address atrocities not just in specific contexts, but to establish a court of last resort to deal with the most egregious of international crimes. Through the remarkable cooperation between the United Nations, its Security Council, and sovereign states, these tribunals and courts were brought into being, representative of mankind's hope that the rule of law was more powerful than the rule of the gun.

What you will come to understand and appreciate in this historic book is how four individuals' pioneering efforts helped to shape these extraordinary bodies. As secretary general of the United Nations (1997–2006), I played a role in the creation of these tribunals and courts, but their administration and functioning depended on the independence and integrity of those who served in them, especially the prosecutors. Hearing their experiences firsthand through the narratives in this text illuminates the immense challenges and triumphs of these unique individuals in their pursuit of justice. I have always supported the need for an international body of law to prevent and hold accountable those who would commit mankind's worst crimes. It is my hope that the experiences found in this book will be but the first steps in what may be a long but worthwhile journey toward justice for mankind.

At the end of the day, the bright red thread woven into the fabric of modern international criminal law is politics. If there is a political will to do so, mankind can face down the beast of impunity. What follows shows what good that political will can do, as well as hard work, perseverance, and a little bit of luck.

Kofi A. Annan
Geneva
May 2017

Preface

This extraordinary book project began over a glass of wine during the annual International Humanitarian Dialogs at the world famous Chautauqua Institution in 2015. Each year, most of the world's international chief prosecutors gather to reflect upon the various issues and challenges pertaining to modern international criminal law. The prosecutors are all friends, and the meetings are informal and collegial. One evening, sitting together on the famous porches of the Athenaeum Hotel while we sipped our wine, I asked my colleagues, somewhat rhetorically, whether any one of us ever actually had asked for the unique job of being a chief prosecutor of an international war crimes tribunal? Not one of us actually asked for, sought out, or applied for the positions we would eventually fill in Yugoslavia, Rwanda, Sierra Leone, or Cambodia, even as prosecutors of the International Criminal Court.

As it turns out, as we went around telling our selection stories, we all got what we called "the phone call." Unexpected, surprising, and/or "out of the blue," so to speak, we received that call asking us whether we would consider being a chief prosecutor. Four of us got the call not only to be prosecutors, but also to help create a brand new tribunal.

After we all left Chautauqua, as I flew home to Maggie Valley in North Carolina, I realized that there have only been five individuals who have created an international justice mechanism. Four of us exist in the modern era. The first was Robert H. Jackson, who had passed decades earlier. As I continued to mull this over, I came to the realization that no chief prosecutor has ever written about how they created the prosecution office of their tribunals. Wouldn't it be amazing if I could get my colleagues who created the five modern international tribunals to write about that experience in a book? Hence the idea of *The Founders* was floated by those founding chief prosecutors, and each agreed to write a chapter on their experiences in the creation of the tribunals in Yugoslavia, Rwanda, Sierra Leone, the ICC, and Cambodia. As one of those founders for the tribunal in Sierra Leone, I would write that chapter.

Of course these important experiences needed context, so I reached out to the best and brightest in the field of international criminal law to help edit and write those contextual chapters. This book contains amazing chapters on the role that Robert H. Jackson played in creating the cornerstones for our modern international criminal law paradigm written by Michael P. Scharf; Leila N. Sadat tracks the evolution of the general principles that make up modern international criminal law; William Schabas provides the reader an overview of the early investigatory steps related to the Balkans, as the international community considered the creation of its first modern international tribunal; Hans Corell, so instrumental in helping to create each of the modern tribunals as UN Legal Counsel, was invited to introduce this volume; and *The Founders* finishes with the important perspectives about the founding of the tribunals by David J. Scheffer, the architect of the United States' role in modern international criminal law and some of the tribunals themselves, such as the Special Court for Sierra Leone, the Extraordinary Chambers in the Courts of Cambodia, and the International Criminal Court.

We all met over breakfast in September 2016 at Nuremberg, Germany, for the tenth annual International Humanitarian Law Dialogs. It is from this meeting that there was mutual agreement to write *The Founders*. All agreed that Richard J. Goldstone would compose a chapter on the creation of the Yugoslav and Rwandan tribunals, I would cover the Special Court for Sierra Leone, Luis Moreno Ocampo would write about the International Criminal Court, and Robert Petit would report on the Extraordinary Chambers in the Courts of Cambodia. All of us felt that context was very important, and so the topical arrangement was conceived, as well as who should write those chapters. Thus you now have before you *The Founders*.

I gratefully acknowledge the steady and professional guidance of my fellow editors, Leila N. Sadat and Michael P. Scharf. Their experience in the details of writing a book such as this was invaluable. Of course there were a myriad of students and research assistants involved, as always, in the background, but whose work was critical in the creation of this book. Special recognition goes to Colin Tansits, our project secretary, who patiently helped to put the manuscript into a presentable form. Other students who helped immensely were Casey Kooring and Sean Mills. All are from Syracuse University College of Law.

I want to acknowledge the vision of John Berger and his team at Cambridge University Press, who enthusiastically agreed to publish for the first time the experiences of all four founding chief prosecutors in one book. This was not meant to be just an academic work, but a book that would highlight the human dynamic of bringing justice to victims of atrocity. It's edgy, it's honest, and it's frank. The authors, hopefully, were at the vanguard of mankind's ability to hold accountable those who prey on their own citizens and nibble away at the edges of civilization. *The Founders* will show that we started something amazing.

David M. Crane
Maggie Valley, North Carolina

PART I

Putting It All in Context

Introduction

Hans Corell

It was with great expectations that I accepted the invitation to write the introduction to a book in which the main part would be personal reflections and perspectives by the founding chief prosecutors of the International Criminal Tribunal for the Former Yugoslavia (ICTY); the International Criminal Tribunal for Rwanda (ICTR); the Special Court for Sierra Leone (SCSL); the International Criminal Court (ICC); and the Extraordinary Chambers in the Courts of Cambodia (ECCC). I was deeply involved in the establishment of all these courts or tribunals, and I therefore looked forward with great interest to the contributions by the prosecutors, as well as the contributions by the other authors, who I had come to know over the years.

The reason for this invitation is of course my involvement with the creation of these institutions. It materialized through a series of coincidences. When I graduated from law school back in 1962, my plan was to become a judge in my own country, Sweden. I therefore immediately took up a position as a law clerk in a circuit court in the countryside. This was the first step in a 10-year period during which I would serve, first, as a law clerk and, later, as a judge in two circuit courts and in two courts of appeal. The main focus of the work in these courts was criminal law. In 1972, I was asked to join the Ministry of Justice to do legislative work. After 13 years in this Ministry, the last three years as the chief legal officer, I became the legal adviser of the Ministry for Foreign Affairs in 1984.

In January 1994, when I had served in this position for over nine years, I received a telephone call from UN Secretary General Boutros Boutros-Ghali, who invited me to join his team as under-secretary general for legal affairs and the legal counsel of the United Nations. For 10 years, from March 1994 to March 2004, I held this position at the crossroads between law and politics – three years with Boutros Boutros-Ghali and seven years with Kofi Annan.

During my time as legal adviser of the Ministry for Foreign Affairs, I represented my country in many international contexts. Among my obligations was also to be the head of the legal department in the Ministry and to supervise our work in the sixth (Legal) Committee of the United Nations General Assembly. As a matter of fact, my obligations spanned from human rights to the law of the sea. By way of example, during all these years, I was the agent of my government before the European Court of Human Rights.

With respect to international criminal law, a crucial moment came in August 1992, when the Conference on Security and Cooperation in Europe (CSCE), now the Organization on Security and Co-operation in Europe (OSCE), appointed me a war crimes rapporteur in Bosnia and Herzegovina and Croatia. In accordance with the rules, the two states would appoint a second rapporteur. The two rapporteurs would then nominate a third rapporteur. The two states nominated my colleague Helmut Türk, who was the legal adviser in the Ministry for Foreign Affairs in Austria. It goes without saying that in nominating a third rapporteur we had to look for a woman. We found a very competent colleague in Gro Hillestad Thune, the Norwegian member of the Council of Europe Commission of Human Rights.

The three of us started working immediately. We visited Croatia between September 30, and October 5, 1992. Two days later, on October 7, 1992, we delivered our first report, suggesting among other things that a committee of experts from interested states should be convened as soon as possible in order to prepare a draft treaty establishing an international ad hoc tribunal for certain crimes committed in the former Yugoslavia.[1] This, our first report, is referred to in William Schabas' contribution on the UN Commission of Experts established pursuant to Security Council Resolution 780 (1992). As CSCE rapporteurs, we had several very positive contacts with the members of the Commission.

For security reasons we were not able to visit Bosnia and Herzegovina, and thus no action had been taken by the CSCE with respect to our proposal for a committee of experts. On November 24, 1992, we offered to make an interim report on Bosnia and Herzegovina analyzing the relevant penal law, and to draft a convention establishing an international *ad hoc* tribunal to deal with war crimes and crimes against humanity committed in the former Yugoslavia. On December 15, 1992, the CSCE Council accepted our proposal, foreseeing continuing consultations in the matter with the UN Commission of Experts.

On February 9, 1993, my two co-rapporteurs and I presented our final report.[2] In this report, we proposed that a war crimes tribunal for the former Yugoslavia should be established on the basis of a convention. A treaty was the only legal avenue

1 Report by Rapporteurs (Corell-Türk-Thune) under the CSCE Moscow Human Dimension Mechanism to Croatia of Oct. 7, 1992, available at www.havc.se/res/SelectedMaterial/19921007cscereportoncroatia.pdf.

2 Proposal for an International War Crimes Tribunal for the Former Yugoslavia by Rapporteurs (Corell-Türk-Thune) under the CSCE Moscow Human Dimension Mechanism to Bosnia-Herzegovina and Croatia of February 9, 1993, available at www.havc.se/res/SelectedMaterial/19930209csceproposalwarcrimestribunal.pdf.

for the CSCE. At the same time, the question of establishing such a court was discussed in the UN Security Council. The CSCE therefore immediately forwarded our proposal to the United Nations. On February 22, 1993, the Security Council decided to establish the International Criminal Tribunal for the Former Yugoslavia (ICTY), mainly on the basis of the report just delivered by the UN Commission of Experts. I thought that this was a very positive development when, on May 25, 1993, the Council adopted Resolution 827 (1992) approving the Statute of the ICTY.

On March 6, 1994, I took up my position as the UN Legal Counsel, while the ICTY was in the process of being established. A month later, on April 6, 1994, the genocide in Rwanda broke out, and I became involved in the establishment of another tribunal, the International Criminal Tribunal for Rwanda (ICTR). As these two ad hoc tribunals started their work, in 1998, I was the representative of the secretary general at the Rome Conference that adopted the Rome Statute of the ICC. Later, I chaired the UN delegations when we negotiated the agreements establishing the Special Court for Sierra Leone (SCSL) and the Extraordinary Chambers in the Courts of Cambodia (ECCC). When the Rome Statute entered into force in 2002, I was also involved in the first phase of the establishment of the International Criminal Court (ICC).

The first contribution in the book is by Leila Nadya Sadat. In a very limited space she provides a learned and very enlightening description of the journey of international criminal justice over the past century. This part is of utmost importance since it will assist readers by providing a genuine background on the efforts that led to the creation of the tribunals described in the book. She is very well placed to make this contribution because of her knowledge and experiences in the field of international criminal law.

As a matter of fact, in 2008 she launched the Crimes Against Humanity Initiative with the aim of working toward a global convention on crimes against humanity.[3] As a result, the question of elaborating such a convention is now on the agenda of the UN International Law Commission with Sean Murphy as the Commission's special rapporteur on the subject matter. Even though crimes against humanity is among the crimes defined in the Rome Statute of the ICC, it is important to have a specific convention on these crimes for several reasons: one being that it will facilitate co-operation among states in combating these crimes.

In her contribution, Leila Sadat points to the many difficulties that remain in establishing international criminal justice. As a matter of fact, she maintains that the difficulties cannot be overestimated.

A major problem that Leila Sadat focuses on is the fraught relationship that the ICC has with the UN Security Council. She maintains that the Council has neither backed the ICC with the power that it could have exerted in the cases that were

[3] Reference is made to http://law.wustl.edu/harris/crimesagainsthumanity/.

brought before the ICC in situations that the Council had referred to the prosecutor. Nor has the Council been able to avoid the temptation of blocking the referral of situations to the prosecutor through the use of the veto. I completely share this view, and I have constantly maintained that the Council has to use the same yardstick when it applies the Rome Statute in these situations.[4]

Toward the end of her contribution Leila Sadat maintains that justice works best when it is consistently and even-handedly applied and that this requires faith, focus, financing and commitment by world leaders. Just as the personnel of these new institutions have been asked to do their jobs, it is now the turn of the politicians of the world to do theirs. In my view, this is a fundamental requirement for establishing the rule of law at the national and international level. I will revert to this question toward the end of this introduction.

Reading Michael P. Scharf's excellent contribution on Robert H. Jackson and the Nuremberg Tribunal reminded me of Telford Taylor's *The Anatomy of the Nuremberg Trials*. The book had just been published when I was appointed war crimes rapporteur in 1992, and I read it with great interest and admiration. This deepened my interest in the trials of the International Military Tribunal and also of the personalities involved in the trials, in particular, Chief US Prosecutor Robert H. Jackson. I have been privileged to learn more about him in later years, after I became a member of the board of directors of the Robert H. Jackson Center in Jamestown, NY. Through the annual International Humanitarian Law Dialogs, initiated by David M. Crane and held in Chautauqua, NY, I have also been privileged to meet regularly with the present international prosecutors. In 2016, the Dialogs were held on 29 and 30 September in Nuremberg in connection with the seventieth anniversary of the judgments of the International Military Tribunal – a very solemn occasion at which Michael Scharf also spoke.

The insightful contribution by William Schabas on the Balkan investigation and the UN Commission of Experts established by Security Council Resolution 780 (1992) is very important in understanding the complex background to the establishment of the ICTY. As I have already explained, there were several very positive contacts between the members of the UN Commission and the CSCE rapporteurs. As a matter of fact, on January 24, 1993, before completing our final report, we met with three of the members of the UN Commission, namely Chairman Fritz Kalshoven, Cherif Bassiouni and William Fenrick. We further had consultations with Bassiouni on legal and technical issues the day after. As it appears from our final report, during our talks, the members of the Commission expressed the view that the

4 *See, e.g.*, Hans Corell, *The Mandate of the Security Council in a Changing World*. In: *International Law and Changing Perceptions of Security*. Eds. Jonas Ebbesson, Marie Jacobsson, Mark Klamberg, David Langlet and Pål Wrange. Leiden/Boston: Brill/Martinus Nijhoff Publishers (2014) (pp. 39–58), available at www.havc.se/res/SelectedMaterial/20142224ilperceptionsofsecurity.pdf.

Commission was not mandated to occupy itself with the question of the establishment of an international criminal court. However, they demonstrated a profound interest in the establishment of such a court, and as CSCE rapporteurs, we were able to draw on their thinking in this field.

Against this background it is also of great importance to read William Schabas' description of the Balkan investigation as a background to the contribution by Richard J. Goldstone.

The first contribution from the founding prosecutors comes from Richard J. Goldstone. It reminds me of the worry that we felt in the UN when the Venezuelan prosecutor, who had been appointed chief prosecutor of the ICTY in October 1993, resigned only three days after he had taken up his position in January 1994. So, when I arrived in the UN in March 1994, there was no chief prosecutor in the ICTY. This was of great concern to us, and the search for a suitable candidate was ongoing. We should also remember that this was happening at the same time as the genocide in Rwanda. When I was informed that Richard Goldstone had been mentioned as a candidate, I was extremely pleased. At long last, the ICTY would become operational.

No doubt, the chief prosecutor would face tremendous challenges. Basically, with the exception of the lessons from the Nuremberg trials, organizing the work in the Office of the Prosecutor would be like navigating in uncharted waters.

When Richard Goldstone makes reference to the first trial, the *Tadić* case, I recall that some thought that this case was not prominent enough to be the first case to be dealt with by the ICTY. My immediate reaction when I heard this argument was that under no circumstances should the UN, and in particular the Office of Legal Affairs, express opinions about who should be prosecuted before an international court. The prosecutor is independent and must go where the evidence leads him or her. As a matter of fact, based on my own experiences from the judiciary in my country, I thought that it was wise to start with a case that was not too complicated and that would allow the different organs of the tribunal to develop their working methods. I therefore note with sympathy Richard Goldstone's hindsight reflection that it was an advantage having a middle-level defendant as the first to face trial in the ICTY.

Richard Goldstone's reference to the establishment of the ICTR reminds me of the resistance that we experienced from the government of Rwanda during the establishment of this tribunal. As a non-permanent member of the Security Council at the time, Rwanda had voted against the establishment of the tribunal, in part because it was not authorized to apply the death penalty. In November 1994, I was therefore sent to Rwanda to convince President Bizimungu, Vice President Kagame and Prime Minister Twagiramungu that they should cooperate with the tribunal. I will never forget my security officers' remark when we flew over the country: "There are now more houses than people down there." That was a genocide exploding in my face!

David J. Scheffer's reference to issues of corruption and maladministration within the ICTR – though not involving the chief prosecutor – reminded me of all the work we had to carry out in the UN Secretariat to deal with this. It took a long time before we had identified individuals who could run the tribunal's registry properly.

The pioneering efforts by Richard Goldstone, the other prosecutors and others who served in the ICTY and ICTR deserve respect. No doubt, this has contributed to raising the awareness of the importance of establishing justice in order to gain peace. These efforts have now become part of the rule of law paradigm that is a precondition for creating peace and security in the world.

Also, the establishment of the two tribunals is an interesting example of how an international treaty can be construed based on how realities develop. The fact that the members of the UN Security Council thought that it was within their competence to establish the two tribunals is a very important development in international law. It is also against this background that Article 13 (b) of the Rome Statute should be understood. According to this provision, the ICC may exercise its jurisdiction with respect to a crime referred to in Article 5 in the Statute in accordance with its provisions "if – – – [a] situation in which one or more of such crimes appears to have been committed is referred to the Prosecutor by the Security Council acting under Chapter VII of the Charter of the United Nations." In this way, the competence that the Council asserted in 1993 and 1994 is confirmed also in the Rome Statute of the ICC.

David M. Crane's reflections and perspectives on the SCSL is fascinating reading. It is a firsthand illustration of the complexities that an international prosecutor is faced with when opening an investigation in a particular situation. It is also highly instructive as a description of the dilemmas that the ICC Prosecutor has to deal with in the situations that he or she encounters. David Crane's contribution also reminds me of my positive experiences when negotiating the agreement between the UN and Sierra Leone on the establishment of the SCSL.

For my part, I have no doubt whatsoever that the government of Sierra Leone was deeply committed to creating a genuine, independent and impartial tribunal. My counterpart was Solomon Berewa, then Minister of Justice. He was very cooperative and fully understood that an agreement with the UN must observe the standards that apply with respect to criminal justice under international law. In particular, since the court would have both national and international judges, he fully understood that the majority of the judges in the chambers had to be international judges. As a matter of fact, when the government of Sierra Leone made its first nomination of judges in the court, their proposal included a judge from another country.

Furthermore, if someone had suggested to me when I signed the agreement with Solomon Berewa on January 16, 2002 that Charles Taylor would stand trial before the SCSL, I would not have believed it. And yet, this is what happened.

There is one situation that I have often revisited over the years, namely a meeting with a group of traditional chiefs in Sierra Leone, a few of them women, who wanted to see me. One of the reasons was the discussion concerning the court's personal jurisdiction, which in the final agreement was limited to "persons who bear the greatest responsibility for serious violations of international humanitarian law and Sierra Leonean law."[5] During my first visit to Freetown, I had seen terrible things: children who were mutilated, with maybe a hand or a foot cut off. I was made aware that the perpetrators were often very young and that they might have been victims themselves in a sense – taken from their families, maybe drugged and taught to commit these atrocities. The question was if these children should also be brought to justice.

In the meeting, one of the chiefs rose in a dignified manner and asked what he should tell his people, who were aware that there were so many perpetrators among them, when the UN offered a court that could only try a few persons. I thought for a moment and then said that this was the position of the UN, and that it would simply not be possible to bring all these perpetrators to justice. Even the best organized criminal justice system would crumble if it had to hear so many cases. I then referred to Nelson Mandela and the manner in which he had dealt with the situation in South Africa when he finally came out of prison: the Truth and Reconciliation Commission. In Sierra Leone, there was already an agreement at the national level that there would be a Truth and Reconciliation Commission and that this Commission would work in parallel with the Special Court! The Chief looked in silence at his colleagues around the table for a few moments. And then they all slowly nodded, likewise in dignified silence.

There is one element in David Crane's contribution that is of particular interest to me: his remark that competent judges at the international level remain a challenge. Based on my own courtroom experience, I can only emphasize this element. I have developed my thoughts about this in another context, and in my view, to elect persons to the ICC who have no courtroom experience whatsoever is simply not appropriate – no matter what other qualifications these candidates may have.[6]

Another striking part in David Crane's contribution is his recollection of his departure from Sierra Leone after his successor Desmond de Silva took over. In the helicopter carrying him across the bay to Lungi Airport, he said a prayer to get him safely to the airport, as a couple of these helicopters over the years had simply stopped working and dropped into the bay. He was terrified. I had exactly the same experience when I had performed my very last official function as the UN legal

[5] Statute of the Special Court for Sierra Leone, Art. 1, ¶ 1 (Jan. 2002), available at www.rscsl.org/Documents/scsl-statute.pdf.

[6] Hans Corell, *Reflections on the Role of International Prosecutors and the Judges of the International Criminal Court*. In: *Foreword to: International Prosecutors*. Eds. Luc Reydams, Jan Wouters and Cedric Ryngaert. Oxford University Press (2012) (pp. v–xi), available at www.havc.se/res/SelectedMaterial/internationalprosecutors_prelims.pdf.

counsel, namely representing Secretary General Kofi Annan at the inauguration of the SCSL courthouse in Freetown in March 2004. Like David, I made it to the airport in the helicopter. But sadly, a few days later I heard that it had fallen out of the sky, and the pilot and the soldiers onboard had lost their lives.

Luis Moreno Ocampo's contribution brings back many memories of the intense work involved in the creation of the ICC during the 1990s. The basic draft of the Rome Statute was provided by the International Law Commission, which is serviced by the Codification Division of the UN Office of Legal Affairs. The work was then pursued by the sixth (Legal) Committee of the General Assembly. In the summer of 1998, the Rome Conference for the establishment of the ICC was convened. As the representative of the secretary general at the conference, I had excellent support from Executive Secretary Roy S. Lee and Secretary of the Committee of the Whole Mahnoush H. Arsanjani. The conference was a great success. On July 17, 1998, the Rome Statute was adopted. The requirement for entry into force was 60 ratifications. These were received in record time. On July 1, 2002, the ICC Statute entered into force, and the judges were sworn in on 11 March 2003.

On April 21, 2003, Luis Moreno Ocampo was elected ICC prosecutor by the Assembly of States Parties to the Rome Statute. With respect to his contribution, I noted with particular interest the key policies for implementing the mandate of the Office of the Prosecutor: "a) complementarity, b) focusing on those bearing the greatest criminal responsibility, and c) maximize the Office of the Prosecutor contribution to the prevention of future crimes."

As regards the policy to fully respect the principle of complementarity this is of course one of the cornerstones in the Rome Statute. It is obvious that the primary objective of dealing with the crimes defined in the Rome Statute is that justice is done at the national level. At the same time, it is obvious that the national justice system may not function properly in areas where these grave crimes have been committed.

In my view the situation in Libya is an example of this dilemma. On February 26, 2011, the UN Security Council adopted Resolution 1970 (2011) referring the situation in Libya since February 15, 2011 to the ICC prosecutor. Under the Rome Statute, states have the right to challenge the admissibility of cases brought before the ICC. While the ICC retains the authority to determine whether it has the jurisdiction to try a case, a challenge may be raised if, for example, a state with jurisdiction claims that it is investigating and prosecuting the case.

After a preliminary examination of the available evidence surrounding the charges against Saif al-Islam Gaddafi and Abdullah al-Senussi, ICC Prosecutor Luis Moreno Ocampo concluded that there was no "genuine national investigation or prosecution" taking place to satisfy the criteria for deference to national authorities. Libyan officials, for their part, argued that the trials of Gaddafi and Senussi were of national importance and should be conducted in Libya. However, during the process both the Libyan government and the Office of the Prosecutor asked the Pre-Trial Chamber to declare the case against al-Senussi inadmissible before the ICC. The ICC Pre-Trial Chamber determined that competent domestic authorities in Libya were conducting domestic proceedings against al-Senussi and that Libya was neither unwilling nor unable to fulfil its responsibilities vis-à-vis international law. Therefore, the Pre-Trial Chamber ruled that the case against al-Senussi was inadmissible before the ICC. With respect to the details of the case, reference can be made to a study by Academie Diplomatique Internationale and the International Bar Association.[7]

To me it is very difficult to understand how the Pre-Trial Chamber could come to the conclusion that courts in a country that has been under a dictatorship for decades are able to try cases against main actors of this regime. Is it really possible to find professional, independent and impartial judges who are able to hear cases against actors of this kind in such a country? I do not think so. It is therefore of greatest importance that the principle of complementarity is applied with utmost caution in situations like the one in Libya. Reference can also be made here to the chapter by David Scheffer.

With respect to the policy to focus on those "most responsible," I think that this is the proper way to proceed. At this stage in the development of international criminal justice this is important. It is at this level that the violence committed is orchestrated, and it is therefore crucial that the prosecutor focus on those who are ultimately responsible for the atrocities. At the invitation of the John Marshall School of Law, I have developed my own thoughts on this topic.[8]

Lastly, with respect to the policy of contributing to prevention of future crimes, this must of course be the fundamental objective of the criminal justice system at both the national and international levels.This is also why it is so important that the same yardstick is used, in particular when the UN Security Council decides whether to apply or not to apply Article 13 (b) of the Rome Statute. It is sad to note that the Council falls short in this respect. The examples mentioned by Luis Moreno Ocampo are telling. Why Darfur and Libya, but not the Middle East or Burundi?

With respect to the different cases referred to, I have followed the situation in Kenya with particular attention in view of the fact that I had the privilege of assisting Kofi Annan in his capacity as chairman of the Panel of Eminent African Personalities. This Panel was established by the African Union in 2008 after the disastrous election in 2007 that generated the violence that led to the Kenyan cases

7 Academie Diplomatique Internationale and the International Bar Association: *International Justice and Diplomacy Case Studies*, forthcoming. *See also* Mark S. Ellis, *Trial of the Libyan regime – An investigation into international fair trial standards*, Nov. 2015, available at www.ibanet.org/Article/NewDetail.aspx?ArticleUid=759f1431-4e10-450d-998e-21349fd8bf26.

8 Hans Corell, *International Prosecution of Heads of State for Genocide, War Crimes and Crimes Against Humanity*. In: *The John Marshall Law Review* [43:xxv 2009] (pp. xxv–xli), available at www.havc.se/res/SelectedMaterial/20090916headsofstate.pdf.

before the ICC. For six years, this panel was engaged in supporting the Kenya National Dialogue and Reconciliation.

In an article published in 2014, I expressed my concerns about these cases.[9] The point I made was that the Kenyan cases before the ICC went wrong from the very beginning, and there was a serious risk that they might become unmanageable at the trial stage. This has now come true.

The investigation produced two main cases, originally with six suspects, involving charges that included the following crimes against humanity: murder, deportation or forcible transfer of population, persecution, rape, and other inhumane acts. However, the charges were either not confirmed or were withdrawn concerning all these six suspects.

The problems that I foresaw have also been confirmed by the present ICC Prosecutor Fatou Bensouda. The following is a quote from an interview with her in *Foreign Affairs* in 2017:

> In the Kenya cases, three people have already been indicted for interfering with witnesses. Arrest warrants have been issued against them. But Kenya, which has the obligation to surrender them, is not doing that. In the Kenya situation, what we have seen was really unprecedented. The level of witness tampering and obstructing the court has resulted in either having to withdraw the case, as I did in the Kenyatta case [against Kenya's president, Uhuru Kenyatta], or one of the judges declaring a mistrial, as in the Ruto case [against Kenya's deputy president, William Ruto].[10]

It is my firm conviction that the lesson that the ICC must draw from these cases is what I was taught as a law clerk many years ago: if someone is going to be indicted as a suspect for very grave crimes, by definition this person should be arrested and put in detention on remand. Otherwise, he or she will try to evade the trial and may also engage in interfering with the evidence.

With respect to the contribution on the ECCC by Robert Petit, I am not surprised at his criticism of the manner in which this court was set up. He even suggests that "if anyone had wanted to create an institution destined to fail he or she would have been hard-pressed to find a better model than that envisioned for the ECCC."[11] For my part I am of the firm opinion that the ECCC should never be used as a model for any future effort of this nature.

As head of the UN delegation negotiating the agreement with Deputy Prime Minister Sok An, I was extremely concerned. As a matter of fact, about a month after the agreement on the SCSL was signed in January 2002, Secretary General Kofi Annan decided to withdraw from the negotiations with the government of

[9] Hans Corell, *Challenges for the International Criminal Court*. In: *The Winter 2014 Issue of the International Judicial Monitor*, available at www.judicialmonitor.org/archive_winter2014/specialreport1.html.

[10] *The International Criminal Court on Trial – A Conversation with Fatou Bensouda*. FOREIGN AFFAIRS 48–53 (Jan./Feb. 2017).

[11] *See* Petit, Chapter 7, this volume, at 126.

Cambodia. We had simply lost confidence in the process, which had gone on for several years.[12]

However, on December 18, 2002 we were forced back to the negotiating table by the General Assembly through Resolution 228. As I have explained in other writings, in some respects our hands were tied, which is also reflected in the agreement between the UN and the government, signed on June 6, 2003. The following is a quote from my address at the sixth annual International Humanitarian Law Dialogs in 2012:

> Let me just say that, as a professional judge, I was extremely concerned when the U.N. Secretariat was forced back to the negotiation table by the U.N. General Assembly in December 2002. In some respects our hands were tied. Now, some of the things I warned against have actually occurred. I am sure that today even people without courtroom experience realize that the solution chosen for the ECCC should not be used as a model for any future effort of this nature. The U.N. imprint should not be given to institutions over which the organization does not have full administrative control.[13]

Robert Petit also says that he came to find that in Cambodia, the level of political interference, perceived or real, was beyond anything he had previously experienced and refers to the "ultimate disagreement" that he and his Cambodian co-prosecutor had over who to prosecute. For my part, I certainly foresaw this during the negotiations, which were the most difficult that I have ever conducted. This is why I must go into some detail in my comments on the ECCC.

First, I must be very clear about the fact that, during the negotiations, we never discussed who should be prosecuted for the simple reason that international law requires an independent prosecutor to decide this. I also kept in mind a communication from Prime Minister Hun Sen to the United Nations in 1999 in relation to a trial of a Cambodian citizen at the national level. In this communication to the UN he said that he had "no rights whatsoever to charge this or that person, or to pre-determine how many people will stand trial."[14] From Robert Petit's contribution it is, however, very clear that this is precisely what happened.

This is also why there are, as he says, "some clear oddities with the statute starting with a conflict resolution mechanism that obviously foresaw fundamental

[12] Part of the explanation appears in my op-ed in the *International Herald Tribune* of June 19, 2002, available at www.globalpolicy.org/component/content/article/163/28839.html.

[13] Hans Corell, *Reflections on International Criminal Law over the Past Ten Years*. Keynote Address at the Sixth Annual International Humanitarian Law Dialogs, held at Chautauqua, N.Y., on Aug. 26–28, 2012, pages 56–58, available at www.havc.se/res/SelectedMaterial/20120827corellkeynoteicl.pdf.

[14] Identical letters dated March 19, 1999 from the Permanent Representative of Cambodia to the United Nations addressed to the Secretary-General and to the President of the Security Council: Annex: Declaration of Prime Minister Hun Sen of the Kingdom of Cambodia on the Issue of the Trial of Ta Mok, UN Doc. A/53/867, S/1999/298 (Mar. 19, 1999) at 2 (citing Mok as an exception), available at www.un.org/en/ga/search/view_doc.asp?symbol=S/1999/298.

disagreements between the internationals and their national counterparts."[15] The reason for these oddities is the so called super-majority that was introduced in the process from the outside. The supermajority is regulated as follows in Articles 3 and 4 of the ECCC agreement.

A decision by the Trial Chamber, composed by three Cambodian judges and two international judges, shall require the affirmative vote of at least four judges. A decision by the Supreme Court Chamber, composed by four Cambodian judges and three international judges, shall require the affirmative vote of at least five judges. This means that if there is no unanimity, at least one international judge would have to agree with the majority decision. Let me quote what I have said about this in the past:

> It was also extremely difficult for me, as head of the U.N. delegation, to keep the negotiations on track, not least because many were involved, partly behind the scenes. One particular problem was the introduction of the super-majority idea brought in from outside. As a judge, I saw this as extremely problematic. It may be that one can handle this feature in the judgment itself. But a judge knows that a court hands down a magnitude of interlocutory decisions in a major trial. How does one deal with a super-majority there? The Co-Prosecutors and the Co-Investigating Judges were other complicating factors (see in particular Chapters 2, 5, and 6). In my opinion, the tribunal should have been an international tribunal with a single prosecutor and a majority of international judges.[16]

This brings me to the co-prosecutors and the co-investigating judges. The General Assembly resolution meant that the UN delegation had to accept this madness. But how should one deal with situations where the national and international co-prosecutors or co-investigating judges were in disagreement? This is why we invented the Pre-Trial Chamber, composed of three national and two international judges. As I have explained in detail to two researchers, the only task of this chamber was to settle such differences.[17] The fact that this chamber has been given other tasks in the internal ECCC rules is in my view not in conformity with the agreement between the UN and the government.

As I told the researchers, it is an irony that we find a positive effect of the super-majority rule here. According to Article 7 of the agreement, a decision of the Pre-Trial Chamber, against which there is no appeal, requires the affirmative vote of at least four judges. In order to stop a prosecution before the ECCC, at least one international judge on the Pre-Trial Chamber would have to support such a decision. Otherwise the prosecution would go ahead in accordance with Article

[15] *See* Petit, Chapter 7, this volume. [16] *See supra* note 6.

[17] John D. Ciorciari and Anne Heindel, *Experiments in International Criminal Justice: Lessons from the Khmer Rouge Tribunal*, 35 MICH. J. INT'L. L. 358–442 (2015), available at www.mjilonline.org/wordpress/wp-content/uploads/2015/04/35.2.Experiments-in-International-Criminal-Justice-Lessons-from-the-K.pdf.

7, paragraph 4: "If there is no majority, as required for a decision, the investigation or prosecution shall proceed."

I saw no other way of protecting the integrity and the dignity of the proceedings than to use the super-majority rule here. Irrespective of the final outcome, at least there would be a public hearing of the case in question before the ECCC. And afterward the general public would be in a position to form an opinion as to whether the final judgement was just.

The lesson from the ECCC process should be that it is important that those involved at the political level listen to people with courtroom experience. I know that some are trying to put the blame for the manner in which the ECCC were created on the UN Office of Legal Affairs. In my view this is utterly unfair. We realized that the manner in which the government wanted to shape the ECCC was not acceptable. Kofi Annan understood this and withdrew from the negotiations. Now we know what happened and can see the result. Robert Petit's description proves the point. The trial of the Khmer Rouge leaders should have been entrusted to an international court designed along the lines of the SCSL, or there should have been a truth and reconciliation commission.

Furthermore, after the signing of the agreement on June 6, 2003, it took an inordinate time before the ECCC would become operational. It is noteworthy that it took until the autumn of 2005 until my successor Nicolas Michel could contact Robert Petit to inform him that he had been shortlisted for the post of international co-prosecutor with the ECCC.

For my part, the ECCC have been a delicate issue for the simple reason that I have no doubt whatsoever that the international judges and prosecutors would do their very best to contribute to a positive result and manage this institution as best as they could. And despite the ECCC's structural flaws and functional challenges, I am sure that many Cambodians have welcomed the trials and think that the ECCC have had positive effects in Cambodia. Reference can also be made here to what David Scheffer says in his contribution.

At the same time, I have a very clear memory of my meeting with representatives of the non-governmental organizations in Cambodia during the negotiations. They were not interested in a court. What they wanted was a truth and reconciliation commission that could explain what had happened to their near and dear. But the government was not interested in such a commission.

The final chapter in the volume is by David Scheffer. It is a very enlightening and thoughtful contribution, which should be read in view of the fact that, for many years, he represented his country dealing with matters relating to international criminal justice. In 2012–2017 he also served as the UN secretary general's special expert on UN Assistance to the Khmer Rouge Trials. This means that he has special knowledge about the political realities in connection with decision-making regarding these matters at the national and international level. His contribution should therefore be read with great attention, in particular by politicians.

The main focus in this contribution is the cost of international criminal justice, which he describes as a favorite boogeyman for the critics of the tribunals. It is therefore interesting to take part of all the figures that he details with respect to the costs for justice both at the national and international level, and also the comparison of this cost with other expenditures, not least when it comes to military spending.

It is easy to agree with him that any commitment to the rule of law does not come cheaply, but compared to other societal costs it is a bargain. For my part, I have always maintained precisely this and that the preventive effect of the national criminal justice system must be transferred to apply also at the international level. Another similarity is that the system is implemented not only to punish those who commit crimes, but in particular to achieve crime prevention.

It is against this background one should view the role of the UN Security Council. If the Council could join hands in situations where it is obvious that the Council must exercise its responsibility to protect, it would send a very powerful signal around the world and contribute to preventing the kind of conflicts that generate the atrocities that international criminal justice has to deal with.

David Scheffer's description of the funding of the tribunals is very important. In his view, the reality is that governments and their taxpayers probably will keep balking at spending strained public monies on such ventures. In his view, it will therefore become increasingly necessary in future years to create new funding sources from the private and non-governmental sectors. In this context he also refers to the funding of the SCSL and the ECCC through voluntary contributions.

This reminds me that, when we prepared the report to the Security Council about the SCSL, I forgot to advise Secretary General Kofi Annan about the constitutional problem that funding through voluntary contributions entail. Within the Secretariat, we concluded that the intention of the Council was that the SCSL would be financed from voluntary contributions from UN member states. The secretary general's view was that the only realistic solution was financing through assessed contributions, in other words contributions decided by the General Assembly, and he provided reasons for this opinion. I have, in another context, expressed regret that we did not advise the secretary general to include in his report yet another argument in favor of assessed contributions, namely the constitutional argument.[18] One should make a comparison with funding of courts at the national level. If national courts were funded by different donors and not from taxes or similar official revenues, what credibility would they have? This reasoning should actually be applied at the international level as well.

David Scheffer also believes that there will be a continuing need to build hybrid tribunals if national courts do not meet the challenge of accountability. This is

[18] *See supra* note 12.

probably true. This could be through either regional treaty arrangements among interested nations, as suggested in 1993 by the CSCE rapporteurs for Bosnia and Herzegovina and Croatia before the Security Council took the initiative. It could also be achieved by treaty between the United Nations and one or more relevant governments. If the latter approach is utilized it is my sincere hope that the SCSL will be used as a model and not the ECCC. In case there is a regional treaty arrangement, I believe that this could actually be supported by the UN Security Council adopting a resolution under Chapter VII of the UN Charter, ordering states to assist this court. This is what I had in mind, if the CSCE alternative had been adopted back in 1993.

Finally, in a more general perspective the lesson that must be drawn from the establishment of these international tribunals and courts is that international criminal justice is an absolutely necessary component in order to establish the rule of law at the national and international level. Leila Sadat stresses that it is now the turn of the politicians of the world to do their job. Luis Moreno Ocampo says that the twenty-first century needs national leaders with global vision. David Scheffer stresses that it is important to ensure that lawmakers understand the value of achieving accountability for atrocity crimes, not only as an imperative requirement in societies built on the rule of law, but also as a primary tool in preventing further atrocities, which are manmade calamities that always cost societies far more to rectify than to prevent.

I could not agree more. Ever since I left the United Nations in 2004, I have constantly focused on the need for the rule of law and statesmanship, not least by those who represent the permanent five members of the UN Security Council. The world needs statesmen and stateswomen who understand that they must contribute to creating a world society where humans can live in peace and dignity with their human rights protected.

Against this background I am closing by quoting the following five recommendations from the Final Communiqué of the 26th Annual Plenary Meeting of the InterAction Council of Former Heads of State and Government in 2008:

Therefore, the InterAction Council recommends:

- Insisting that states observe scrupulously their obligations under international law, in particular the Charter of the United Nations and encouraging the leading powers to set an example by working within the law and abiding by it, realising that this is also in their interest;
- Affirming the commitment to settle international disputes through peaceful means and urging states to accept the compulsory jurisdiction of the International Court of Justice;
- Acknowledging that there are situations that require the Security Council to act with authority and consequence in accordance with the principle of the responsibility to protect;

- Calling for universal ratification of the Rome Statute of the International Criminal Court and the full cooperation with the Court on the part of all states;
- Calling for all states to devote resources to education on global ethics, the foundations of international law and the meaning of the rule of law at the national and international level[19]

The result of this meeting is that there is now available a short guide for politicians on the rule of law.[20] The guide is freely accessible for downloading and printing from the web in 23 languages, with more to come.

The person who gave us the idea of elaborating this guide was former Chancellor Helmut Schmidt of Germany. It is important that the main actors at the political level in the world are aware of their responsibility for the rule of law both at the national and international level. A crucial component of the rule of law is to establish criminal justice and deal with the impunity that threatens international peace and security. It is therefore also necessary that politicians understand the important role that prosecutors play in this work.

This book is a valuable contribution to the efforts of enlightening persons at the political level, as well as the general public, about many things that have to be kept in mind in establishing international criminal justice. Despite the challenges it is worth the struggle. The rule of law must be the cornerstone upon which civilization advances. What you will read next is how part of that cornerstone was put in place.

19 Available at http://interactioncouncil.org/final-communiqu-29.

20 *Rule of Law – A Guide for Politicians*. A guide elaborated under the auspices of the Raoul Wallenberg Institute of Human Rights and Humanitarian Law at Lund University, Sweden, and the Hague Institute for the Internationalisation of Law (HiiL), the Netherlands, available at http://rwi.lu.se/what-we-do/academic-activities/rule-of-law-a-guide-for-politicians-2/.

1

International Criminal Justice

The Journey from Politics to Law

Leila N. Sadat

The establishment of international criminal courts and tribunals is a relatively new phenomenon. As judicial bodies, they endeavor to operate with all the objectivity, neutrality, and commitment to the rule of law that their mandates require and their statuses confer. Yet they operate in a highly complex sociopolitical environment. They attract controversy and criticism because they typically apply international law directly to high-ranking and powerful people – presidents, prime ministers, military officers, and others with influence and importance. These individuals, if convicted, may be imprisoned or even, in the case of the Nuremberg trials, executed. So the stakes in any international criminal law case are high.

The judges of these courts and tribunals, and the quality of their trial management and jurisprudence, is an important component of determining the impact and success a given tribunal will have and the respect it will acquire. Yet the prosecutors who bring the cases forward are the "engines" of this emerging system of international criminal justice as well as its "face." Thus, they often bear the brunt of critiques levied against these tribunals. Because international criminal courts and tribunals are charged with a mandate of applying the law in conflict situations that involve weighty questions of war and peace, as well as human survival, they inevitably occupy "a small center in a whirling international vortex" in which almost everything they do "has political implications."[1]

Since the 1990s, several international courts and tribunals have been established to try individuals responsible for the commission of war crimes, crimes against humanity, genocide, and even terrorism. The prosecutors of those institutions, some of whom are featured in this book, have charged more than 300 individuals with the commission of atrocities that span nearly two decades of conflict on nearly every continent, and one of their successors has ongoing investigations on the others.

[1] Patricia A. Wald, *Running the Trial of the Century: The Nuremberg Legacy*, 27 CARDOZO LAW REV. 1559, 1581–82 (2006).

These institutions have, in a way, been tasked with taking *political judgments* about the inappropriateness of certain behaviors committed by states and non-state actors, such as the levying and conduct of war and attacks upon civilians, and turning them into precedents establishing the *illegality* of individuals acting within these atrocity zones. The demand for accountability has been felt at the national level as well – high profile cases brought against former Chilean dictator Augusto Pinochet and, more recently, former Chadian leader Hissène Habré, demonstrate that the thirst for justice and accountability evidenced by the relatively recent creation of international criminal courts and tribunals is part of a far-ranging and profound global trend.[2]

Yet the international community has not easily accepted either the need for or the desirability of this transformation. To paraphrase Justice Robert H. Jackson, the US Chief Prosecutor at the Nuremberg Trial, it has required almost herculean self-restraint for state power to bend to reason. It took two devastating world wars, which were themselves the culmination of centuries of human atrocities, before the international community finally, and reluctantly, cried "stop," and tentatively agreed that some actions were so inherently destructive of human values that the individuals committing them could be said to have committed a *crime*.

As the stories of the prosecutors chronicled in this book demonstrate, this journey from politics to law is far from complete. International criminal courts and tribunals are not yet fully accepted features of the international political landscape, and they continue to face challenges to their political legitimacy, their independence, and even their existence. Lack of funding, problems of state cooperation, difficulties in arresting defendants, challenges stemming from uneven support for their institutions, and significant criticism of their work by the media, governments, defendants, and academics often made and continue to make their jobs extraordinarily difficult.

In spite of these difficulties, after 1993 international criminal justice became a major feature of the international legal landscape. The ad hoc international criminal courts and tribunals, which were the first created and are now either closing or have closed, left several major legacies: *first*, the significant corpus of international criminal jurisprudence created by their work, jurisprudence that creates legal precedent for future courts and other stakeholders to follow; *second*, their effect upon the lives that they touched, whether it is the individuals tasked with working at them in some capacity, the victims or witnesses involved in their proceedings, or even the defendants they incarcerated or acquitted; and *finally*, through their concrete examples, the operation of the *ad hoc* tribunals provided the momentum needed to finally establish a permanent International Criminal Court, and undoubtedly assisted in that court achieving, in record time, the sixty ratifications required to

2 *See, e.g.*, KATHRYN SIKKINK, THE JUSTICE CASCADE: HOW HUMAN RIGHTS PROSECUTIONS ARE CHANGING WORLD POLITICS (2011).

bring it into existence. This chapter will chronicle the journey from politics to law over the past 100 years. It concludes with some thoughts about some of the current predicaments facing international criminal justice today.

In 1914, through a series of bizarre and extraordinary events, the world's great powers were drawn into a war that lasted more than four years and killed up to an estimated 21 million people, more than half of whom were civilians.[3] World War I initially pitted the Allied countries of Russia, France and the United Kingdom against the Central Powers of Germany and Austria-Hungary. In time, the United States and Japan would enter the war on the Allied side, with Bulgaria and the Ottoman Empire joining the Central Powers.[4] The warring states used methods and means of warfare that produced horrific casualties and inflicted painful deaths upon combatants and civilians alike; particularly awful was the use of poison gas,[5] a violation of the Hague Declaration Concerning Asphyxiating Gases and the Hague Convention on Land Warfare that had been drawn up and signed only a few years prior;[6] equally terrible was the ethnic cleansing and genocide of Turkey's Armenian population, which is estimated to have resulted in over one million deaths.[7]

The Great War was not the first conflict begun by European powers: the nineteenth century saw conflict from beginning to end, including the Napoleonic wars, the famous Battle of Solferino in 1859, and the invasion of Paris by Prussian forces in 1870. The United States experienced conflict firsthand during the same period as a consequence of its civil war, which resulted in an estimated 750,000 dead.[8] The use of modern weaponry, however, rendered the Great War more punishing, more heinous, and more shocking than any conflict that had gone before, and as it progressed, the idea surfaced that what had happened was not simply the continuation of "politics by other means," as Prussian military historian Carl von Clausewitz might have argued, but instead a cataclysmic event, at least some aspects of which were *unlawful* – indeed, *criminal*. The public demanded that someone be held responsible.

3 World War I Killed, Wounded and Missing, ENCYCLOPEDIA BRITANNICA, available at www.britannica.com/event/World-War-I/Killed-wounded-and-missing.

4 World War I: 1914–1918, ENCYCLOPEDIA BRITANNICA, available at www.britannica.com/event/World-War-I.

5 Laurence Norman, *Chemical Weapons*, WALL STREET J., http://online.wsj.com/ww1/chemical-weapons.

6 Hague Declaration (IV, 2) of 1899 Concerning the Prohibition of the Use of Projectiles the Sole Object of Which Is the Diffusion of Asphyxiating or Deleterious Gases, July 29, 1899, *reprinted in* 1 AM. J. INT'L L. SUPP. 159 (1907); Hague Convention (II) of 1899 with Respect to the Laws and Customs of War on Land, July 29, 1899, 32 Stat. 1803; Hague Convention (IV) of 1907 Respecting the Laws and Customs of War on Land, Oct. 18, 1907, 36 Stat. 2277.

7 *The Armenian Genocide Resolution Unanimously Passed by the Association of Genocide Scholars of North America*, ASS'N OF GENOCIDE SCHOLARS (June 13, 1977), available at www.genocidescholars.org/sites/default/files/document%;09%5Bcurrent-page%3A1%5D/documents/IAGSArmenian%20Genocide%20Resolution%20_0.pdf.

8 Guy Gugliotta, *New Estimate Raises Civil War Death Toll*, NY TIMES (Apr. 2, 2012), available at www.nytimes.com/2012/04/03/science/civil-war-toll-up-by-20-percent-in-new-estimate.html.

The awkwardly named Commission on the Responsibility of the Authors of the War and on Enforcement of Penalties, which was created by the Allies after the war, found that responsibility for the war emanated from a "dark conspiracy against the peace of Europe," fomented by Germany and Austria in the first place, seconded by Bulgaria and Turkey. The Commission proposed the creation of an international "high tribunal" for the trial of "all enemy persons alleged to have been guilty of offences against the laws and customs of war and the laws of humanity."[9] This was an innovation, for although the parties to the conflict had signed the Hague Conventions of 1899 and 1907, those treaties required only the payment of reparations as the remedy for breach; prevailing ideas about absolute state sovereignty made it difficult to imagine that international law could hold *individuals* accountable for violations of their country's treaty obligations. Thus it was perhaps unsurprising that the US members of the Commission dissented, arguing that although the actions of the Central Powers may have been *immoral*, they were not *illegal*.[10] They argued that they were unaware of any "international statute or convention making a violation of the laws and customs of war – not to speak of the laws or principles of humanity – an international crime, affixing a punishment to it, and declaring the court which has jurisdiction over the offence."[11]

A compromise was reached and the Treaty of Versailles provided for a special tribunal to try Wilhelm II of Hohenzollern, the German emperor, for the "supreme offence against international morality and the sanctity of treaties." However, the Netherlands refused to extradite the German kaiser for trial – he was, after all, Queen Victoria's grandson – [12] and only a handful of others were handed over to a German court in Leipzig. Most of those were acquitted, and the whole effort was generally considered a fiasco.[13]

The idea of an international criminal jurisdiction, however, captured the imagination, and proposals for the establishment of a permanent international criminal court issued from jurists and legal organizations, particularly in Europe.[14] US scholars and some of their British colleagues were decidedly less enthusiastic about the idea (one prominent international lawyer suggested it was "delusion[al]").[15] The United States and Europe also largely parted company regarding the construction of the postwar international system when the United States Senate rejected the League of Nations treaty.[16] Yet, when war came again to Europe in the 1930s, and the suffering and

9 *Commission on the Responsibility of the Authors of the War and on Enforcement of Penalties: Report Presented to the Preliminary Peace Conference*, 14 AM. J. INT'L L. 95, 123 (1920).

10 *Id.* at 128. 11 *Id.* at 146.

12 BBC History, Wilhelm II, available at www.bbc.co.uk/history/historic_figures/wilhelm_kaiser_ii.shtml.

13 Mathew Lippman, *Nuremberg: Forty-Five Years Later*, 7 CONN. J. INT'L L. 1 (1991).

14 Leila Nadya Sadat, *The Nuremberg Paradox*, 58 AM. J. COMP. L. 151, 166–69 (2010).

15 J.L. Brierly, *Do We Need an International Criminal Court*, 8 BRITISH Y.BK. INT'L. L. 81–88 (1927).

16 JOHN MILTON, JR., BREAKING THE HEART OF THE WORLD: WOODROW WILSON AND THE FIGHT FOR THE LEAGUE OF NATIONS (2001).

slaughter began once more to mount, the Allied Powers determined that the perpetrators of the war would be punished. They issued declarations to this effect in 1942[17] and 1943,[18] promising that

> Those German officers and men and members of the Nazi party who have been responsible for, or have taken a consenting part in ... atrocities, massacres and executions, will be sent back to the countries in which their abominable deeds were done in order that they may be judged and punished according to the laws of these liberated countries ... without prejudice to the case of the major criminals, whose offenses have no particular geographical localization and who will be punished by the joint decision of the Governments of the Allies.[19]

This was the basis for what became the Nuremberg and later the Tokyo trials, conducted by the Allied Powers in 1945 and 1946, which brought the accused up on three charges: crimes against peace, war crimes, and crimes against humanity. These trials created a precedent for the establishment of today's international criminal courts and tribunals.

As Michael Scharf in the next chapter suggests, the decision to hold trials after the war was not a foregone conclusion. The quartet of Allied Powers (France, the Soviet Union, the United States, and the United Kingdom), bickered about whether or not to hold a trial at all and, once the decision was made to hold one, who should be charged and what procedural rules should apply.[20] Even within the United States, there was a real dispute regarding whether the trial was a good idea,[21] and following the Nuremberg trial, American lawyers were divided over whether it had been a useful or productive exercise. Although Courtroom 600 in the Nuremberg Palace of Justice, in which the trial was held, has become a place of commemoration, that is a recent development. Germans did not readily accept the results of the trials when they were held;[22] rather, most Germans denied any knowledge of the atrocities, and particularly the Holocaust, after the war. According to some observers, it was not until the Adolf Eichmann trial held by Israel in the 1960s that German interest in the trial appears to have surfaced.[23] Interestingly, Germany is now one of the nations most committed to international criminal justice and the success of the International Criminal Court.

[17] The *St. James Declaration*, Resolution by Allied Governments Condemning German Terror and Demanding Retribution (Jan. 13, 2942) *in* British and Foreign Papers, 1940–1942, at 1072 (Her Majesty's Stationary Office).

[18] The *Moscow Declaration*, Declaration of German Atrocities, Nov. 1, 1943, 3 Bevans 816, 834, DEPT. STATE BULLETIN (Nov. 6, 1943), at 310–11.

[19] *Id.* [20] TELFORD TAYLOR, THE ANATOMY OF THE NUREMBERG TRIALS (1992).

[21] BRADLEY F. SMITH, THE AMERICAN ROAD TO NUREMBERG: THE DOCUMENTARY RECORD 1944–1945, at 5–12 (1982).

[22] MICHAEL P. SCHARF, BALKAN JUSTICE: THE STORY BEHIND THE FIRST INTERNATIONAL WAR CRIMES TRIAL SINCE NUREMBERG (1997); Christoph Burchard, *The Nuremberg Trial and Its Impact on Germany*, 4 J. INT'L CRIM. JUST. 800, 800–29 (2006).

[23] Leila Nadya Sadat, *The Nuremberg Trial, Seventy Years Later*, 15 WASH. U. GLOBAL STUD. L. REV. 575, 582 (2016).

The geopolitical environment at the end of the war was difficult as well. Just two days prior to the signing of the treaty that would create the international military tribunal at Nuremberg, the *Enola Gay* was winging its way through the sky en route to dropping an atomic bomb on Hiroshima, and one day after its signature, a second bomb incinerated Nagasaki. Because the four Allied Powers had a vested interest in not pursuing charges that would show them in a poor light, they did not include charges relating to aerial bombardment at Nuremberg, and the Russians insisted on accusing the Germans of the Katyn Forest massacre – which Russian forces had actually carried out. In terms of the activities of the International Military Tribunal for the Far East, established by military proclamation to try Japanese defendants, its judgment was issued over a stinging dissent by the Indian judge who objected to the exclusion of Allied crimes and the lack of judges from the vanquished nations on the bench, complaints that were compounded by the doubtful procedural fairness of the trial itself.[24] These allegations of "victor's justice" plagued the Nuremberg trial and continue to resonate today as individuals indicted by the International Criminal Court point to the unfairness of others similarly situated who remain free from judicial inquiry due to the Court's limited jurisdiction.

Yet even with these deficiencies, the Nuremberg trial and the notion of international human rights and criminal justice it expounded were revolutionary. The idea that human beings could assert rights held under international law against their governments was an innovation, as was the notion that leaders could be held responsible for violations. It is also generally accepted that the decision to hold a trial, and the accomplishment of the task to a high level of professionalism and distinction, represented a real achievement. It may have been an American "show"[25] in terms of the material support and size of the various participating prosecutorial teams, but it built upon decades of European thought and legal analysis.[26] The Nuremberg trial significantly advanced the journey of international criminal justice from politics to law. But the question remained whether Nuremberg would simply be a one-off historic event, or whether it would have enduring salience in the postwar era. It is to this question that this chapter now turns.

The decision to hold war crimes trials was taken contemporaneously with the San Francisco Conference establishing the United Nations. The principles of Nuremberg are thus deeply intertwined "with the organization of the United Nations as the twin foundations of an international society ordered by law."[27] This is evidenced by the UN Charter's prohibition on the use of force against the

[24] Neil Boster & Robert Cryer, The Tokyo International Military Tribunal: A Reappraisal 17, 323–27 (2008).

[25] Elizabeth Borgwardt, A New Deal for the World: America's Vision for Human Rights 233 (2005).

[26] Sadat, *Nuremberg Paradox*, *supra* note 14.

[27] Taylor, *supra* note 20, at 42.

territorial integrity and political independence of member states,[28] and in the provisions of the charter on human rights.[29] Indeed, modern human rights law – like modern international criminal law – rests upon the Nuremberg foundation. The corollary of the notion that individuals have duties under international law, expounded by the International Military Tribunal at Nuremberg, is that they may also acquire rights thereunder.

The Nuremberg Principles were prepared by the International Law Commission and presented to the General Assembly after the war,[30] and at least some of the "law" of the charter and judgment found its way into new global treaties on apartheid, genocide, the laws of war, and torture,[31] although aggression and crimes against humanity were never made the subject of similar specialized conventions.[32] Understood broadly, the Nuremberg Principles eschew collective responsibility in favor of individual criminal responsibility; provide that no human being (even a head of state or other responsible government official) is above the law with respect to the most serious crimes of concern to humanity as a whole – war crimes, crimes against humanity, and the crime of aggressive war; and that reliance upon internal law is no defense against crimes for which an individual may have responsibility under international law.[33]

At the international level, therefore, the Nuremberg Principles became, in theory, a critical legal underpinning of the new world order. Politics, however, impeded

28 UN Charter Art. 2, para. 4.

29 *Id.*, Arts. 55 & 56. *See also* MARY ANN GLENDON, A WORLD MADE NEW: ELEANOR ROOSEVELT AND THE UNIVERSAL DECLARATION OF HUMAN RIGHTS (2001).

30 Int'l Law Comm'n, Report of the International Law Commission Covering Its First Session, April 12 – June 9, 1949, UN GAOR, 4th Sess., Supp. No. 10, UN Doc. A/925 (1949).

31 International Convention on the Suppression and Punishment of the Crime of Apartheid, Nov. 30, 1973, 1015 UNTS 243; Convention on the Prevention and Punishment of the Crime of Genocide, Dec. 9, 1948, 78 UNTS 277; Convention for the Amelioration of the Condition of the Wounded in Armies in the Field, Aug. 22, 1864; Hague Convention (II) With Respect to the Laws and Customs of War on Land, July 29, 1899; Hague Convention (IV) Respecting the Laws and Customs of War on Land, Oct. 18, 1907; Geneva Convention (I) for the Amelioration of the Condition of the Wounded and Sick in Armed Forces in the Field, Aug. 12, 1949, 75 UNTS 31; Geneva Convention (II) for the Amelioration of the Condition of Wounded, Sick and Shipwrecked Members of Armed Forces at Sea, Aug. 12, 1949, 75 UNTS 85; Geneva Convention (III) Relative to the Treatment of Prisoners of War, Aug. 12, 1949, 75 UNTS 135; Geneva Convention (IV) Relative to the Protection of Civilian Persons in Time of War, Aug. 12, 1949, 75 UNTS 287; Convention Against Torture and Other Cruel, Inhumane or Degrading Treatment or Punishment, Dec. 10, 1984, 1465 UNTS 85.

32 There is now underway an effort to draft and have adopted a new global treaty on crimes against humanity. This initiative was begun at Washington University School of Law in 2008 by the author, *see* LEILA NADYA SADAT, FORGING A CONVENTION FOR CRIMES AGAINST HUMANITY (2d. ed., 2013), and is now being carried forward at the United Nations International Law Commission. *See Summaries of the Work of the International Law Commission, Crimes Against Humanity*, International Law Commission, available at http://legal.un.org/ilc/summaries/7_7.shtml. *See also* M. Cherif Bassiouni, *"Crimes Against Humanity": The Need for a Specialized Convention*, 31 COLUMB. J. TRANSNAT'L L. 457 (1994).

33 Leila Nadya Sadat, *Shattering the Nuremberg Consensus: U.S. Rendition Policy and International Law*, 3 YALE J. INT'L AFF. 65, 66 (2008).

their implementation. The permanent members of the UN Security Council were often divided, which meant that the International Law Commission had difficulty advancing its work on a draft code of crimes and a statute for an international criminal court.[34] The Nuremberg Principles were also often honored in the breach as states pursued what they believed to be in their national interests without paying them much mind. The United States invaded Vietnam; the Soviet Union invaded Afghanistan. Neither government appeared to understand – or perhaps to care – that the Nuremberg Principles applied to these wars.[35] French scholar Claude Lombois likened the Nuremberg precedent to a "dormant volcano": quiescent, but capable of eruption at any moment.[36]

That moment came in the 1990s, as the former Yugoslavia erupted in war and the Rwandan genocide sickened and shocked the world. As public demands for justice and accountability mounted, the Security Council, suddenly freed from Cold War politics, reached for the Nuremberg precedent and established, for the first time since 1945, two new international criminal tribunals: the International Criminal Tribunal for the Former Yugoslavia (ICTY) to address crimes committed in the territory of the former Yugoslavia and the International Criminal Tribunal for Rwanda (ICTR) to address the crimes committed in Rwanda. The politics surrounding the creation and operation of these tribunals has been exhaustively documented by others, including some of the authors in this volume;[37] suffice it to say that they faced tremendous political and logistical challenges, particularly in their first few years. The Yugoslavia and Rwanda Tribunals had similar, but not identical, jurisdictions to their forebearer, although neither tribunal included crimes against peace in its statute, limiting their jurisdictions to genocide, war crimes, and crimes against humanity.[38] The Yugoslavia Tribunal, in particular, was the first court to be established in the middle of an armed conflict it had been tasked to investigate for the commission of atrocity crimes, a "novel experiment of dual-track justice and warfare,"[39] that would become the model for the International Criminal Court once established.

[34] Leila Nadya Sadat, *The Proposed Permanent International Criminal Court: An Appraisal*, 29 Cornell Int'l L.J. 665, 667 (1996) (formerly Wexler).

[35] *See* Taylor, *supra* note 20, at 636 (outlining the US position on both invasions and their relation to the Nuremberg Principles); Jean Allain, *The Continued Evolution of International Adjudication*, *in* Looking Ahead: International Law in the 21st Century 50, 55 (Can. Council of Int'l Law ed., 2012) (discussing popular opposition to the conflicts in Vietnam and Afghanistan based on the Nuremberg Principles); Benjamin B. Ferencz, *The Nuremberg Principles and the Gulf War*, 66 St. John's L. Rev. 711, 719–20 (1992) (discussing the willingness of heads of state to ignore the Nuremberg Principles).

[36] Claude Lombois, Droit Pénal International 162 (1979).

[37] *See, e.g.*, David Scheffer, All the Missing Souls: A Personal History of the War Crimes Tribunals (2012).

[38] Statute of the International Criminal Tribunal for the Former Yugoslavia, SC Res. 827, Annex, UN Doc. S/RES/827 (May 25, 1993); Statute of the International Criminal Tribunal for Rwanda, SC Res. 955, Annex, UN Doc. S/RES/955 (Nov. 6, 1994).

[39] Scheffer, *supra* note 37, at 19.

Although both of the ad hoc tribunals suffered some of the same human difficulties experienced at Nuremberg, they were ultimately able to establish themselves as credible and successful international institutions, trying scores of defendants and creating important precedents that have added depth to our conceptual and practical understanding of international criminal justice and the substantive law of war crimes, crimes against humanity, and genocide, as well as international criminal procedure.[40]

Their establishment was followed by the creation of other international criminal courts and tribunals, some of which are discussed in this volume: the Special Panels for East Timor in 2000; the Special Court for Sierra Leone in 2002; the Extraordinary Chambers in the Courts of Cambodia in 2003; and the Special Tribunal for Lebanon in 2007. Although often criticized as too expensive and, in the case of the Yugoslavia and Rwanda Tribunals in particular, remote from the regions they served, the establishment of these international criminal courts and tribunals fueled the resurgence of the movement for the establishment of a permanent international criminal court, the dream begun in the ashes of World War I nearly 70 years earlier.

On July 17, 1998, a treaty for the permanent International Criminal Court (ICC) was adopted after years of difficult discussions and five long, hot weeks of grueling negotiations in Rome. The ICC Statute is much longer and more complicated than the statutes of earlier international criminal tribunals, and the jurisdictional regime and procedure of the Court much more complex. In particular, the ICC – unlike the ICTY, the ICTR and the Nuremberg Tribunal itself – is based upon the principle of "complementarity," meaning that the Court is intended as a court of last, not first, resort and will hear only cases in which states are unable and unwilling to proceed.[41] Thus, under the Court's complicated admissibility rules, any state – even one not party to the statute – can divest the Court of jurisdiction by opening an investigation into a case in which jurisdiction is sought by the Court.

Cases can be sent to the Court either by a state party, the Security Council or the prosecutor acting *proprio motu* – on her own initiative; in the latter case, a Pre-Trial

40 The International Criminal Tribunal for the Former Yugoslavia has indicted 161 persons, of whom 83 have been sentenced, 1 is in trial, and an additional 6 cases are currently on appeal: *Key Figures of the Cases*, INTERNATIONAL CRIMINAL TRIBUNAL FOR THE FORMER YUGOSLAVIA, available at www.icty.org/sid/24. The International Criminal Tribunal for Rwanda has indicted 93 individuals with 59 convictions; proceedings have concluded with respect to 85 persons; 8 are fugitives who remain at large: *Key Figures of the Cases*, MECHANISM FOR INTERNATIONAL CRIMINAL TRIBUNALS, http://unictr.unmict.org/en/cases/key-figures-cases. *See also* Leila Nadya Sadat, *The Contribution of the ICTR to the Rule of Law, in* PROMOTING ACCOUNTABILITY UNDER INTERNATIONAL LAW FOR GROSS HUMAN RIGHTS VIOLATIONS IN AFRICA 118 (Charles Chernor Jalloh & Alhagi B. M. Marong eds., 2015); Yaël Ronen, *The Impact of the ICTY on Atrocity-Related Prosecutions in the Courts of Bosnia and Herzegovina*, 3 PENN ST. J. L. & INT'L AFF. 113 (2014) (discussing the importance of ICTY jurisprudence in the national courts of Bosnia and Herzegovina).

41 Rome Statute for the International Criminal Court, Preamble & Art. 17.

Chamber must authorize the opening of the investigation under Article 15 of the statute. The Security Council has the power to refer situations to the Court with no jurisdictional restrictions, whether or not the state of the potential accused's nationality or the territorial state (where the crimes were committed) has ratified the statute. In the other two situations, however, a referral can be made only if the territorial state or the state of the accused's nationality is a party to the Rome Statute. The Court has three crimes in its statute: genocide, crimes against humanity, and war crimes; and at the end of 2017, the Court's Assembly of States Parties decided to "activate" the Kampala Amendments on the crime of aggression, making that crime justiciable at the Court as well.

The International Criminal Court has 123 states parties as at this writing.[42] The Court currently has 11 situations under examination involving 10 countries, and 8 additional situations in the "preliminary examination" phase. Two of the Court's active situations – in Libya and Darfur, Sudan – were referred to it by the Security Council, but have been very difficult in terms of investigation and trial. The other situations were mostly referred by the territorial states themselves – this is true of the situations in Uganda, the Democratic Republic of the Congo, Mali, and the Central African Republic – or the referrals were made *proprio motu* by the prosecutor with the consent of the territorial state (in the Côte d'Ivoire and Georgia cases) or, as it transpired, against the will of the territorial state in the Kenya case.[43]

The Court, like the ad hoc tribunals before it, has had a somewhat rocky start, with the first trial (the *Lubanga* case) taking a long time and being criticized for its narrow charges and evidentiary problems. It has also had difficulty procuring needed financial resources; problems arresting its defendants;[44] states accusing it of being "anti-Africa" given the large number of first cases and situations coming from African states;[45] threats and tampering with witnesses and refusal of states to cooperate in providing evidence to the

42 Burundi withdrew in October, 2017. South Africa and the Gambia had also indicated their intentions to withdraw, but those objections have now themselves been withdrawn.

43 *The Court Today*, INT'L CRIM. COURT, available at www.icc-cpi.int/iccdocs/PIDS/publications/TheCourtTodayEng.pdf; *Prosecutor v. William Samoei Ruto, Henry Kiprono Kosgey and Joshua Arap Sang*, ICC-01/09–01/11–19, Application on Behalf of the Government of the Republic of Kenya Pursuant to Article 19 of the ICC Statute (Mar. 31, 2011), available at www.icc-cpi.int/CourtRecords/CR2011_03107.PDF; Identical letters dated March 4, 2011 from the Permanent Rep. of Kenya to the United Nations addressed to the Secretary-General and the President of the Security Council, UN Doc. S/2011/116 (Mar. 8, 2011).

44 *See, e.g.*, Human Rights Watch, UNFINISHED BUSINESS: CLOSING GAPS IN THE SELECTION OF ICC CASES (2011); Somini Sengupta, *Omar al-Bashir Case Shows International Criminal Court's Limitations*, NY TIMES (June 15, 2015), available at www.nytimes.com/2015/06/16/world/africa/sudan-bashir-international-criminal-court.html?_r=0.

45 Adam Taylor, *Why So Many African Leaders Hate the International Criminal Court*, WASH. POST (June 15, available at 2015), www.washingtonpost.com/news/worldviews/wp/2015/06/15/why-so-many-african-leaders-hate-the-international-criminal-court/?utm_term=.08cad7b4c703.

prosecutor;[46] weathering a bruising attack by the United States, which went so far as to adopt anti-ICC legislation and to threaten countries ratifying the statute with the loss of all financial and military assistance if they did not sign ICC immunity agreements with the United States;[47] problems with creating an effective, efficient trial process, especially given the additional layer of the new Pre-Trial Chamber; and complaints about court personnel both inside and outside the Court.

Notwithstanding these difficulties – which could discourage even the staunchest supporters of the Court – the ICC has had some real achievements and has not only survived, but thrived in its first 15 years of existence. It has indicted more than three dozen individuals, concluded proceedings against more than a dozen individuals, and has several cases at trial. Uganda, which was the first situation referred to the Court due to the terror inflicted by the Lord's Resistance Army in the north of the country, is now peaceful; and although the prosecutor was forced to withdraw the Kenya cases due to evidentiary issues and non-cooperation, Kenya's elections following the ICC's intervention were relatively peaceful as well. Although the Court itself cannot be directly credited with bringing about peace in the countries in which it is operating without more empirical evidence of the same, at the very least the fears expressed of disastrous interference with ongoing peace processes in the Ugandan and Kenyan situations clearly did not materialize.

Significant convictions have been issued in cases tried against individuals involved in the situations relating to the Democratic Republic of the Congo, the Central African Republic, and Mali; and many of the operational difficulties the Court experienced in its early years appear to be diminishing with the passage of time. There remains pushback from some states parties, particularly from the African region, which was evidenced by stirring and highly critical interventions from several African states during the ICC's fifteenth Assembly of States Parties in November 2016, but these sentiments were not uniformly shared, and many African states spoke forcefully in favor of the Court and the values of peace and justice it represents to their countries. As one member of civil society remarked during a seminar held on the occasion of the dedication of the Court's permanent premises in April 2016, given the large number of Africans working in high positions at the Court itself and with the Court, the criticism seems more likely due to the fact that "the Court is working" rather than evidence of structural bias against African nations by the Court.

46 *Briefing Paper: Witness Interference in Cases Before the International Criminal Court*, Open Soc'y Justice Initiative (Nov. 2016), www.opensocietyfoundations.org/sites/default/files/factsheet-icc-witness-interference-20161116.pdf; *Prosecutor v. Uhuru Muigai Kenyatta*, ICC-01/09–02/11–1037, Second Decision on Prosecution's Application for a Finding of Non-Compliance under Article 87(7) of the Statute (Sept. 19, 2016).

47 American Servicemember's Protection Act of 2002, 22 USC §§ 7401–7433.

At the same time, the Syria situation and the North Korean situation remain painfully outside the reach of the ICC because Russia and China are willing to veto resolutions that could refer those cases to the Court. Likewise, the United States remains outside the reach of the Court in many cases because it is not a party to the statute and is often (but not always) conducting its operations on the territory of non-states parties. This raises not only the specter, but the reality, of double standards, and gives individuals accused by the ICC the same argument that the Nuremberg and Tokyo defendants raised: that the "justice" dispensed by the Court is victor's justice only, not the kind of evenhanded application of the law that would be expected from a court exercising universal jurisdiction over international crimes. Indeed, the biggest problem remaining is undoubtedly the rocky relationship the Court has with the Security Council, which has neither backed the cases it has referred with the power it could have, nor has it been able to avoid the temptation of blocking the referral of situations through the use of the veto – like Syria – that clearly should be before the ICC.

This chapter has chronicled the fractious journey of international criminal justice over the past century. It has been a journey of fits and starts, progressing often suddenly and unexpectedly at times, and languishing during others. To the extent that progress has been made, at least some credit goes to the prosecutors who are the subject of this book, as well as to the many others that have toiled away diligently at these international criminal courts and tribunals or have supported them from the outside. These courts and tribunals have always faced – and will continue to face – real challenges. Whether it is skepticism and disbelief from academics and politicians,[48] frontal attacks from defendants and governments, or simply lack of consistent and sufficient funding, one cannot overestimate the difficulties that remain. These problems are compounded by the current hostility between Russia and the United States that has once more paralyzed the Security Council; and the refusal of several major powers to ratify the ICC Statute. The Nuremberg experience showed that it took decades for the trials to be accepted by the German people; it remains to be seen whether the result will be the same in the former Yugoslavia, Rwanda, or any of the ICC's current situation countries.

Justice works best when it is consistently and evenhandedly applied. This requires faith, focus, financing, and commitment by world leaders. Only they have the capacity to turn the dream of an effective, functioning system of international criminal justice into a reality. Prosecutors can bring cases. Judges can manage trials

48 *See, e.g.*, Ralph Zacklin, *The Failings of Ad Hoc International Tribunals*, 2 J. INT'L CRIM. JUST. 541 (2004); Mark Kersten, *Seeing the Forest for the Trees: The International Criminal Court and the Peace-Justice Debate*, ABA-ICC PROJECT: INT'L CRIM. JUST. TODAY (July 20, 2016), available at www.international-criminal-justice-today.org/opinion/seeing-the-forest-for-the-trees/; JENNIFER K. ELSEA, CONG. RESEARCH SERV., RL31495, U.S. POLICY REGARDING THE INTERNATIONAL CRIMINAL COURT (2006). *See also* Mark J. Osiel, *The Demise of International Criminal Law*, HUMANITY JOURNAL, June 10, 2014, http://humanityjournal.org.

and issue judgments. But only states can ratify treaties and fund the institutions they establish. Just as the personnel of these new institutions have been asked to do their jobs, often under difficult and trying circumstances, it is now the turn of the politicians of the world to do theirs. As I wrote many years ago, the establishment of the International Criminal Court in the summer of 1998 effected an "uneasy revolution" in international law and politics, one that has been contested by the great powers ever since its creation.[49] The International Criminal Court, and the creation of the international criminal courts and tribunals featured in this volume, "represents one of the world's most elaborate experiments in enforcing legal restrictions on violence."[50] One hopes that the members of the Security Council will become more restrained in their use of the veto (as has been proposed by a large group of states),[51] assist with funding and arrests as appropriate, and, ultimately, one day join the International Criminal Court so as to put "international law squarely on the side of peace."[52]

49 Leila Nadya Sadat, *The New International Criminal Court: An Uneasy Revolution*, 88 GEO. L. J. 381 (2001) (with S. Richard Carden).

50 DAVID BOSCO, ROUGH JUSTICE: THE INTERNATIONAL CRIMINAL COURT IN A WORLD OF POWER POLITICS 177 (2014).

51 There is an effort to impose a "responsibility not to veto" on the five permanent members of the Security Council in cases involving the commission of atrocity crimes. *See, e.g.*, Letter dated Dec. 14, 2015 from the Permanent Representative of Liechtenstein to the United Nations addressed to the Secretary-General, UN Doc. A/70/621 (Dec. 14, 2015).

52 REPORT TO THE PRESIDENT BY MR. JUSTICE JACKSON, OCT. 7, 1946, *reprinted in* U.S. DEPT. OF STATE, INTERNATIONAL CONFERENCE ON MILITARY TRIALS, LONDON, 1945, at 432, 439 (Pub. No. 3080) (1949), available at www.loc.gov/rr/frd/Military_Law/pdf/jackson-rpt-military-trials.pdf.

2

The Cornerstone

Robert H. Jackson and the Nuremberg Tribunal

Michael P. Scharf

History's first international criminal court was the Nuremberg Tribunal, created by the victorious Allies after World War II to prosecute the major German war criminals. After the Nuremberg trials, half a century would pass before the International Criminal Tribunal for the former Yugoslavia, the International Criminal Tribunal for Rwanda, the Extraordinary Chambers in the Courts of Cambodia, the Special Court for Sierra Leone, and ultimately the International Criminal Court (ICC) would be established. This book tells the stories of those modern tribunals through the firsthand narratives of their founding chief prosecutors. But to understand the context of those chronicles, one must begin with the tale of Robert H. Jackson, the chief US prosecutor of the Nuremberg Tribunal. Jackson died in 1954, but this chapter channels his spirit through his and others' contemporaneous reporting of the role he played in negotiating the Charter of the Nuremberg Tribunal and prosecuting the first case ever to be tried by an international criminal tribunal.[1]

Recently, on the seventieth anniversary of the judgment of the Nuremberg Tribunal, I was invited to speak at a historic conference in Nuremberg featuring the US attorney general and the founding chief prosecutors of the several modern international criminal tribunals whose chapters appear in the pages of this book. The opening session took place in Courtroom 600 at the Palace of Justice, the very venue where Jackson prosecuted the Nazi leaders after World War II. The venerable courtroom is now a museum piece, restored to its 1945 splendor. Standing at the podium where Jackson gave his legendary opening speech, I felt transported back to those heady times, when international justice was a lofty experiment for the ages.

Despite the passage of time, the events that prompted the formation of the Nuremberg Tribunal in 1945 are probably more familiar to most than those which

[1] Michael Scharf gratefully thanks CWRU Law student Sabrina Morris for her helpful research assistance for this chapter.

led to the creation of the ad hoc tribunals and ICC at the end of the twentieth century. Between 1933 and 1940, the Nazi regime established concentration camps in which Jews, Communists, and opponents of the regime were incarcerated without trial; it progressively outlawed the Jews, stripped them of citizenship, and made marriage or sexual intimacy between Jews and German citizens a criminal offense; it forcibly annexed Austria and Czechoslovakia; it invaded and occupied Poland, Denmark, Norway, Luxembourg, Holland, Belgium, and France; and then it set in motion "the final solution to the Jewish problem" by establishing death camps such as Auschwitz and Treblinka, where six million Jews were exterminated.

As Allied forces pressed into Germany and an end to the fighting in Europe grew near, the Allied powers faced the task of establishing an acceptable procedure for dealing with the surviving Nazi leadership. The initial step in that direction was the establishment in 1942 of the United Nations War Crimes Commission. The phrase "United Nations" had been adopted by the alliance of Britain, the United States, the Soviet Union, China, and 22 other nations united against the Axis Powers – Germany, Italy, and Japan. The War Crimes Commission was supposed to investigate and collect evidence of war crimes, but it had no investigatory staff and no resources. So instead, the Commission turned its attention to the academic exercise of determining whether launching an aggressive war should be considered a crime under international law; whether atrocities committed by a government against its own citizens should be regarded as an international crime; and whether an international tribunal should be created for the trial of war crimes. Unfortunately, the members of the Commission were so evenly divided on these matters that no consensus was ever reached.

As the end of the war was nearing, the issue of war crimes trials was bumped up to the highest political levels. The British government initially opposed the establishment of any tribunal for the trial of the civilian and military leaders of Nazi Germany on the ground that their "guilt was so black" that it was "beyond the scope of judicial process."[2] British Prime Minister Winston Churchill, therefore, proposed the summary execution of the major Nazis on the basis of a political decision of the Allies. This came to be referred to in government circles as the "Napoleonic precedent," since the one-time emperor of the French had, after his defeat at Waterloo in 1815, been exiled to St. Helena without trial by political decision of the victorious governments of Britain, Austria, and Russia.[3] The Soviet premier, Joseph Stalin, also favored the Napoleonic precedent, and reportedly had his subordinates draw up a list of 50,000 Nazi war criminals for execution. At a banquet attended by Franklin Roosevelt and Churchill, Stalin proposed a toast, stating, "I drink to the quickest possible justice for all German war criminals. I drink to the justice of a firing squad ... Fifty thousand must be shot."[4]

[2] Telford Taylor, The Anatomy of the Nuremberg Trials (1992), at 29. [3] *Id.*

[4] Joe J. Heydecker & Johannes Leeb, The Nuremberg Trial 77–78 (R.A. Downie trans., 1962).

Surprisingly, President Roosevelt appeared willing to go along with this approach.[5] But its prospects perished with Roosevelt's death in April 1945. Upon taking office, President Harry Truman made it clear that he opposed summary executions. Instead, at the urging of US Secretary of War Henry Stimson, Truman pushed for the establishment of an international tribunal to try the Nazi leaders. The Soviets declared that they could go along with such a judicial approach so long as the tribunal's task was "only to determine the measure of guilt of each particular person and mete out the necessary punishment."[6] But the United States responded that "if we are going to have a trial, then it must be an actual trial."[7]

President Truman ultimately convinced his British, French, and Soviet counterparts that the establishment of an international tribunal would serve several shared objectives. First, judicial proceedings would avert future hostilities that would likely result from the execution, absent a trial, of German leaders. Legal proceedings, moreover, would bring German atrocities to the attention of all the world, thereby legitimizing Allied conduct during and after the war. Finally, such a trial would permit the Allied powers, and the world, to exact a penalty from the Nazi leadership rather than from Germany's civilian population.[8]

For the task of negotiating the charter of the world's first international criminal tribunal and trying the major Nazi perpetrators, the United States turned to Robert H. Jackson, a successful trial attorney who had served from 1934 to 1936 as general counsel of the Bureau of Internal Revenue, from 1936 to 1938 as assistant attorney general, from 1938 to 1940 as solicitor general, from 1940 to 1941 as attorney general, and since 1941 as an associate justice of the US Supreme Court.[9] As a Supreme Court justice, Jackson won acclaim for his bold dissent in the controversial case of *Korematsu v. the United States*, in which the majority upheld the internment of Japanese Americans during World War II. On April 13, 1945, the day after President Roosevelt's death, Justice Jackson delivered a keynote speech at the annual conference of the American Society of International Law, in which he laid out his thinking about how an international trial for the captured German leaders should be undertaken. The thoughtful speech convinced the administration that Jackson was their man for Nuremberg.[10]

A few days later, on April 26, 1945, President Truman offered Jackson the opportunity to take a leave from the Supreme Court and represent the United States as negotiator and prosecutor of history's first international criminal tribunal. The

[5] On September 15, 1944, President Roosevelt approved a memorandum supporting Churchill's plan for the German leaders and agreeing to "concert with him a list of names" for execution. TAYLOR, *supra* note 2, at 31.

[6] TAYLOR, *supra* note 2, at 59. [7] *Id.*

[8] Kevin R. Chaney, *Pitfalls and Imperatives: Applying the Lessons of Nuremberg to the Yugoslavia War Crimes Tribunal*, 14 DICKINSON J. INT'L L. 62 (1995).

[9] Robert Jackson, *Nuremberg in Retrospect: Legal Answer to International Lawlessness*, 35 AMERICAN BAR ASSOCIATION JOURNAL 813, 815 (Oct. 1949).

[10] TAYLOR, *supra* note 2, at 44–45.

challenge that Jackson accepted was formidable. In Jackson's words, "many well-wishers thought it a quixotic undertaking beyond our power to accomplish."[11]

There were no statutes, rules, or precedents to draw from. As Jackson said, "while substantive law could be gleaned from scattered sources, there was no codification of applicable law."[12] To make things more complicated, "the prosecution must be conducted in four languages by lawyers trained in four different legal systems," Jackson said.[13] At the time, it was not even clear what hard evidence would be available. Jackson noted that "very little real evidence was in our possession, the overwhelming mass of documents being still undiscovered and their existence largely unsuspected."[14] As to the venue for the trial, Jackson quipped, "we did not even know whether a court-house that could house such a trial was still standing in Germany, or if so, where it was to be found."[15] And to make matters worse, rather than support Jackson's historic undertaking, he faced opposition from his fellow Supreme Court justices, who publicly "beefed about a man leaving the Supreme Court to do a political job" and described the mission as "Jackson's lynching expedition."[16] But despite the challenge and opposition, "Justice Jackson did not hesitate as to where his duty lay."[17]

Shortly after agreeing to take on the task, Jackson and his counterparts from the United Kingdom, France, and Russia, gathered in London to draw up a charter for the International Military Tribunal to try the German civilian and military leadership for war crimes, the crime of waging a war of aggression, and crimes against humanity.[18] Nuremberg was chosen as the site of the Tribunal for symbolic reasons – for it was there that the Nazi Party had staged its annual mass demonstrations and that the anti-Semitic Nuremberg Laws had been decreed in 1935.[19]

Of his days in London, Jackson wrote, "I doubt whether a more novel or challenging task ever was set before members of the legal profession."[20] The 15 negotiating sessions from June 26 to August 8, 1945 leading up to the adoption of the Charter of the Nuremberg Tribunal ranged from turbulent to tumultuous. The problem was that the negotiators brought to the table their own legal conceptions and the experiences of their respective legal systems: the Common Law adversarial system as it had evolved differently in England and in the United States, and variations of the Civil Law inquisitorial system employed in France and Russia. The task of creating an entirely new judicial entity acceptable to the four parties that would blend elements from the two systems proved an incredible challenge for the

[11] Jackson, *supra* note 9, at 815. [12] *Id.* [13] *Id.* [14] *Id.* [15] *Id.*

[16] Felix Frankfurter, Felix Frankfurter Reminisces 222 (1960).

[17] Lord Shawcross, Mr. Justice Jackson: Four Lectures in His Honor 98 (1969).

[18] Agreement for the Prosecution and Punishment of Major War Criminals of the European Axis (London Agreement), signed at London, Aug. 1945, 82 U.N.T.S 279, 59 Stat. 1544, E.A.S. No. 472 (entered into force, Aug. 8, 1945); Charter of the International Military Tribunal (annexed to the London Agreement) [hereinafter Nuremberg Charter].

[19] Taylor, *supra* note 2, at 61. [20] Jackson, *supra* note 9, at 815.

negotiators. "With dissimilar backgrounds in both penal law and international law it is less surprising that clashes developed at the Conference than that they could be reconciled," wrote Jackson in the preface to his report containing a summary of the Charter's negotiation history.[21]

Under the Continental system, most of the documentary and testimonial evidence is presented to an examining magistrate, who assembles it in a dossier, copies of which are provided to the defendant and to the court prior to trial. The court, either on its own motion or at the request of one of the parties, will question witnesses directly, and cross-examination by opposing counsel is unusual. There is no rule against hearsay evidence, and trials in absentia are permitted. In the Anglo-American system, in contrast, the indictment contains only a summary of the facts alleged, and the evidence is presented in open court by the lawyers who examine and cross-examine the witnesses. Most importantly, under the adversarial system, the defendant has a right to confront his accusers – a right that limits use of hearsay evidence and ex parte affidavits, and requires the presence of the accused at trial.

The charter that Jackson and his fellow negotiators eventually came up with represented a blend of the two systems. Mixing elements from both systems, the Nuremberg Charter required, contrary to the Anglo-American practice, that the indictment "shall include full particulars specifying in detail the charges against the defendants," and that there be "documents" submitted with the indictment. But, contrary to the Continental practice, it did not require that the prosecution present all of its evidence with the indictment. Also contrary to Continental practice, defendants could testify as witnesses on their own behalf, but in contrast to Anglo-American practice, defendants could be compelled to testify by the Tribunal, and they were permitted to make an unsworn statement at the end of the trial.[22]

Jackson and the other negotiators agreed, moreover, that the technical rules of evidence developed under the common-law system of jury trials to prevent the jury from being influenced by improper evidence would be unnecessary for a trial where no jury would be used.[23] Accordingly, the Nuremberg Charter adopted the principle that the Nuremberg Tribunal should admit any evidence that it deemed to have a probative value and should not be bound by technical rules of evidence, such as the notion of "hearsay." Commenting on the evidentiary and procedural compromises, Jackson wrote,

> The only problem was that a procedure that is acceptable as a fair trial in countries accustomed to the Continental system of law may not be regarded as a fair trial in common-law countries. What is even harder for Americans to recognize is that trials

21 Robert H. Jackson, *Report of Robert H. Jackson, United States Representative to the International Conference on Military Trials*, v–vi (US Govt. Prt. Office, 1949).

22 Taylor, *supra* note 2, at 64.

23 Robert H. Jackson, *Report of Robert H. Jackson, United States Representative to the International Conference on Military Trials* xi (US Department of State: 1945).

which we regard as a fair and just may be regarded in Continental countries as not only inadequate to protect society but also as inadequate to protect the accused individual.[24]

One particularly controversial compromise was made in the area of the Tribunal's substantive law, which ultimately resulted in depriving the Tribunal of jurisdiction over the Nazis' prewar atrocities against the Jews. Jackson had proposed inclusion of a charge of conspiracy to commit any of the crimes within the jurisdiction of the Tribunal in order to reach prewar Nazi outrages against German Jews, which could not be treated as war crimes but which could be punishable as initial steps in a conspiracy to commit war crimes after the war had begun. The other parties were reluctant to accept this proposal, particularly since the Anglo-American concept of conspiracy was not recognized in any of the Continental European legal systems at that time. At the Soviet's insistence, the proposed language was amended to make the conspiracy charge applicable only to the crime of initiating a war of aggression. Jackson accepted the revision but then sought to ignore it by persuading the other Nuremberg prosecutors to include in the indictment a charge of conspiracy to commit all three of the offenses contained in the Nuremberg Charter. Jackson's attempt at an end-run around the limited notion of conspiracy contained in the Charter proved unsuccessful, however. In its judgment, the Nuremberg Tribunal narrowly interpreted the wording of the Charter and ruled that the notion of conspiracy only applied to the crime of aggression, thus precluding a general finding that prewar atrocities were punishable.

Despite this and other compromises, Jackson felt that he had achieved the major goals he had set for the negotiations. As one of the senior members of his staff explained, "He had a declaration that initiating aggressive war was a crime, he had the agreement to establish an international tribunal, and the trial would take place in Nuremberg, in the American Zone of Occupation, where he would be, comparatively speaking, on home ground."[25] In the following weeks, the international prosecutors reached agreement on the list of defendants, the charges, and the division of labor, and within just five months, the trial was ready to commence on the morning of November 20, 1945. It was now time, as Jackson put it in his report to the president, "to establish incredible events by credible evidence."[26]

The Nuremberg trial started with Jackson's opening statement, which has gone down in history as among the most elegant and powerful words ever uttered by a lawyer. Jackson began, "The privilege of opening the first trial in history for crimes against the peace of the world imposes a grave responsibility." He then put the trial in perspective, saying, "The wrongs which we seek to condemn and punish have been so calculated, so malignant, and so devastating, that civilization cannot tolerate their being ignored, because it cannot survive their being repeated."

[24] Robert H. Jackson, *Report of Robert H. Jackson*, *supra* note 23, at x–xi.

[25] Taylor, *supra* note 2, at 77. [26] Taylor, *supra* note 2, at 54.

Jackson then pointed out what was most extraordinary about holding a trial for such crimes: "That four great nations, flushed with victory and stung with injury, stay the hand of vengeance and voluntarily submit their captive enemies to the judgment of the law is one of the most significant tributes that Power has ever paid to reason."

Next, Jackson confronted head on the question of "victor's justice." He began by recognizing that the criticism had validity, but emphasized that there was no real choice: "The nature of these crimes is such that both prosecution and judgment must be by victor nations over vanquished foes. The worldwide scope of the aggressions carried out by these men has left but few real neutrals." To overcome this problem, he urged the Tribunal to be scrupulously fair. "We must never forget that the record on which we judge these defendants is the record on which history will judge us tomorrow. To pass these defendants a poisoned chalice is to put it to our lips as well." Therefore, he said, "We must summon such detachment and intellectual integrity to our task that this Trial will commend itself to posterity as fulfilling humanity's aspirations to do justice."

Nuremberg was the first trial in which leaders were held individually to account for the actions undertaken by the state. The trial was subject to extensive radio and news coverage, and it was hoped that the trial would discredit the Nazi leaders and pave the way for the eventual reintegration of Germany. Thus, in words meant for the German people at large, Jackson said, "We would also make it clear that we have no purpose to incriminate the whole German people." He explained,

> If the German populace had willingly accepted the Nazi program, no storm troopers would have been needed in the early days of the Party and there would have been no need for concentration camps or the Gestapo. The German, no less than the non-German world, has accounts to settle with these defendants.

Then, previewing the case before the judges, Jackson promised that the prosecution would establish "undeniable proofs of the incredible events" and that

> the catalog of crimes will omit nothing that could be conceived by a pathological prince, cruelty, and lust for power. Against their opponents, including Jews, Catholics, and free labor, the Nazis directed such a campaign of arrogance, brutality, and annihilation as the world has not seen since the pre-Christian era.

After describing the major crimes in broad terms, Jackson said that these wrongs had "aroused the sleeping strength of imperiled civilization" and that "its united efforts have ground the Nazi war machine to fragments," but at a terrible price. "The struggle has left Europe a liberated yet prostate land where a demoralized society struggles to survive."

Finally, Jackson's opening speech reached its moral crescendo. "The real complaining party at your bar is Civilization." He went on: "Civilization asks whether law is so laggard as to be utterly helpless to deal with crimes of this magnitude by criminals of this order of importance. It does not expect that you can make war impossible." Then, quoting the words of Rudyard Kipling's poem, "The Old Issue," Jackson said,

> It does expect that your juridical action will put the forms of international law, its precepts, its prohibitions and, most of all, its sanctions, on the side of peace, so that men and women of good will, in all countries, may have "leave to live by no man's leave, underneath the law."[27]

To those who observed and wrote about the Nuremberg trial, one of the most dramatic moments of the trial was the face-off between Jackson and Hermann Goering, the highest-ranking defendant on trial. Goering was not only Hitler's powerful second in command, but he had been a World War I military hero, and despite Germany's defeat, he was still a popular figure in Germany on the eve of the trial.

An unrepentant Goering testified on his own behalf three months into the trial, March 13–18, 1946. Jackson was determined to use his cross-examination of Goering to discredit the Nazi kingpin and the entire Nazi enterprise. In public remarks on the eve of the trial, Jackson lamented that "I have yet to hear one of these men say that he regretted that he had a part in starting the war. Their only regret is at losing it."[28] As Judge Sir Norman Birkett, the UK alternate judge on the Tribunal explained in his memoir, "If the leader of the surviving Nazis could be exposed and shattered, and the purposes and methods of the Nazi government revealed in their horrible cruelty, then the whole free world would feel that this trial had served its supreme purpose."[29]

Goering, in turn, was convinced that the trial would be the last chapter of his life, and that what he would say, and how he would say it, would deeply mark his historical "image."[30] If Goering managed to out-duel Jackson in the courtroom, Judge Birkett wrote, it would "restore German belief in their leaders, and the verdict will be regarded by the German people as excessively unjust."[31] The stakes could not have been higher.

Jackson had spent almost as much time preparing for his cross-examination of Goering as he had writing his masterful opening statement. However, rather than start by confronting Goering with the Holocaust decrees that bore Goering's signature as he originally planned, Jackson decided at the last minute to begin his cross-examination with flattery. "You are perhaps aware that you are the only man living who can expound to us the true purposes of the Nazi Party and the inner workings of its leadership?" he asked in his first question. In his mémoire, Jackson explained his strategy, saying that he decided to begin in this manner in order to "induce him to

[27] Quotations in the preceding section come from Jackson, Opening Address to the International Tribunal, Nov. 10, 1945.

[28] Eugene C. Gerhart, AMERICA'S ADVOCATE: ROBERT H. JACKSON 402 (1958).

[29] TAYLOR, *supra* note 2, at 340. [30] *Id.* at 329. [31] *Id.* at 330.

display his Nazi attitudes as much as possible, instead of humiliating him."[32] But the tactic ended up backfiring terribly.

Jackson followed up by asking Goering a series of questions that Jackson thought should be answered with a simple "yes" or "no" in the American and British style. One by one, these questions were designed to inextricably lead Goering down the primrose path, culminating in his ruin. But this was not an ordinary court and Goering was not an ordinary defendant, and so the presiding judge, Sir Geoffrey Lawrence from the UK, told Jackson that the defendant would be allowed great leeway to answer questions at length. This bench ruling was preceded by a whispered conversation between US Judge Francis Biddle and Judge Lawrence, and Jackson was convinced that this was Biddle's way of getting even with Jackson for perceived past slights. Biddle had succeeded Jackson as both solicitor general and attorney general, and the two had had a complicated and sometimes acrimonious relationship.

But the ruling should not have surprised Jackson. One of the senior members of Jackson's prosecution staff, Telford Taylor, has stated that Jackson clearly opened the door to this ruling in phrasing his first question as he had done. According to Taylor, "Goering was doing exactly what Jackson had asked him to do, and what broke Jackson's self-control was that his witness was answering too articulately and unashamedly."[33]

Whatever prompted it, the ruling completely undermined Jackson's strategy and emotionally unhinged the chief prosecutor. As Judge Birkett later wrote, "The cross-examination had not proceeded more than ten minutes before it was seen that Goering was the complete master of Mr. Justice Jackson."[34] Taylor later wrote that his boss "paid dearly for his tactical blunder, in both public prestige and his own discontent."[35]

The Nuremberg Tribunal rendered its judgment on September 30 and October 1, 1946. From a juridical standpoint, the weaknesses of Jackson's cross-examination of Goering had little effect on the trial's outcome. This was largely because testimony was mere window dressing in a trial that, according to the Tribunal's judgment, turned almost entirely on incriminating documents of the defendant's "own making, the authenticity of which has not been challenged." Goering was convicted on all counts. The Tribunal also found 18 of the other 21 defendants guilty on one or more charges. Goering and eleven other defendants were sentence to death, three were sentenced to life imprisonment, and four were given terms of 10–20 years. Goering ended up taking his own life by swallowing a smuggled-in cyanide capsule on the eve of his execution.

Opinion polls conducted in Germany after the Nuremberg Trial indicated that, despite the convictions, 80 percent of the West German people did not believe the

[32] *Id.* at 335. [33] *Id.* at 342. [34] *Id.* at 341. [35] *Id.* at 343.

findings of the Nuremberg Tribunal and considered the proceedings to be nothing but "acts of political retribution without firm legal basis."[36] In a then-classified 1953 State Department report, the US government concluded that the Nuremberg trials had failed to "reeducate West Germans."[37]

Yet, these polls were not known to Robert Jackson who, in his final report to President Truman,[38] provided an optimistic summary of what had been accomplished at Nuremberg. In describing the work that went into preparing for the trial; the staggering number of participants; the amount of testimony, documentary, and film that was entered into evidence, Jackson said, "It is safe to say that no litigation approaching this in magnitude has ever been attempted."

In the conclusion of his report, Jackson says, "the vital question in which you and the country are interested is whether the results of this trial justify the heavy expenditure of effort." To Jackson, the Nuremberg trial attained six notable accomplishments.

First, Jackson felt it significant that the Nuremberg Charter, which he negotiated, had unambiguously declared crimes against humanity and waging aggressive war as crimes under international law. What's more, these were crimes for which leaders and heads of state could be liable before an international tribunal. In his words, "It is a basic charter in the International Law of the future." Elsewhere, Jackson further explained, "I shall not be surprised if a distant day will recognize this legal condemnation of oppressions and aggressions as civilization's chief salvage from the Second World War."[39] A few months after the judgment was rendered, the newly created UN General Assembly unanimously adopted the principles of the Nuremberg Charter, which continue to be cited as the bedrock of international criminal law today.

Second, Jackson's report to the president emphasized the importance of establishing these principles in a judicial precedent. "No one can hereafter deny or fail to know that the principles on which the Nazi leaders are adjudged to forfeit their lives constitute law – and law with a sanction," he wrote. Jackson conceded that "it would be extravagant to claim that agreements or trials of this character can make aggressive war or persecution of minorities impossible," but he argued "we cannot doubt that they strengthen the bulwarks of peace and tolerance."[40]

Third, Jackson observed that the Nuremberg Charter devised "a workable procedure for the trial of crimes which reconciled the basic conflicts in Anglo-American, French, and Soviet procedures." Jackson felt that the procedures proved that international trials were possible and should be pursued again as history requires in the

36 Peter Maguire, Law and War: An American Story 241, 246 (2000). 37 *Id.*

38 *Justice Jackson's Final Report to the President Concerning the Nuremberg War Crimes Trial*, 20 Temp. L. Q. 338 (1946–1947).

39 Robert H. Jackson, The Nuremberg Trial: Civilization's Chief Salvage from World War II, Remarks delivered at the University of Buffalo Centennial Convocation, Buffalo, NY 114–117 (Oct. 4, 1946).

40 *See* Jackson, *supra* note 21.

face of mass atrocity. In a speech given a few days after the Nuremberg judgment, Jackson explained, "And what we may someday hope for is some permanent forum where the victims of persecution may invoke protection of the law before instead of after it culminates in war, as those whose civil rights are violated in the United States may resort to the Courts for protection."[41] Thus, Jackson became one of the first advocates for the establishment of a permanent international criminal court that would apply the principles of Nuremberg to all countries across the globe.

Fourth, in his final report Jackson lauded the orderly and dispassionate way the trial was conducted. Jackson had once said that "Courts try cases, but cases also try courts."[42] To Jackson, "the example of leaving punishment of individuals to the determination of independent judges, guided by principles of law, after hearing all of the evidence for the defense as well as the prosecution," could do much to "strengthen the process of justice in many countries."[43]

Fifth, Jackson commented on the importance of the documentary record produced by the trial: "We have documented from German sources the Nazi aggressions, persecutions, and atrocities with such authenticity and in such detail that there can be no responsible denial of these crimes in the future and no tradition of martyrdom of the Nazi leaders can arise among informed people."

Finally, Jackson underscored that the Nuremberg trial served as a cautionary tale for any country tempted to take the first steps down the road toward dictatorship. "The record discloses," he wrote, "the early symptoms of dictatorship and shows that it is only in it incipient stages that it can be brought under control." Jackson concluded, "The Nuremberg trial has put that handwriting on the wall for the oppressor as well as the oppressed to read."

Jackson recognized that the Nuremberg trial had engendered a great deal of criticism in the United States and in other countries. Criticisms of victor's justice, unclean hands, application of *ex post facto* law, and unfair procedures were leveled on the trial by journalists, academics, politicians, and even Jackson's fellow Supreme Court justices.[44]

In his report to President Truman and in other writings, Jackson answered those criticisms in three ways. Initially he reminded the critics that, as the world's first international war crimes trial, Nuremberg was operating in uncharted territory. In Jackson's words, "many mistakes have been made and many inadequacies must be confessed [but] I am consoled by the fact that in proceedings of this novelty, errors and missteps may also be instructive to the future."[45]

Next, he compared Nuremberg to the alternative that had been proposed – executions without trial. As Jackson put it, "Whatever defects may be charged to

41 *Id.* 42 TAYLOR, *supra* note 2, at 45. 43 *See* Jackson, *supra* note 21.

44 These criticisms are summarized in Michael P. Scharf, *Have We Really Learned the Lessons of Nuremberg*, 149 MILITARY LAW REVIEW 65–71 (1995).

45 *Justice Jackson's Final Report*, *supra* note 37.

the Nuremberg trial, its danger as precedent and its offensiveness to American ideals of justice, liberty and law are as nothing compared to the dangers from killing or punishing people for political crimes by executive order."[46]

And ultimately, Jackson defended Nuremberg by pointing out that the defendants were given rights that they never accorded their victims: "Whatever criticisms may be made of the trial, we have never to face the claim that we executed any persons without giving them full opportunity to meet accusation with every means of defense."[47]

Jackson ended his report to the president by saying that Nuremberg "was perhaps the greatest opportunity ever presented to an American lawyer."[48] It was an opportunity that few others in history have ever had. To history's other founding international prosecutors, Jackson was a trailblazer, a cautionary tale, and an inspiration.

[46] Robert H. Jackson, *Justice Jackson Weighs Nuremberg's Lessons*, NY TIMES 12, 59–60 (June 16, 1946).
[47] Robert H. Jackson, *The United Nations Organization and War Crimes*, AMERICAN SOCIETY OF INTERNATIONAL LAW 196–203 (1952).
[48] *See* Jackson, *supra* note 21.

3

The Balkan Investigation

William Schabas

The direct ancestor of the International Criminal Tribunal for the Former Yugoslavia – the institution that confirmed the rebirth of international criminal justice – was the Commission of Experts. Comprised of five members, several of them specialists in international law, the Commission's establishment was mandated by the Security Council. Resolution 780, adopted unanimously on October 6, 1992, was charged with investigating "grave breaches of the Geneva Conventions and other violations of international humanitarian law committed during the conflict in the former Yugoslavia."[1]

It was the most robust measure that had then been taken by the United Nations in order to deal with a conflict whose beginnings dated back more than a year. The conflict had featured battles and atrocities over a period of several months as Slovenia, and then Croatia, broke away from Yugoslavia to become independent states. The worst of the conflict, in Bosnia and Herzegovina, where the three main ethnic groups were more balanced in numbers and where no single one could claim a majority, was only then getting underway. Desperate but unsuccessful political initiatives to address the crisis had been launched since 1991. But it was only in mid-1992 that the Security Council began to use the language of international criminal justice. In August 1992, it adopted a resolution that said perpetrators "will be individually [held] responsible."

The August Resolution had been provoked by stunning revelations of atrocities in the Omarska concentration camp. The Resolution referred to "reports of mass forcible expulsion and deportation of civilians, imprisonment and abuse of civilians in detention centres, deliberate attacks on non-combatants, hospitals and ambulances, impeding the delivery of food and medical supplies to the civilian population, and wanton devastation and destruction of property."

This wasn't the first time international law had turned its attention to the Balkans. One of the very earliest international fact-finding or expert commissions of inquiry

[1] S.C. Res. 780, ¶ 2 (Oct. 6, 1992).

was set up in 1913, at the dawn of the First World War. An unofficial body backed by the young Carnegie Endowment, it investigated violations in the conflicts that afflicted the territory of what would later be called "Yugoslavia." The Commission's report invoked two of the Hague Conventions of 1899 and 1907 as a basis for concluding that war crimes had been perpetrated by various forces in the conflict. Cherif Bassiouni has written that the atrocities documented by the Commission of Experts bear a "haunting resemblance" to those in the report of the 1913 Carnegie Commission.

After the First World War there were calls for international prosecution of war crimes. A Commission on Responsibilities set up by the Preliminary Peace Congress compiled evidence of atrocities, including rapes, torture, killing of hostages and "denaturalization," a notion akin to what is today the crime of genocide, perpetrated by the Austrians and their allies in the Balkans. Greece, Serbia and Romania managed to convince the Commission that the peace treaty with Bulgaria should provide for an international criminal court to prosecute individual perpetrators. However, the measure was vetoed by the French prime minister after the Americans objected.

And then there was the Nuremberg trial in 1945 and 1946. It did not focus on the Balkans at such, of course, but in its more general treatment of Nazi atrocities throughout the occupied continent the region was not neglected. The International Military Tribunal heard evidence of the mass murder of hostages, perpetrated in Yugoslavia by the Gestapo. In its judgment, it noted Hitler's instruction to his generals that Yugoslavia was to be destroyed with "unmerciful harshness."

Thus, when the Security Council flagged the perpetration of war crimes in the Balkans in October 1992, the initiative to investigate atrocities in that sorry region was not being cut from whole cloth. International criminal law was only just awakening from its 40-year hibernation. The invasion of Kuwait by Iraq in 1990 had prompted calls for an international criminal tribunal to try the crime of aggression as well as for a fact-finding commission similar to what was called for in Resolution 780, but neither initiative bore fruit. A related idea, that of a "truth commission," was also starting to appear on the international radar screen. A UN-backed initiative that was led by a distinguished American judge, Thomas Buergenthal, had recently completed its study of atrocities in El Salvador. All of this contributed to a context in which, as Victor Hugo wrote, nothing could stop an idea whose time had come.

In August 1992, Tadeusz Mazowiecki, the special rapporteur on the former Yugoslavia who had been appointed by the UN Commission on Human Rights, produced a report that proposed the establishment of an international commission of inquiry. Within the Department of State, a young international lawyer, Michael Scharf, was preparing draft language for a Security Council resolution whereby such a body would be authorized.

During the negotiations of the text of Resolution 780, the United Kingdom, France and Russia agreed on setting up a fact-finding body, but wanted to call it a "committee." The United States insisted that the body be called a "commission," apparently having in mind the precedent of the United Nations War Crimes Commission. That institution had begun its work in London in early 1944 and was seen, then and now, as a precursor to the International Military Tribunal.

Under Resolution 780, the secretary general was charged with implementing the will of the Security Council. The Resolution did not specify the size of the Commission of Experts. Secretary General Boutros-Ghali chose to appoint a "Magnificent Five," all of them men, something that would be unthinkable today. Nor did they represent the five geographic groups in the United Nations, as is the tradition, but care was taken to ensure that none of them were from a permanent member of the Security Council.

Three of them were distinguished academics: Frits Kalshoven, of Leiden University in the Netherlands; Torkel Opsahl, of the University of Oslo; and Cherif Bassiouni, an Egyptian national working at DePaul University in the United States. Each was a distinguished scholar in what were then still relatively obscure fields, international humanitarian law, and international human rights law, at least by comparison with the present day. The other two members were William Fenrick, an accomplished Canadian military lawyer; and Keba M'Baye, a Senegalese judge who had served on the International Court of Justice. Kalshoven was named chairman of the Commission.

The Commission of Experts was frustrated from the start, and throughout its work, both by its lack of appropriate funding and by an apparently uncooperative United Nations bureaucracy characterized by extreme caution and even inertia. But it also had to contend with serious concerns, both within the UN and from powerful states and international personalities, that by focussing upon justice the Commission of Experts might complicate efforts to negotiate peace. Some thought that an effective fact-finding commission, with the means to document violations of international law, could get in the way of political compromise.

Even before the Commission first met, it attracted attention from other bodies concerned with investigation of atrocities in the Balkan conflict. Acting upon a report prepared by a three-person committee set up by the Conference on Security and Cooperation in Europe, which included the Swedish judge Hans Corell, the Conference's Committee of Senior Officials recommended, in early November 1992, that "[t]he United Nations Commission of Experts should give particular attention to the principle of personal responsibility for war crimes and examine how this principle could be put into practice by an *ad hoc* tribunal."[2]

[2] *See* Hans Corell, *Evaluating the ICC Regime: The Likely Impact on States and International Law*, Training Course organized by T.M.C. Asser Institute, Science Alliance and No Peace Without Justice, at 4, http://legal.un.org/ola/media/info_from_lc/romestatute_dec00.pdf.

The Commission began meeting in Geneva, in November 1992, in one of the conference rooms of the old Palais des Nations, originally built as the headquarters of the League of Nations. Provided with only limited information from member states, and without yet having undertaken its own fact-finding, the Commission of Experts focussed on the legal dimension of its task. This was something for which the members were well suited, given their undoubted and widely acknowledged expertise.

Ironically, as the Commission of Experts was convening in December 1992, the US secretary of state was delivering a dramatic speech in another of the conference rooms down the corridor in the same building. In the final weeks of his cabinet term within the Bush administration, Lawrence Eagleburger named several individuals whom he said should be held personally responsible, including Radovan Karadžić, Ratko Mladić, Slobodan Milošević, Vojislav Šešelj, and Adem Delić. They were described as individuals who should be prosecuted for war crimes, and indeed, they all would later stand in the dock before the International Criminal Tribunal for the former Yugoslavia.[3]

In January 1993, the Commission began taking steps to address the inadequacy of its funding. It proposed that the United Nations set up a trust fund into which member states could make voluntary contributions, a seemingly simple matter. Lawyers inside the United Nations opposed the idea, arguing that it had not been specifically contemplated by the Security Council resolution.

In March, the General Assembly agreed to create a trust fund. Almost immediately, the United States contributed half a million dollars. Later, under the creative leadership of Cherif Bassiouni, additional resources were tapped from governments as well as from private sources, notably philanthropic foundations with a human rights orientation.

The Commission of Experts presented its first interim report to the United Nations Security Council in early February 1993. The report attempted a definition of "ethnic cleansing," a rather new term that was appearing increasingly in journalistic sources, popular accounts and political debates. For the Commission, "ethnic cleansing" consisted of "rendering an area wholly homogenous by using force or intimidation to remove persons of given groups from the area." Its definition was later endorsed by the International Court of Justice in its February 2007 judgment in the *Bosnia v. Serbia* case.

The Commission concluded that "ethnic cleansing" had been perpetrated "by means of murder, torture, arbitrary arrest and detention, extra-judicial executions, rape and sexual assaults, confinement of civilian population in ghetto areas, forcible removal, displacement and deportation of civilians, deliberate military attacks or

[3] *See* David Binder, *Bush Warns Serbs Not to Widen War*, NY Times (Dec. 28, 1992), available at www.nytimes.com/1992/12/28/world/bush-warns-serbs-not-to-widen-war.html.

threats of attacks on civilian areas, and wanton destruction of property."[4] For the Commission, these were both war crimes and crimes against humanity and, potentially, even genocide.

The Commission of Experts was not the first to use the language of international criminal law to describe the Balkan conflict. But the prestige of its members, and especially the great authority they possessed in the relevant areas of international law, cloaked its findings in gravitas. This was not a case of inexpert politicians or journalists throwing around provocative language, often in a demagogic context. Rather, eminent scholars in the field, sitting as members of an official United Nations Commission, had made authoritative preliminary findings.

The February report of the Commission considered the establishment of an ad hoc international criminal tribunal that might be charged with prosecuting the crimes it was then identifying. The Commission of Experts said that "it would be for the Security Council or another competent organ of the United Nations to establish such a tribunal,"[5] adding that such a move would be "consistent with the direction" that the work of the Commission had taken. The Commission was not the first body to propose an international tribunal, but by adding the weight of its view to the debate, it may well have tipped the scales.

Within days, the Security Council adopted Resolution 808 whereby it "[d]ecide [d] that an international criminal tribunal shall be established for the prosecution of persons responsible for serious violations of international humanitarian law committed in the territory of the former Yugoslavia since 1991."[6] Three months later, in May 1993, the Security Council adopted the Statute of the International Criminal Tribunal for the Former Yugoslavia (ICTY).[7]

Nearly half a century had passed since the establishment of the first generation of international criminal courts, at Nuremberg and Tokyo. In May 1993, when the Security Council actually established the Tribunal, nobody would have expected that the ICTY would not conclude its operations until December 2017, and even then before its prosecutions were entirely finished. A successor institution known as the Mechanism for the International Criminal Tribunals would then be required for the final appeals and retrials, and for future unforeseen developments such as the arrest of remaining suspects and the discovery of new evidence.[8]

Adoption of Security Council Resolution 827 in May did not immediately shift the center of gravity to the new ICTY. It would take nearly a year for the tribunal to become fully operational. Judges weren't elected until November 1993, and eight

4 *See* Letter Dated May 24, 1994 from the Secretary-General to the President of the Security Council, S/1994/674 (May 27, 1994), available at www.icty.org/x/file/About/OTP/un_commission_of_experts_report1994_en.pdf.

5 Interim Report of the Commission of Experts Established Pursuant to Security Council Resolution 780 (1992), UN Doc S/25274, para. 74.

6 S.C. Res. 808, ¶ 1 (Feb. 22, 1993).

7 S.C. Res. 827 (May 25, 1993).

8 United Nations Mechanism for International Criminal Tribunals, available at www.unmict.org/en.

more months would pass before a prosecutor, Richard Goldstone, took the reins. In the meantime, the Commission of Inquiry pursued its important work. This had been understood by the Security Council. The preamble of Resolution 827 stated that

> pending the appointment of the Prosecutor of the International Tribunal, the Commission of Experts established pursuant to resolution 780 (1992) should continue on an urgent basis the collection of information relating to evidence of grave breaches of the Geneva Conventions and other violations of international humanitarian law as proposed in its interim report.[9]

As well as confirming the Council's confidence in the work of the Commission of Experts, this also underscored the vital relationship between the Commission and the Tribunal. Cherif Bassiouni would later describe the Commission of Experts as "the first stage in the establishment of the Tribunal."[10]

Frits Kalshoven resigned from the Commission of Experts in September 1993, openly protesting the lack of political support from major governments, including France and the United Kingdom. He pointed to the failure to provide any logistical or financial assistance, complaining that it was unacceptable for the Security Council to vote to create a body and then deny it the means to implement its decision. Regrettably, nearly a quarter of a century later, the problem persists. A few weeks after Kalshoven's gesture, the Norwegian member of the Commission, Torkel Opsahl, died suddenly.

But far from withering under the impact of these two blows, as some cynical observers predicted at the time, the Commission was suddenly invigorated by the appointment of Cherif Bassiouni as chairman. It was in many ways the finest hour for the great Egyptian international lawyer, who had done so much throughout his career of many decades to keep the flame of international justice alight. A polyglot and polymath, Bassiouni had been teaching international law at DePaul University in Chicago since the 1960s. In the early 1970s, he took on the leadership of the International Institute of Higher Studies in Criminal Sciences, known since 2016 as the Siracusa International Institute. Over the years, international experts gathered periodically for conferences and expert panels at the Institute's seat in Siracusa, on the Italian island of Sicily, to discuss and debate issues of international criminal law and human rights.

Bassiouni immediately took steps to address the funding challenges, defying the entreaties of senior lawyers within the United Nations system. He also enlisted pro bono professionals and legions of law students who were thrilled to direct their energies to real problems in one of the world's great crises. By early 1994, the Commission had collected some 65,000 documents that were catalogued and organized in a data base located in Chicago, as well as a computerized archive comprising hundreds of hours of testimony.

9 S.C. Res. 827 (May 25, 1993). 10 *Id.*

Another commissioner, William Fenrick of Canada, directed a series of 34 field investigations. These included the excavation of several mass graves in the conflict region. Later, Fenrick migrated to the International Criminal Tribunal, together with one of his deputies on the Commission of Experts, Payam Akhavan. Both became valued senior staff members of the Office of the Prosecutor in the early days of its activities. In this way, much of the institutional memory and expertise of the Commission, acquired before the ICTY existed but principally during the first year when it was not fully functional, was informally transferred to the Tribunal.

The Commission was also energized by the addition of two women members, appointed to replace Kalshoven and Opsahl. Dutch legal academic Christine Cleirin took charge of investigations into rape and sexual assault, directing a team of 40 women lawyers, psychologists, and interpreters. More than 200 victims or witnesses to sexual and gender-based violence were interviewed by the Commission. Hanne Sophie Greve, a Norwegian judge, conducted an investigation into the ethnic cleansing of Prijedor, something that was later documented in the judgments of the ICTY. When Prosecutor Richard Goldstone initiated proceedings against Tadić in November 1994, the written application relied upon evidence gathered by the Commission of Experts.

In the case law of the ICTY itself, the Commission seems to have made more of a mark for its legal conclusions and analysis than for its very substantial factual findings. Perhaps that is because the Commission's report could not readily have been admissible as evidence. The facts it uncovered had to be subject to independent proof during the trials. On the other hand, the views of the Commission of Experts on matters like command responsibility, a notion about which the post–Second World War proceedings were rather thin, proved both helpful and persuasive. The doctrine of command responsibility, set out in Article 7 of the ICTY Statute permits the conviction of a military and even a civilian superior for the acts of subordinates to the extent that the superior should have known that the crimes might be committed. The Commission's conclusions about the admissibility of circumstantial evidence and the mental element of international criminality also influenced the case law of the ICTY.

In December 1993, the Commission was informed by the legal advisor to the secretary general that its mandate was to conclude at the end of April 1994, a ruling that was inconsistent with the Security Council's instruction that the Commission continue its work until a prosecutor was appointed. In a technical sense, a prosecutor had been appointed by then, although he never really took up the job. The fledgling office had to await the arrival of Richard Goldstone, in July 1994.

Welcoming its final report and the voluminous annexes, Secretary General Boutros-Ghali said,

> The material and information collected and recorded in the data base, now transferred to the Tribunal, will not only assist in the prosecution of persons responsible for serious violations of international humanitarian law, but will constitute a permanent documentary record of the crimes committed in the former Yugoslavia, and thus remain the memorial for the hundreds of thousands of its innocent victims.[11]

Amen.

[11] Letter from Boutros Boutros-Ghali, Secretary-General of the United Nations to M. Cherif Bassiouni, President, International Human Rights Law Institute, DePaul University, January 4, 1995.

PART II

The Founders

4

The International Criminal Tribunals for the Former Yugoslavia and Rwanda

Richard J. Goldstone

After graduating from Witwatersrand University School of Law in 1962, I practiced for 17 years at the Johannesburg Bar. My practice was almost exclusively in the field of commercial law. As a young barrister, I did my share of pro bono criminal defenses in the High Court, but that was the extent of my criminal trial experience, save for a long and complex commercial fraud trial that lasted for some nine months in Durban. In 1977, during that trial my application for senior status (the English Bar equivalent of Queen's Counsel) was granted[1].

Between 1978 and 1980, I accepted three short acting appointments on what was then called the Transvaal Supreme Court (today called the Gauteng High Court). During the first half of 1980, I was invited by the minister of justice to accept a permanent appointment on the Court. This presented me with an excruciatingly difficult decision. From my student days I had been involved in activities designed to bring to an end the evil system of apartheid. I had served as the president of the student council at the University of the Witwatersrand that had actively opposed attempts by the government to segregate what it regarded as a "white university." I had also served on the executive committee of the National Union of South African Students (NUSAS), an organization that was also strongly anti-apartheid and an anathema to the government. As a form of retribution, for some years the apartheid government denied me a passport.

A few anti-apartheid lawyers had accepted appointments to the bench with the intention of ameliorating the harsh application of the racially oppressive laws that then applied to the black majority. One of them, John Didcott, was a role model. He was a former leader of the student council at the University of Natal and a member of the Executive Committee of NUSAS. He quickly made a name for himself as the author of well-written opinions that castigated racist laws and for issuing astute

[1] Much of this chapter is based upon the reflections contained in *For Humanity: Reflections of a War Crimes Investigator* (Yale University Press, 2000).

decisions that had the effect of blunting some of the harsh consequences of some oppressive laws. Another important consideration that persuaded me to take a judicial appointment was the work that was being performed by the Legal Resources Centre (LRC), a national organization that was based on the Legal Defense Fund of the National Association for the Advancement of Colored People in the United States of America (the LDF). There was also Lawyers for Human Rights that provided thousands of pro bono counsel to black South Africans who were being brought to court under apartheid laws. Friends and colleagues who were involved in those organizations encouraged lawyers who were opposed to racial oppression to accept appointments to the bench. They preferred to have sympathetic judges rule on their cases. During my term on the High Court, I was able to deliver opinions that substantially ameliorated the effects of some apartheid laws.

In 1989, I was appointed to what was the highest court in South Africa, now called the Supreme Court of Appeal. In the following February, the then president, F.W. de Klerk announced that the system of apartheid was to end with the release of Nelson Mandela, who had spent 27 years in prison, together with other leaders of freedom organizations, and the unbanning of the freedom movements that had been proscribed since 1960.

During 1990, I headed two judicial commissions of inquiry. The most important of them looked into the shooting by the South African Police into a crowd of tens of thousands of peaceful protestors outside the township of Sebokeng, not far from Johannesburg. I found that the police had acted without any lawful justification and that the government was liable to pay damages to the families of those killed and to those who had been injured. The other commission of inquiry related to the death in police cells of the partner of Nelson Mandela's daughter Zindzi. I held that he had taken his own life and that the South African Police were not responsible for his unfortunate death.

The transition to democracy was a difficult one and, to the surprise of most South Africans, was accompanied by substantial violence. During the four years of the transition, more than 15,000 people (mostly black) were killed in political violence. It was Nelson Mandela's view that the violence had been precipitated by rogue elements in the security forces for whom the end of apartheid and the introduction of majority rule were quite unacceptable. He called this "the third force." This theory was hotly denied by de Klerk and his government. The violence continued and threatened to derail the negotiations designed to reach agreement on a democratic constitution for post-apartheid South Africa. Eventually, in October 1991, with the support of all the participants to the negotiations, and with much trepidation, I accepted the appointment to lead another judicial commission of inquiry – this one into the causes of the violence. Between October 1991 and April 1994 my commission conducted 40 investigations into situations of violence. Its activities and its findings achieved both national and international recognition, including support from the Security Council of the United Nations.

Immediately after South Africa's first democratic elections in April 1994 and the inauguration of Nelson Mandela as president, my wife, Noleen, and I enjoyed a well-earned vacation in Italy. On our return to Johannesburg, I was informed by the new minister of justice, Dullah Omar, that the Mandela Cabinet had decided that I should be invited to be one of the 11 justices of the new Constitutional Court that was to be established under our new constitution. This was obviously a wonderful offer, and I had no hesitation in accepting it. On the following day, out of the blue, I received a faxed message from Antonio Cassese, the first president of the International Criminal Tribunal for the Former Yugoslavia (ICTY). He inquired whether I would be prepared to accept nomination by the secretary general of the United Nations as chief prosecutor of the ICTY. This was an offer that held little appeal for me. In the first place, it would have made me unavailable for the Constitutional Court. Perhaps more important, it would require experience in areas that were quite outside my expertise. I had never been a prosecutor, and I knew next to nothing about the laws of armed conflict and very little about the former Yugoslavia and the war that had been raging there since 1991.

I was drafting a polite refusal to President Cassese when I received two calls – the first from Noleen. I informed her of the "amusing" offer from Cassese. Her immediate response was that it would be so wonderful to live in The Hague for a few years and get away from the police security that I had had to accept in the face of serious death threats that accompanied my commission activities and had continued into the democratic era. I agreed that it would be a wonderful experience but not at the cost of accepting a position for which I was wholly unqualified.

The second call followed almost immediately. It was from President Mandela. He told me that he understood that I had received the invitation from the United Nations. I confirmed that and informed him that I was in the process of refusing it. He asked me why I was not interested in the position, and I explained my reasons to him. He responded by saying that I should be in no hurry to send my refusal as he had just spoken with the secretary general of the United Nations, Boutros Boutros-Ghali, and had informed him that I would accept the position! With some shock, I inquired about my position on the Constitutional Court. He said that South Africa was greatly indebted to the United Nations for its efforts to end apartheid and that we should not turn down the first request to a South African to accept an important position in the United Nations. For that reason, he added, the Cabinet had decided earlier that day to amend our Constitution to make it possible for me to take time away from court without forfeiting my seat. He had informed the secretary general that I would be available not for the full four-year term provided in the Security Council Statute for the ICTY[2] but for two years, after which I was to take up my seat on the Constitutional Court. Well, I was hardly in position to decline the "request" from President Mandela, and I responded positively to President Cassese.

[2] ICTY Statute, Art. 16, ¶ 4 *The Prosecutor.*

I soon discovered the background to the strange invitation I had received from Cassese. The ICTY had been established by a resolution of the Security Council in May 1993. The Statute that was adopted by the Council provided that the Tribunal's 11 judges were to be elected by the General Assembly from a shortlist of 22 provided to it by the Council. This was a subtle way to involve the General Assembly in setting up the ICTY. The chief prosecutor was to be appointed by the Security Council. A nomination for the position was to be submitted to the Council by the secretary general. The Council agreed that the appointment would be made by consensus – that meant that each of the 15 members of the Council would, in effect, have a veto over the appointment.

In October 1993, the secretary general nominated and the Security Council unanimously appointed as the chief prosecutor Ramon Escovar Salom, the attorney general of Venezuela. It was not until January 1994 that he took up his position. The delay was caused by the fraud trial he was conducting against a former president of Venezuela. The former president was convicted, and Salom eventually arrived in The Hague. Just three days after his arrival, he resigned to take up the position of minister of internal affairs in Venezuela. Fortunately, during his extremely short tenure, he did appoint a deputy prosecutor. He was Graham Blewitt, an experienced Australian prosecutor who had recently headed the Nazi war crimes investigations that had been launched by the Australian Government.

There was then an unseemly political block on the Security Council process of appointing a successor to Salom. Between January and June of 1994, the Security Council vetoed no fewer than eight nominees put forward by the secretary general. Russia vetoed five, presumably because they came from NATO member nations. The United Kingdom vetoed a nominee from the United States on the basis that he was a Muslim and that that was not a good idea because of the high number of Muslim victims in Bosnia and Herzegovina. The United Kingdom felt that it would also be calculated to further cause resentment in Serbia, which had, in any event, rejected the ICTY. In retaliation, Pakistan vetoed a nominee from the United Kingdom as well as the then attorney general of India. By this time, the judges of the ICTY were beside themselves with frustration and even anger. They had already been in The Hague for some eight months, and there was no prosecutor in place and no work being prepared for them in the Office of the Prosecutor (OTP). The judges were discussing amongst themselves the likelihood that they might have to resign en masse if no chief prosecutor was appointed by the end of July 1994.

During June 1994, Cassese attended a human rights conference in Paris. He discussed the problems surrounding the appointment of a chief prosecutor with a senior judge of the Conseil d'Etat, Roger Arrera. Arrera advised Cassese that if a South African supported by Nelson Mandela was nominated by the secretary general, there was little if any likelihood that any member of the Security Council might vote against it. The idea appealed to Boutros-Ghali, and that was how an unqualified nominee came to be nominated as effectively the first chief prosecutor of the ICTY. My appointment was confirmed unanimously by the Security Council the following day.

I pause to draw attention to the way in which somewhat petty politicking by members of the Security Council delayed for many months the delivery of justice for the many thousands of victims of serious war crimes in the former Yugoslavia. Those victims and survivors must have felt acknowledged when the Security Council in May 1993 recognized their victimhood by establishing the first ever truly international war crimes court. It is difficult to imagine their feelings of frustration and resentment when the politics of the Security Council members caused an unseemly delay and even threatened the very existence of the war crimes tribunal.

Very soon I was introduced to the murky world of United Nations bureaucracy. On the day I informed Cassese that I was in a position to accept the nomination as the chief prosecutor, our telephone woke us at about 12.30 a.m. It was Deputy Legal Advisor of the United Nations Ralph Zacklin. After introducing himself, he asked if I was prepared to accept the position as prosecutor of the ICTY. I asked if he was aware of the time in South Africa and, that some hours before, I had indicated to President Cassese my willingness to accept the appointment. In response he said that he was aware of the time but that the Security Council was urgently to vote on the nomination and that President Cassese did not have authority to issue the invitation on behalf of the secretary general. He added that he did have such authority. That was my rather rude introduction to the world of the United Nations.

Soon after the Security Council made the appointment, it was agreed that I would take up the office of chief prosecutor on August 15, 1994. In the meantime, I was invited to visit New York to meet with the secretary general and to be briefed by members of the Office of Legal Affairs (OLA). I would then go on to The Hague and meet with Graham Blewitt and a skeleton staff of about 40 people who had been assembled during the months of delay by the Security Council. Twenty-three of them had been "donated" by the US government, and others came from Australia and a few other countries. Apart from Blewitt, the others had not been regularly appointed. Under the Statute for the ICTY, only the chief prosecutor could make appointments to the OTP.[3]

Zacklin had informed me that I should make my own travel arrangements, including business class air travel, from Johannesburg to New York and Amsterdam. He assured me that I would be reimbursed on my arrival in New York. I acted on that assurance. However, soon after arriving in New York I was informed that there were no funds available to reimburse my travel expenses and that hopefully I would be reimbursed a few days later in The Hague. This was the first inkling I had of the parlous financial position of the United Nations at that time. The United States was withholding its dues, which had caused a serious fiscal

[3] ICTY Statute, Art. 16, ¶ 5 *The Prosecutor.*

situation for the organization. Fortunately, by the time I arrived in The Hague, sufficient funds were available for the reimbursement of my travel expenses.

I was fortunate indeed to have Graham Blewitt as my deputy. Apart from his legal acumen and prosecutorial experience, he was an outstanding office administrator and was responsible for the structure that we adopted for the OTP. At our first meeting, he rather hesitantly showed me a diagrammatic sketch of what he had in mind. He was relieved when I told him that I was more than happy to rely on his expertise in an area in which I had none at all. I met with the skeleton staff in The Hague and was impressed with their professional experience and the friendship that they extended to me. They included experienced lawyers, investigators, and computer technicians.

My first day in office in The Hague was August 15, 1994. At that time the ICTY employed a public relations director who worked for all three organs of the Tribunal – the judges, the Office of the Prosecutor, and the registry. He was an experienced French journalist by the name of Christian Chartier. During my term as chief prosecutor, Chartier gave me much helpful advice with regard to the media. I knew from my South African experience the important role that the media plays with regard to justice and the courts. Without media attention, the work of criminal courts would have little meaning or importance for the public. I knew when I arrived in The Hague that because of the delay in the appointment of a chief prosecutor, the media, especially in Europe and North America, had written off the ICTY as a failure. It was said by some to be a "fig leaf" designed to hide the shame of Western nations, which had done little of consequence to stop the war that was the cause of so many victims in the former Yugoslavia. Some serious commentators even suggested that the Tribunal was intentionally designed to fail.

On that first day in office, Chartier informed me that he had committed me to an interview that same afternoon with Mike Wallace of the popular TV program *60 Minutes*. He was doing a segment he had already entitled "An Act of Hypocrisy." He also informed me that Wallace had a reputation of being a fearsome interviewer and that I should be prepared for a difficult experience. Much to my relief, Mike Wallace turned out to be both extremely well informed and friendly. My interview came at the end of the program, and I did my best to put a positive spin on my appointment and expressed my determination to ensure that investigations and prosecutions would be efficiently managed.

During my short visit to New York, I was told by Zacklin that I should be wary of a man called Cherif Bassiouni, a leading US/Egyptian expert on international criminal law from De Paul University in Chicago. Bassiouni had led a team of experts appointed by the Security Council to advise whether war crimes had been committed in the former Yugoslavia. It was his report that led to the resolution that established the ICTY. According to Zacklin, Bassiouni had had a stormy relationship with the Secretariat, had aspired to hold the position of chief prosecutor, and would do what he could to injure me and the Tribunal. He added that Bassiouni was media savvy and I should keep a careful lookout for him. I decided that if there was any truth in Zacklin's allegations, I should take steps to speak to and, if possible, meet with Bassiouni. Accordingly, I called him in Chicago and invited him to spend a few days in The Hague and take the small staff already assembled through the report he had furnished to the Security Council. He immediately and enthusiastically accepted the invitation. Not many days later, I met Cherif Bassiouni at Schiphol Airport. We immediately hit it off, and from that day to the present time, we have enjoyed a warm friendship. Bassiouni is one of the best lecturers I have ever heard, and the staff in my office benefited tremendously from his interaction with them. Contrary to the advice I received in New York, Bassiouni did all he could to support me and the work of the OTP.

There were immediate serious problems that I had to face during my first days and weeks in The Hague. An immediate problem was an arcane United Nations rule that was called "the 13 percent rule." It provided that any gift to the United Nations from any source had to be accompanied by a cash payment of 13 percent of the cost of the gift. That struck me as being rather ridiculous, but it was soon explained to me that there was a good rationale to back it up. When the United Nations accepts a gift, it almost invariably has to use funds to utilize it. Such an expenditure is not included in the UN budget, and if it was to be expended, the funds would perforce have to come from unallocated revenue. The source of funding for the UN comes from all of its member states. If wealthy nations were free to make gifts to the UN programs they fancied, the effect would be to force the world body to use funds outside of its budget. So in the case in point, the 23 gifted individuals sent by the United States to the OTP, would require funds to be spent in providing offices, secretarial support, and, in the case of investigators, the funding of travel to many parts of Europe and especially the former Yugoslavia.

In this case, the United States was adamant in refusing to pay what would come to some millions of dollars in addition to paying the substantial amounts involved in providing the 23 personnel. There was an impasse, and the decision taken by the United Nations Secretariat was that unless the United States paid the money, no further supporting funds would be made available to the persons sent by the United States to The Hague. The result of that would have been that most of the individuals would not have been able to continue with their work and would have had to return home. It took an urgent visit to UN Headquarters in New York to obtain a waiver from the Secretariat of the application of the 13 percent rule for that year. A similar decision was also made a year later. My successor, Louise Arbour, was not as fortunate in 1997, and a number of the US personnel had to leave the ICTY. Some were placed in regular UN slots.

On the advice of Graham Blewitt, we set up seven teams of investigators, each one having a number of investigators, one or two lawyers, and an information analyst.

The procedure for issuing indictments was time-consuming and thorough. However, it proved to be efficient and successful. A draft indictment was prepared by the investigation team. Accompanied by all the supporting documents and memoranda, the draft indictment was submitted to a meeting of all the lawyers in the OTP. They would debate the indictment and consider whether the charges were justified by the evidence, make suggestions for improvements, and sometimes conclude that the indictment was not justified at all or in part. At the conclusion of the discussion, the decision of the meeting, including a minority view if there was one, was conveyed to Graham Blewitt and me for a final decision. Neither Graham nor I participated in the aforementioned discussions. We wished to be able to consider the draft indictment with open minds. On a few occasions, we would agree, one way or another, with a minority view. Whatever decision we took on indictments, our full reasons would be furnished to the relevant members of the OTP. As I explained to our colleagues, we were running a transparent office but not necessarily a democratic one!

When we signed off on a draft indictment, it would be submitted, as required by the Statute, to one of the trial chamber judges for confirmation. That judge invariably called for discussion with senior members of our office and on occasion would request further information or might suggest an amendment to the indictment. When confirmed by the judge, the indictment would be issued. On some occasions, the judge might, at my request, keep the indictment sealed to avoid the defendant evading arrest. Graham Blewitt and I took pride in the fact that every one of the indictments we issued was confirmed by the judge to whom it was submitted.

Soon after I became chief prosecutor, I met with Madeleine Albright, the United States permanent representative to the United Nations. She was an enthusiastic supporter of the ICTY, and she appointed her then senior adviser, David Scheffer, to be my guide and adviser in Washington, DC. David and I struck up a warm friendship, and our careers have crisscrossed ever since. During important meetings with the US government during my term as chief prosecutor for both ad hoc tribunals, David was my guide and friend. I am indeed delighted that David is contributing a chapter to this volume.

An important development in the early months of the life of the ICTY was an agreement with the US government for the furnishing of confidential intelligence information to our office. Most of the negotiations leading to that agreement were conducted with the then legal advisor of the Central Intelligence Agency, Elizabeth Rindskopf.[4] The US government was prepared to supply my office with intelligence information on the condition that it would not be shared with any person outside the few members of the OTP who were cleared to receive it. This meant that it could not

[4] Elizabeth Rindskopf subsequently became a most successful dean of the McGeorge Law School in Sacramento, California. We became good friends and for some years I served on her international advisory board.

be disclosed to the defendant or even the judges. It meant, too, that the information could not be used against a defendant, but only as a source that could assist in leading to the discovery of other sources of information. Finally, it also meant that any exculpatory evidence that might be disclosed in confidence would have to be shared, with the consent of the supplier of the information, with the defendant.

The immediate problem presented by this approach was that keeping the information confidential would have been inconsistent with the obligation of the prosecutor, under the rules of the Tribunal, to share all relevant information with the defendant upon his or her first appearance before the court. This, in turn, at my request, led to a rule change. Unlike the International Criminal Court (ICC), rules of procedure were left by the ICTY Statute to the judges to make and thus to amend.[5] This meant that rules could be changed without delay by a plenary session of the judges. The rule change I requested led to Rule 70(B).[6] It provided that if the prosecutor is in possession of information that has been provided to the prosecutor on a confidential basis and which has been used solely for the purpose of generating new evidence, that initial information and its origin may not be disclosed by the prosecutor without the consent of the person or entity providing the initial information. Similar rules were made for the International Criminal Tribunal for Rwanda (ICTR) and for the ICC. It has enabled international prosecutors to obtain crucial evidence. This included intercepted telephone conversations between President Slobodan Milošević and Radovan Karadžić that was used in the trials against each of them.

Soon after my arrival in The Hague, I was informed by a senior UN official in New York that, during the following November, I should expect to appear before the Advisory Committee on Administrative and Budgetary Questions (ACABQ). This is a subsidiary organ of the General Assembly. It is an expert committee and consists of 16 members elected by the General Assembly for a period of three years, on the basis of a broad geographical representation. Members serve in a personal capacity and not as representatives of member states. The Committee examines in detail all budgets submitted to the Secretariat and reports on them to the General Assembly. It is an exception for the General Assembly to approve line items that are rejected by the ACABQ. I was informed that the hearing before the Committee

5 ICTY Statute, Art. 15 *Rules of procedure and evidence* ("The judges of the International Tribunal shall adopt rules of procedure and evidence for the conduct of the pre-trial phase of the proceedings, trials and appeals, the admission of evidence, the protection of victims and witnesses and other appropriate matters.").

6 ICTY Rules of Procedure and Evidence, Rule 70(B) *Matters not Subject to Disclosure* ("If the Prosecutor is in possession of information which has been provided to the Prosecutor on a confidential basis and which has been used solely for the purpose of generating new evidence, that initial information and its origin shall not be disclosed by the Prosecutor without the consent of the person or entity providing the initial information and shall in any event not be given in evidence without prior disclosure to the accused.").

would be a nightmare and that I had better be well prepared to present the budget of the OTP. The acting registrar of the ICTY, Theo van Boven, would be defending the budget of the registry and the judges' chambers. I was left under no doubt that I should not expect a successful result from the ACABQ if no indictment were issued prior to the November meeting.

By the end of October 1994, Graham Blewitt and I were of the firm view that there was sufficient evidence to support only one indictment, that against Dragan Nikolić. He was a 46-year-old Bosnian Serb who was indicted by the ICTY on November 4, 1994.[7] He wasn't apprehended until April 2000. By the time he appeared before the trial chamber, he faced some 80 counts of crimes against humanity and war crimes. Nikolić was a camp commander in the Bosnian Serb–controlled town of Vlasenica.

Not without justification, in the context of the war crimes committed in the former Yugoslavia, Nikolić was regarded by the media as "a small fish." There was tremendous pressure on me to indict some of the leaders. Nikolić was perhaps not the most appropriate person to be the first indicted by the first ever truly international criminal court. However, the advice I had received proved to be correct and made a substantial difference to the attitude of the ACABQ when I appeared before it soon after the issuance of the indictment. Indeed, the members of the ACABQ hardly referred to the line items in our budget and spent most of the two-day meeting discussing the philosophy of international criminal justice and the role of the ICTY in the context of the war that was then still raging in the former Yugoslavia. In the end, we received approval for the whole of the budget and that was of cardinal importance for the progress of our work.

A huge frustration during my term of office was the failure to obtain the arrest of the defendants we indicted. I was quite shocked that the UN troops in Bosnia were not prepared to arrest indicted war criminals. The justification for their supine attitude was that arrests were the work of the police and not the army. The real reason, as was made clear to me at meetings in Washington, DC, was that military leaders did not wish to provoke retaliation from Serb supporters of their popular nationalistic leaders. This was exacerbated after the indictment during July 1995 of both Karadžić and his army chief, Ratko Mladić.[8] Although their whereabouts were known, the UN military remained unpersuaded that they should hunt them down and arrest them. This delayed their eventual trials by some 13 years.

The first arrest for the ICTY occurred in unusual circumstances. Many war crimes were known to have been committed in the Prijedor region of northern Bosnia. Some of them were investigated by the Bassiouni commission and were thus on the radar screen of our investigators in The Hague. Early in 1994, I

7 *Prosecutor v. Dragan Nikolić*, Case No. IT–94–2–I, Indictment (Int'l Crim. Trib. for the Former Yugoslavia Nov. 4, 1994), available at www.icty.org/x/cases/dragan_nikolic/ind/en/nik-ii941104e.pdf.

8 *Prosecutor v. Radovan Karadžić and Ratko Mladić*, Case No. IT–95–5–I, Indictment (Int'l Crim. Trib. for the Former Yugoslavia July 24, 1995), available at www.icty.org/x/cases/karadzic/ind/en/kar-ii950724e.pdf.

learnt that German prosecutors had indicted Duško Tadić on 12 counts of crimes against humanity, 12 counts of grave breaches of the Geneva Conventions, and 10 counts of violations of the customs of war. He had escaped to Germany using a fictitious identity but was recognized by some of his victims. With not a single defendant then in our holding cells in The Hague, it became more than tempting to obtain an order compelling Germany to defer the prosecution of Tadić to the ICTY. Under the Security Council Statute, the ICTY had primacy over domestic courts. The problem that soon emerged was that Germany had no domestic law that enabled its courts to order the transfer of the prosecution of Tadić to the ICTY. After a number of meetings with German Foreign Minister Klaus Kinkel, the German Parliament – with commendable speed – promulgated new legislation that authorized non-German citizens present in Germany to be transferred to the ICTY in The Hague.

The Tadić trial was the first ever before a truly international criminal tribunal.[9] With hindsight, it was an advantage having a middle-level defendant as the first to face trial in the ICTY. Without the media attention that a Milosević or Karadžić would have garnered, the judges and the prosecutors cut their teeth dealing with Tadić.

The first argument raised by Tadić was directed at the legality of the Security Council establishing a criminal court. Nowhere in the UN Charter was such a power to be found. Could the power be implied under the provisions of Chapter VII of the Charter? The primary question was whether the judges could go behind their oaths and find that the very establishment of the Tribunal did not fall within the competence of the Security Council. The trial chamber held that it did not have the competence to question the Tribunal's legality.

In an *obiter dictum*, the trial chamber went on to find that the Council did indeed have the power to establish a criminal tribunal under the powers conferred upon it by the provisions of Chapter VII.[10] It had already determined that the situation in the former Yugoslavia posed a threat to international peace and security. That determination triggered the further provisions that allowed the Security Council to pass binding resolutions on all UN member states that were designed to remove the threat. Those powers included "complete or partial interruption of economic relations and of rail, sea, air, postal, telegraphic, radio, and other means of communication, and the

9 The Nuremberg trial was before a multinational tribunal rather than one of an international character.

10 *Prosecutor v. Tadić*, Case No. 94–1–T, Opinion and Judgement, ¶ 2 (Int'l Crim. Trib. for the Former Yugoslavia May 7, 1997), available at www.icty.org/x/cases/tadic/tjug/en/tad-tsj70507JT2-e.pdf; ("The Security Council, having found that the widespread violations of international humanitarian law occurring within the territory of the former Yugoslavia, including the practice of 'ethnic cleansing,' constituted a threat to international peace and security, exercised its powers under Chapter VII of the Charter of the United Nations to establish the International Tribunal, determining that the creation of such a tribunal would contribute to the restoration and maintenance of peace.").

severance of diplomatic relations."[11] If those measures proved to be inappropriate or inadequate, the Council was empowered "to take such action by air, sea, or land forces as may be necessary to maintain or restore international peace and security." The reasoning was to the effect that if military force could be used to remove the threat to international peace and security, there was no reason why an international court could not be established if it was calculated to end the threat.

On appeal, the appeals chamber held that it did indeed have the jurisdiction to rule on the legality of the Security Council resolution establishing the tribunal and, in effect, the alternative finding by the trial chamber was followed. There was thus, at the outset of the jurisprudence of the ICTY, a link made between peace and justice.

Other novel questions of law arose in the Tadić trial. By a majority of 3–2, the appeals chamber held that if witness protection demanded it, and if not inconsistent with the fair trial rights of the defendant, witnesses could remain anonymous and their identity withheld not only from the public but also from the defendant. Another complex issue was whether the grave breaches of the Geneva Convention ceased to be applicable immediately if a situation of international armed conflict ended and was replaced by a noninternational armed conflict. By a majority of 4–1, the appeals chamber held that indeed it did and that the prosecutor had to establish that, on the date of each alleged violation of the law, the conflict was of an international or noninternational character. The practical consequence was that prosecutors ceased relying on the grave breach provisions. This was especially so in the light of the further holding by the appeals chamber to the effect that under customary international law, the war crimes that were cognizable with respect to international armed conflicts applied also to noninternational armed conflict.

I decided that argument on these issues before the appeals chamber should be made by me as chief prosecutor. It was a daunting prospect. In order to be properly and appropriately prepared I invited Theodor Meron, a professor of international law at New York University,[12] to spend time with me in The Hague. He graciously and generously agreed to do so, and I benefited much from his learning and experience. Together with other senior lawyers in my office, he presided over the "murder board" that grilled me for hours on end in preparation for my appearance before the judges. Indeed, that experience was far less comfortable and more challenging than the real thing!

The Rwandan genocide was perpetrated between April and June 1994. At that time, Rwanda held a nonpermanent seat on the Security Council. The slaughter came to

[11] *Prosecutor v. Tadić*, Case No. 94-1-T, Opinion and Judgement (Int'l Crim. Trib. for the Former Yugoslavia May 7, 1997), available at http://www.icty.org/x/cases/tadic/tjug/en/tad-tsj70507JT2-e.pdf.

[12] Some years later, Theodor Meron became a judge of the ICTY and for two terms served as its President. He is presently the President of the Mechanism for the Criminal Tribunals set up by the Security Council to carry on the work of the ICTY and ICTR after their closure.

an end when the army of the Rwanda Patriotic Front, led by Paul Kagame (who would later become president of Rwanda) put the national army and the militias supporting it to flight. The overwhelming majority of the justice system of Rwanda (its judges and prosecutors) were murdered in the genocide. The new government of Rwanda (under President Pasteur Bizimungu and Deputy President Kagame) formally requested the Security Council to establish an international criminal tribunal for Rwanda. It turned out that what the Rwandan leaders had in mind was a court with an international character sitting in Rwanda and, in effect, replacing the domestic criminal court system that had been destroyed in the genocide. They certainly did not wish to have the equivalent of the ICTY sitting hundreds of miles from the site of the crimes. They also anticipated that the court would have the power to sentence the worst perpetrators to death.

The Security Council could hardly refuse the request for another international criminal tribunal – especially one that came from an African state suffering from the worst genocide since World War II. It had only recently agreed to a European request for such a tribunal. A draft Statute was prepared, and it provided for the Rwanda tribunal to have its seat in Arusha, in neighboring Tanzania. The OTP would be situated in Kigali – after all the great majority of witnesses were in Rwanda. The temporal jurisdiction was to be the calendar year of 1994, and there would be no death sentence. Life imprisonment would be the harshest sentence. The two UN tribunals were to share a common chief prosecutor.

Those terms were quite unacceptable to the government of Rwanda. It was adamant that the tribunal was to sit in Rwanda, have the death sentence, have a longer temporal jurisdiction, and have its own chief prosecutor. The Security Council was not prepared to change those provisions. It was for good reason the tribunal could not be situated in Rwanda – it would have been impossible to guarantee the security of the judges, let alone defense witnesses and counsel. For too many members of the UN, the death sentence was quite unacceptable. The reason for the common prosecutor was to ensure that there were similar practices and procedures in both tribunals. In the face of the Security Council insisting on its terms, Rwanda withdrew its request for the tribunal. However, the Security Council was unprepared to back off and decided that Rwanda would get the ICTR[13] whether it liked it or not. The resolution establishing the ICTR was tabled in the Security Council. Thirteen members voted in favor, one (China) abstained, and one (Rwanda) voted against. So literally overnight, on November 8, 2004, I found myself as the only official appointed to the ICTR. It was my invidious task to set up the OTP in Kigali, the capital of the traumatized country that did not want us.

I was immediately of the view that I should travel to Kigali as soon as possible to meet with Rwandan leaders and to seek their assistance in setting up the OTP. Without that acceptance and assistance, it would just not work. The OLA had been

[13] S.C. Res. 955 (Nov. 8, 1994).

charged by the Security Council with taking all steps to set up the ICTR. I called the office of the UN legal counsel, Hans Corell, only to be informed that he was away from New York and I should speak to his deputy, Ralph Zacklin. I explained to Zacklin why I thought it imperative to visit Rwanda without any delay. He responded that the OLA should send a mission to Kigali before a visit from me would be appropriate. I inquired as to when such a mission would go to Rwanda. He said he did not know and would give it his attention. I called again a few days later to be informed that a mission from OLA would not be going to Rwanda before the following year, 1995. I said that I could not wait that long and an absence could only have a negative effect on the Rwandan leaders. His response was unhelpful, and I said I intended to travel to Kigali the following week. He said that no funds had yet been allocated for the ICTR, and there were thus no funds for a visit by me to Kigali. I asked whether I could raise the funds. His curt response was that I could do as I wished.

Later that week I had a meeting with Swiss Foreign Minister Flavio Cotti. The meeting concerned the ICTY, of which Switzerland was a staunch supporter. After we had discussed issues concerning the ICTY, Minister Cotti inquired about the ICTR. I told him of my problems with OLA. He immediately instructed his assistant to pay 100,000 Swiss francs to the trust fund for the ICTR, which had been established by the secretary general (as he had also for the ICTY). He said that I now had funds for my visit, and he agreed with me that I should make that visit as soon as possible.

Within days, together with two senior member of my office, I was in Kigali. The visit was successful, with the government of Rwanda pledging support for the OTP. The most difficult problem was staffing such an office. It was difficult enough to recruit appropriate experts to The Hague, a comfortable and safe environment in the heart of Europe. Many ICTY staff members were accompanied by their families. Good housing was plentiful and educational facilities were excellent. The United Nations had declared Rwanda to be a "hardship post." This meant that family members were not allowed to join staff members in the country. Security concerns dictated that members of staff had to live in one of two not very pleasant hotels.

A complicating factor was that Rwanda was not prepared to have French or Senegalese nationals in Rwanda, as they suspected them of having been in cahoots with the previous government. Belgium would not allow its nationals to work in Rwanda. The pool of French-speaking experts was effectively narrowed to Francophone Canada. The United Nations decided that it was not safe for me to stay in either of the hotels that were operating, and I was housed at UN army barracks. This was very uncomfortable and not helped by the troops beginning their morning exercises outside my window at about 5:30 a.m.

I became friendly with the special representative of the secretary general, Ambassador Shaharyar Khan of Pakistan, who was a consummate diplomat without whom my difficult task would have been all the more difficult. During the last few of my 14 visits to Kigali, I was the houseguest of Ambassador Khan, and that made those visits far more congenial and enjoyable.

On my return to The Hague after my first visit to Kigali, I found a curt note from Zacklin informing me that it was not appropriate for a senior officer of the United Nations to raise funds from a member state. I took some pleasure in responding to the effect that Switzerland was not a member state![14]

As mentioned earlier, in 1994 and 1995, the financial position of the United Nations was extremely difficult. I had great difficulty in obtaining office equipment and supplies for the Rwanda OTP. For some months, the skeleton staff being assembled in Kigali used Coca-Cola boxes as desks and chairs. Eventually, Kofi Annan, who was then head of peacekeeping at the United Nations, found much of what we required unused in a UN warehouse in Brindisi on the eastern coast of Italy. The United States was helpful in arranging for a transport flight to bring the equipment from Italy to Rwanda.

I appointed Al Breau, a leading French-Canadian police officer, as head of investigations in Kigali. After a few weeks, he informed me that if he had 18 months before any indictments were issued, he could assure me of sufficient evidence to indict all the senior leaders responsible for the genocide. I informed him that if we did not issue indictments within about eight weeks, we would not be operating at all and that our funding would cease. To his credit, with a small and dedicated staff, the investigations section was able to support the early indictments that were issued.

In the early weeks of my term of office in each of the tribunals, I spent considerable time traveling to capitals of relevant European and African countries to which it was clear we would be sending our investigators. I decided that it was not appropriate for an international prosecutor's office to do so without the explicit and implicit consent of the state concerned. With few exceptions, the attitude of governments was that we were welcome to send our investigators and that any required assistance would be forthcoming. Those visits and making those requests enabled me to meet the relevant ministers of foreign affairs and justice. Conducting face-to-face meetings was conducive to obtaining more important assistance when we required it.

The other reason for spending time out of The Hague was the difficult and time-consuming negotiations on the agreement on confidential intelligence information with the US government. Those meetings were held both in The Hague and in Washington, DC.

After some months in office, I realized the importance of a chief prosecutor having complete independence. I was requested to meet with the secretary general in New York. He informed me that he had requested and received from the registrar's office in The Hague the details of my travels from the time I had arrived

[14] Switzerland joined the UN as a member in 2002.

in August 1994. He informed me that I was spending too much time outside my office and that he had received complaints from some permanent representatives that I was spending too much time in Washington, DC, and that there was suspicion that I was receiving instructions from the US government. With some annoyance, I explained the reasons for my travels and in no uncertain terms informed Boutros-Ghali that I proposed to continue to do my work as I thought fit. I also expressed my annoyance that he had obtained details of my travel, as it were, behind my back. I said that in the future if he required that kind of information, he had only to request it from me. I reminded him that the ICTY Statute guaranteed my independence and provided that I was not to accept any orders from any government or any other source and that, I added, presumably included the secretary general. It was not a friendly meeting.

In July 1995, I issued the first of two indictments against Radovan Karadžić, the self-proclaimed president of Republika Srpska, and Ratko Mladić, his army commander.[15] They were charged with crimes against humanity and war crimes. This indictment brought with it tremendous media attention. Again, I was summoned by Boutros-Ghali. His complaint was that I had thought fit to indict Karadžić and Mladić during the continuance of the war in Bosnia and at a time when efforts to mediate peace were under way. He suggested that I should have consulted him before taking that step. I again reminded him of my independence, to which he said he had difficulty with dealing with a member of the UN staff who was not answerable to him.

Boutros-Ghali had clearly touched on the delicate issue of whether justice could interfere with or retard peace. My attitude was that the Security Council had given me a clear mandate to issue indictments against war criminals when sufficient evidence justified such a course. I was not required nor prepared to wait for an indefinite period before for doing so simply because peace negotiations might be in progress. I was not privy to such negotiations and had no idea of their prospects. Again, the secretary general did not take kindly to my attitude. Of course, neither of us knew or could have known that the indictment against Karadžić facilitated the ending of the Balkan War at the Dayton meeting in November 1995. As was made clear by Bosnian President Alija Izetbegović, after the event, there was no way he would have attended the Dayton meeting if Karadžić had been present. It was only a few months after the massacres had taken place in Srebrenica. Karadžić was unable to attend the meeting only because of the indictment and his inevitable arrest by the United States if he had sought to travel to Dayton. So, in the result, the indictment facilitated rather than retarded the peace.

Soon after this incident, there was a third issue with Boutros-Ghali. I had been invited with my wife and another member of the OTP, Gavin Ruxton, and his wife, to attend a special seminar to be held in the Nuremberg courtroom to mark the

[15] *Prosecutor v. Radovan Karadžić and Ratko Mladić, supra* note 8.

fiftieth anniversary of the start of the Nuremberg trial. I was to make one of the opening presentations. A few days before we were to depart for Nuremberg, I received a call from the secretary general's chief of staff, Jean-Claude Aimé. He said that the secretary general understood that I was traveling on the weekend to Nuremberg. I confirmed that. He said he had a message from the secretary general to the effect that I may not make the trip. I was a little surprised and asked for the reason. He said he had no idea, but that was the message. I asked to speak to Boutros-Ghali. Aimé informed me that he was traveling and was expected back some hours later. I asked him to arrange for the secretary general to call me back that evening. When Boutros-Ghali did make contact, I asked him for the reason for the strange message. He explained that the United Nations was technically insolvent, and he had no option but to cancel travel by all UN officials. I asked whether he was aware that the City of Nuremberg was paying all our expenses. He said he was not aware, and that that was different. He wished me a good trip to Nuremberg! I must confess to being amazed at this level of micromanagement of the United Nations by the secretary general. There was no way that I would have let down my Nuremberg hosts, especially on three days' notice. The fact that I had my seat on the South African Constitutional Court being kept warm for me gave me complete independence. This was important for both my actual and perceived independence as chief prosecutor. I might add that the independence of prosecutors was always close to the heart of the UN legal Counsel, Under-Secretary General Hans Corell. His own background as a Swedish judge no doubt informed his understanding of the importance of that independence.

It was difficult to run both OTPs, and especially so with regard to Rwanda, when my main office was in The Hague. I sympathized with the growing claims made by the government of Rwanda to have a chief prosecutor appointed for the ICTR. That did not happen until September 2003, when Hassan Bubacar Jallow replaced Carla del Ponte. What made it more complicated was the difficulty of flying between Kigali and Arusha, where the judges held their plenary sessions. The distance between the two cities is under 500 miles. However, there were no flights between them, and I usually had to fly via Amsterdam or Brussels – many thousands of miles. Late in 1995, the Norwegian government, as a gift to the ICTR, placed a charter aircraft at the disposal of the OTP.

One of the most important negotiations I conducted for the ICTR was with the government of Cameroon. They had arrested Théoneste Bagosora, who was considered to be the mastermind behind the genocide. He was indicted by the ICTR, and an arrest warrant was issued against him.[16] He was also wanted by the government of Rwanda so that he could be put on trial in Kigali. There were important reasons not to defer to the jurisdiction of Rwanda. In the first place, the ICTR had

16 *See Prosecutor v. Theoneste Bagosora*, Case No. ICTR–96–7–I, Amended Indictment (Int'l Crim. Trib. for Rwanda Aug. 12, 1999), http://unictr.unmict.org/sites/unictr.org/files/case-documents/ictr-98-41/indictments/en/990812.pdf.

primacy under the ICTR Statute, and Bagosora was considered to be the leading perpetrator. Secondly, the courts of Rwanda were hardly operating, and there was no prospect of Bagosora receiving a fair trial in Kigali. I had little difficulty in persuading the attorney general of Cameroon that his government was under an international law obligation to give preference to the claim for the transfer of Bagosora to the ICTR. This led to a very difficult meeting with the whole cabinet in Kigali. With great reluctance, the government of Rwanda accepted the fact that I was not prepared to back off in insisting on Bagosora be transferred by Cameroon to Arusha for trial before the ICTR. After substantial delays, Bagosora was transferred to Arusha. At the end of a long trial, he was convicted of crimes including genocide. He was held responsible for the murder of the then prime minister of Rwanda and the 10 Belgian soldiers who were acting as her security guards. The trial chamber sentenced Bagosora to life imprisonment. The appeals chamber reduced the sentence to one of imprisonment for 35 years.

The ICTR was regarded by some media critics as being the "poor relation" of the ICTY. That is not correct. It is true that, at the start of the ICTR, it shared not only the chief prosecutor but also the appeals chamber of the ICTY. There were thus only six trial judges appointed to the ICTR and no appeals chamber judges. After complaints were received from many quarters, including the Rwandan government and the ICTR judges, the appeals chamber was reconstituted to include judges from both tribunals. The financial position of the ICTR was no different from that of the ICTY. There were trust funds established by the secretary general for both tribunals. They received voluntary contributions from member states. The governments of the Netherlands and the United States were particularly generous in giving financial support to the ICTR. At the suggestion of Dutch Minister Jan Pronk and United States Assistant Secretary of State for Human Rights John Shattuck, a successful international fundraising meeting was convened in Kigali during 1995. Around six million dollars were raised at that event.

The early years establishing the ICTY and ICTR laid the foundation for the successes that followed. The ICTR has already closed down, and its jurisdiction has been taken over by the Mechanism for International Criminal Tribunals (MICT), established for that purpose by the Security Council.[17] During its period of operation between 1995 and 2015, the ICTR indicted a total of 95 individuals. Three of them remain at large as fugitives, and if captured they will be tried before the MICT. The ICTR convicted 61 individuals, 37 of whom are currently serving sentences, 20 of whom have completed their sentences, and 4 of whom died while serving their sentences. The Tribunal acquitted 14 defendants and transferred the cases against 10 defendants to national jurisdictions.

With regard to the ICTY, the last trial, that against Ratko Mladić, recently concluded with a guilty verdict. And there is one appeal, that of *Prosecutor v.*

[17] S.C. Res. 1966, ¶ 1 (Dec. 22, 2010) (establishing the Mechanism for International Criminal Tribunals).

Perlić and Others, involving six convicted persons. During its period of operation between 1994 and the present, 161 persons were indicted, proceedings for 154 defendants were concluded, and 83 were sentenced to various terms of imprisonment. The trials of 17 of those arrested were transferred to other courts. There are no fugitives. In other words, all of the arrest warrants issued by the ICTY were executed.

In 1996, when I left the ICTY and ICTR I could not remotely have anticipated the successes that would be achieved by each of the tribunals. There were also the successes of the Special Court for Sierra Leone that are described in Chapter 5 of this volume, which is written by its first chief prosecutor, David Crane. There can be no doubt that the successes of these three criminal tribunals provided the impetus for the diplomatic conference that was called in June 1998 at which the Rome Statute for the ICC was fashioned. Those successes also played a substantial role in the decision by 124 nations to ratify the Rome Statute and become members of the ICC's Assembly of States Parties.

The value of the tribunals to the countries of the former Yugoslavia and Rwanda has been the topic of books and countless media reports, interviews, and academic articles. They certainly brought modern international criminal justice to public attention in many countries around the world. They assisted many of the victims, and survivors find solace and receive important public acknowledgement of their sufferings. They have helped in the recording of a fuller and more accurate history of the relevant events than would have been possible without them. Their retributive role was clearly established. Whether they act as a deterrent and whether they might reduce the number of serious war crimes in the future are more difficult questions and will always remain an elusive topic.

5

The Special Court for Sierra Leone

David M. Crane

I sat at my desk surveying my office. It was clean and empty. It was June 30, 2005. I was leaving for home after three years in West Africa. It was a time of great emotion as I reflected back on those years. This was my last day as chief prosecutor for the world's first hybrid international war crimes tribunal called the Special Court for Sierra Leone.[1] It had been an amazing and historic effort on the part of my team of prosecutors, investigators, paralegals, administrative staff, and even my close protection officers who kept me safe. The entire week had been one of recognition and celebration. Just yesterday I had been made an honorary paramount chief by the Civil Societies of Sierra Leone, replete with robes and other accoutrements.

I was torn on whether I should leave. It was time to go, my work had been done, and the trials of all of the heads of the warring factions in the horror that was the civil war in Sierra Leone were moving forward and largely completed. My prosecution plan was working with an excellent team of trial counsel presenting our cases. I had been away from home too long. My family needed me. Yet my heart was with my client . . . the people of Sierra Leone.

There was a gentle knock on my door and my dear friend and deputy chief prosecutor, Desmond de Silva, came in. "It's time David," he said softly. Desmond was succeeding me as chief prosecutor.

I got up and followed him out the door, glancing back one more time. My close protection security detail closed in around me as I headed for my car to be taken to the heliport at United Nations headquarters on Lumley Beach. It was raining softly. The air was heavy and close, with the all too familiar smells of smoke, diesel fuel, and garbage. It clung to me, enveloped me almost as if to say goodbye. I would not miss the feeling nor the stench.

As I looked around, there in front of me was a guard of honor drawn up outside my office gates. Made up of the Court's security force, they stood at attention. Desmond addressed them. I did too, and I passed by them in review with tears in my eyes. The

[1] S.C. Res. 1315, ¶ 1 (Aug. 14, 2000) (recommending the creation of the Special Court for Sierra Leone).

close protection security detail officer opened my car door, and I turned to Desmond to shake his hand. "Thank you, for this" is all I could say. Desmond stood to attention and saluted me. As a fellow military veteran, I returned that salute and got in the car to start my long journey home. As the caravan turned right on Jomo Kenyatta Road, I watched the Special Court's compound fade into the mist. My job done, I settled back into my seat.

The old Russian MI-8 helicopter was already cranking up when I arrived at the heliport. The blades of the aircraft cut the damp air, stirring up the garbage that lined the field. My chief of protection, Berold Hinds, helped me carry my bags to the helicopter, and then we climbed up and strapped in. As we lifted off and turned toward Lungi Field, the international airport across the bay, I got one more glimpse of the Court complex nestled at the foot of Leicester Peak. Shuddering, the helicopter blades bit into the air, and we headed to the airport. I recall saying a prayer to get me safely to the airport, as a couple of these helicopters over the years had simply stopped working in mid-air and plunged into the bay. I was terrified. To have come all this way, facing all the challenges, and to have this Russian helicopter drop me into the bay off Freetown would be so ironic. I have never been more relieved than when those wheels settled onto the tarmac at the airport.

I was escorted to customs and bag check before I was allowed to board the plane to Brussels and then on to Dulles International Airport near my home in Washington, DC. As I walked toward the plane, some of the Sierra Leonean workers on the field began to clap, and as I got to the stairs to get on my flight, everyone on the field was clapping. I turned to Berold, my constant companion in Sierra Leone, and shook his hand, thanking him for keeping me safe. I then looked around, acknowledged the applause, and went up the step into the cool air-conditioned space of the plane. Settling down in my business class seat, I was handed a cold glass of Champagne. As the plane began to taxi, I reflected on my time in West Africa and how I became a chief prosecutor of an international war crimes tribunal. This is the story of that beginning.

As in the cases of most of my fellow chief prosecutors, I neither sought nor wanted the position I would eventually be offered. I had a successful career in the Senior Executive Service of the US federal government. My wife, Judi, and I both had been in national security positions for decades. We had just settled into our newly built home in Alexandria, Virginia, a suburb of Washington, DC. Our jobs were interesting and exciting, and we fully expected to remain in the area, retiring to North Carolina someday. Then the phone rang at home as we were about to have dinner. I picked up the phone, a bit irritated.

It was early evening August 27, 2001. A member of the Bush administration was on the line asking me if I would be interested in being the nominee by the United States for the position of chief prosecutor of a new war crimes tribunal in West Africa. Startled, I questioned the caller about the position, how serious the United States was with this nomination. (The United States had just "unsigned" the Rome Statute for the International Criminal Court, angering the entire world.) I reluctantly said I might be interested. He thanked me and hung up.

Judi asked me who that was, and I told her as we set the table for dinner. She laughed and said, "You won't get that." I told her that I agreed, laughing. Judi also chuckled, saying "And besides, you are a Democrat." I nodded in agreement. I popped the cork of the Chianti we were having with our Italian dinner and pushed the phone call from my mind. I was a busy man with a great deal on my plate. I oversaw 80 percent of the US Intelligence Community on behalf of the secretary of defense. I had other things to do.

Late in September the War Crimes Office of the State Department called me at my office near the Pentagon and asked me to send my résumé over to them, as they were putting together the nomination package for the chief prosecutor position for what was now being called the Special Court for Sierra Leone. Again, I was surprised and still not that interested. It had been just a few weeks after the 9/11 attacks, the United States was at war, and both Judi and I were extremely busy. I glibly said "Sure," emailed my résumé over to them, and promptly forgot about it. I would hear nothing for two months.

In mid-November 2001, Hans Corell, former under-secretary general of the United Nations, called me and asked me to come to New York to sit down and talk about the position I had been nominated for by the United States. We settled on a date in early December. I flew up on a Sunday night for the Monday morning interview. I walked across the street to the United Nations building from the hotel and headed up to Hans' office on the thirty-fourth floor. He met me in the outer office and introduced me to a few people, including his deputy, Ralph Zacklin. We proceeded into his office, where we chatted for about an hour in an informal interview. Hans was polite and Ralph eyed me skeptically. He was openly hostile. I left the interview angry. It was all quite unsettling. I caught an early flight back to Washington. I told Judi that I was losing what interest I had in the position. She agreed and we moved on with our lives.

During the winter months of 2002, I researched the facts surrounding the 10-year civil war in Sierra Leone and began to learn the players in the process of the creation of the Special Court. I had conversations with many of them, seeking their perspectives and views coming away with the clear feeling that I was not their nominee of choice. I was an American, and this was a strike against me. I would travel back to New York twice more for interviews and discussions without having a sense of where I stood in the selection process.

In early April, the US State Department point of contact called me and told me that the secretary general would most likely pick Ken Fleming, an Australian who was already working with the study group that had gone to Sierra Leone in January to negotiate a treaty establishing this new international court. I was never asked to join that effort, so I was not surprised when they told me it would most likely be Ken

Fleming. I was disappointed but thanked the State Department representative. I took my file on Sierra Leone, put it in one of my filing cabinets, and called Judi to tell her I was not going to be selected. She seemed relieved. I was glad it was over. It had been a long and frustrating six months.

On Friday, April 19, 2002, I drove into work, dropping off Judi at her office and going on to mine a few miles away. It was a clear and bright day, the cherry trees around the tidal basin near the Jefferson Memorial were still pink. I could see them from my window. The gleaming marble of the US capitol building was a perfect backdrop to the trees. My morning meetings complete, I had settled back at my desk to take care of my inbox when I received a phone call from the Office of the Secretary of Defense asking me whether I had seen the internet news. I said I had not. The caller stated that Reuters was reporting that an American had been chosen as the chief prosecutor of the West African court set up to prosecute individuals for war crimes and crimes against humanity. He asked me whether that was me. I told him that I wasn't sure. Surprised and a bit puzzled, I thanked him and hung up. I sat back, my heart pounding. How could this be? Was it me or some other nominee from the United States?

Within two minutes, my secretary, Karen Washburn, told me that someone named Hans Corell was on the line and wanted to speak with me. She forwarded the call to me. "David, this is Hans Corell. Kofi Annan has selected you to be the prosecutor of the Special Court for Sierra Leone. I will be going down to announce this at a press conference in the next few minutes. I do hope you will accept." Stunned, I mumbled yes. He thanked me and hung up. I picked up the phone and called the War Crimes Office at the State Department. They had not heard and, frankly, were as stunned as I was. They told me they would inform Secretary of State Colin Powell. So there it was. I was the new chief prosecutor of the Special Court for Sierra Leone. I called Judi to tell her. She was surprised and said we will chat about it all over the weekend. My world, and hers, had just changed forever.

The next few months were a blur of activity, with briefings, meetings, lunches, discussion groups while I planned how I was going to implement my prosecution strategy, which I had worked on over the winter months of 2002. I dusted it off in earnest and began working the plan. Additionally, I had to assemble an advance team to deploy early to Sierra Leone to lay the groundwork logistically for the setup of the Office of the Prosecutor (OTP).

I also had to begin the process of retiring from the federal government after almost 30 years of service. I was taking a huge risk. I was ending a very successful career on the chance that I might be able to succeed in helping seek justice for the people of Sierra Leone. It was a risk I chose to take, but with some trepidation. I was confident that I could put together a viable plan with a workable organization. I had been doing this most of my career. I had a reputation of creating new organizations and managing them to success, creating three different offices during my career – a legal office, an academic department, and a major intelligence oversight organization.

The creation of a new tribunal was something few individuals have ever done, yet I felt this experience would help. At the end of the day, it did.

A month after my appointment, I convened a briefing on my overall prosecutorial strategy to as many of the constituent parties under the auspices of the United States Institute of Peace (USIP) as I could. My friend Neil Kritz helped set that up for me. At that May briefing, I told members of the new management committee, NGOs, and other government officials how I was going to execute my mandate to include a phased-in creation of the OTP from July 2002 to its full operational capacity in November 2002. They seemed more surprised than impressed, as no one had ever done this before. I thought it was standard procedure, but I was told afterward that this was a first for an international tribunal.

It was during this briefing that I told them about my idea of a town hall program where I would walk the countryside talking to the people about the Special Court but more importantly listening to them tell me what happened there. It was a first-ever concept and was met with some skepticism.

While at the USIP that day I spent an hour talking to William Schabas, one of the newly appointed commissioners for the Sierra Leone Truth and Reconciliation Commission.[2] It was the beginning of a long professional and personal relationship. There had been much concern about whether a truth commission and a war crimes tribunal could work together. It was here that I laid out my policy toward the commission, which included supporting them and pledging not to use any information or evidence they gathered in my criminal investigation. I felt it was not necessary, as I had my own investigative plan and was concerned that my involvement with the commission would prevent witnesses from coming forward to tell their stories to them. We both pledged to get together in Freetown later in the summer.

I retired from the US federal government on June 6, 2002 after serving my country for 30 years as a paratrooper, special operations officer, judge advocate, assistant general counsel, senior intelligence officer, and inspector general – all within the Department of Defense. A week later, Judi and I flew to Utah for a week to hike and relax as we celebrated 30 years of marriage. It was a wonderful week of time together in a beautiful part of the United States.

After our return, we began to prepare our advance team to fly to Sierra Leone in mid-July. I flew to New York for consultations with members of the Security Council, various NGOs, and the legal advisor to the United Nations. I also was introduced to the newly appointed court registrar, Robin Vincent from Great Britain. We had lunch together and began a long personal and professional relationship that lasted for years, but it was sadly cut short by his untimely death in 2011. After our lunch, Robin and I went down to the local Chase Manhattan Bank and

[2] *See* Peace Agreement Between the Government of Sierra Leone and the Revolutionary United Front of Sierra Leone, Art. VI, July 7, 1999, UN Doc. S/1999/777 (July 12, 1999).

deposited $1 in the new Special Court for Sierra Leone bank account. We walked back to our temporary offices in the UN Annex. Robin would leave for Sierra Leone the second week in July, and I would meet him there on or around August 7.

While in New York, my new deputy prosecutor, Desmond de Silva, came from London to meet me and to discuss my strategic plan for setting up the OTP and for implementing my prosecution strategy. We could not have been more different in outlook and background, yet we would be a great team for over three years. We would deploy to Sierra Leone in phases: first, the core team consisting of mysel; my special assistant, Michael Pan; my chief investigator, Alan White; my chief of prosecutions, Frank Fountain; and others. Desmond would follow a month later to form up the Appellate Division.

It was during this visit that I tried to develop a professional and hopefully personal relationship with Hans Corell's deputy, Ralph Zacklin. A man with a taciturn personality, he was disliked. Ralph was adamantly opposed to my selection as chief prosecutor and was commenting publicly that he gave me and the registrar, Robin Vincent, just a few months before we would fail. I asked him to lunch and tried to get to know him and to talk to him about my overall strategic plan as a way to develop any relationship with him.

Any person would have appreciated my reaching out and my promise to work with him and his office. The lunch seemed to go well, and we shook hands, pledging to work together. That pledge by Ralph lasted only as long as he turned the corner back to his office.

I flew back to Washington and, with my advance team of six persons, to include my Chief of Investigations and Prosecutions, attended the Legal Attaché course at the FBI Academy in Quantico, Virginia. Among the courses taught were defensive driving, small arms training, hand-to-hand fighting, and counter-surveillance techniques. We were also fitted for level III protective vests. I would wear mine most of the time when I was in public while in Sierra Leone.

My last few weeks in the United States were spent concentrating on getting my personal affairs in order, saying goodbye to family, and arranging for meetings in London and The Hague in late July. Desmond was arranging meetings at the foreign office, various international NGOs, and dinners as well as receptions.

On July 27, 2002, Judi drove me to Dulles. We hugged goodbye and she drove away. I would not see her for some time. I remember that moment even today and the pain we both felt. I was flying into the worst place on earth to live with a destroyed country and society, no electricity or running water, and rampant disease. Over 1.2 million people had been murdered, mutilated, maimed, and/or raped. Ninety percent of the country was destroyed. I was flying into hell.

At the gate, I met my personal assistant and political advisor Mike Pan. As we boarded the Virgin Atlantic flight to London, I glanced out the window for one last look, wondering what I had gotten myself into. I prayed, "Lord keep me strong, keep me focused, keep me safe."

Our week in London was a success: we established contacts and relationships with Her Majesty's government that would pay great benefits in my plan related to the simultaneous takedown of all of the indictees in one arrest operation across the region sometime in the winter of 2003. I kept this fact closely held.

From London we flew to The Hague where I had meetings with Carla Del Ponte, the prosecutor of the International Criminal Tribunal for the Former Yugoslavia and her team. Our meetings were cordial and in most cases informative and helpful. I sensed a great malaise however and nagging suspicion that there was no overall prosecution strategy.

We flew to Brussels, where we linked up with Alan White, my chief of investigations, who had been on our advanced team. While in Sierra Leone, he had found an old mansion, Seaview, that would be both the temporary home of the OTP and the residence of six senior members of the OTP, including myself. It was on two acres of land, surrounded by a 30-foot-high fence, with blast doors, bulletproof glass, and space on the first floor and in the basement for the OTP. The second floor held our rooms, where I would live for three years.

Al White, Mike Pan, and I took the first SN Brussels flight into Sierra Leone in its history. As we landed, I looked out at a devastated land. Lungi Airport was a grouping of dilapidated buildings, some of them burned out, others collapsing from misuse in the damp humid tropical air of West Africa. Off to the side was a white trailer with the UN symbol that housed the UN transportation office and the location of the helipad for the UN helicopters that shuttled UN personnel to and from UN headquarters in Freetown across the bay to the airfield.

I stepped off the aircraft into a bright tropical sun. It was in the nineties with no breeze. What struck me immediately was the air, which smelled of diesel fuel, burning wood, garbage, human excrement, and the sickly, unmistakable smell of death. As I write this, I can smell and taste it even now.

We walked to the burnt out hangar and customs office. We then went to the UN transportation office to get on the next helicopter back to headquarters. Since we did not have the proper paperwork, the transportation officer refused to give us passage, and we had to catch a commercial helicopter run by Paramount Airways. The helicopter was a dilapidated Russian MI-8 cargo helicopter flown by former Ukrainian air force pilots. We took off, rattling and straining into the sky and landing at their heliport next to UN headquarters. I was met by Robin Vincent. His first words to me were "welcome to hell." As we drove to Keith and Susanne Biddle's home, where we would stay for a few weeks while getting Seaview ready for occupation, I looked out at a vast wasteland. Vultures circled above us, and people bathed in gutters, as there was no running water. And the smell, always that sickly sweet, lingering smell of death.

Freetown is the capital of Sierra Leone. Nestled beneath the Lion Mountain from whence the country gets its name, Freetown was almost too much for the senses. The smells, the colors, the constant movement of tens of thousands of people amidst the honking of horns was overwhelming to a newcomer. The signs of a recent war were everywhere. It seemed to me that everything was damaged or destroyed.

At that moment, the Special Court for Sierra Leone consisted of five people, and we got right to work. We had to clean, provision, and furnish our new headquarters at Seaview. It was right in the middle of rainy season and it was not unusual for it to rain 10 inches in a day. It rained almost every day, all day. Everything was damp and moldy. This did not stop us from assembling furniture together, unloading trucks, and laying on fuel for our generator. We had to hire a house staff and coordinate with the Sierra Leone National Police for gate guards and a security detail.

While we were settling in to the basics of living in Freetown, I began to reach out to the diplomatic community, civil society, and the national government for talks and consultations. We were already in phase three of my strategic plan. I was hiring staff and bringing them on in phases to ensure everyone had a job and that they "hit the ground running." I used a different approach than other UN missions. I built the office around the mission, having them arrive when needed, not the mission around the office where UN staff would arrive with nothing to do and a lot of time to do it. We had no "hall walkers" in the OTP.

As we were busily setting up our office, Alan White came to me and told me that he had received a handwritten note from Gibril Massaquoi, one of the battlegroup commanders of the infamous Revolutionary United Front (RUF), part of the three warring groups in the 10-year horror that was the civil war in Sierra Leone. He wanted to meet secretly with Alan. He felt that he should. We contacted the Keith Biddle, the inspector general of the Sierra Leone National Police, whose home we had stayed at when we first arrived, and set up a meeting to plan security for Alan.

The plan was for Alan to be driven to the bar in Kissey Town to meet up with Massaquoi. There would be police backup in alleyways a block or two from the bar, just in case they were needed. Alan had a 9mm pistol that he carried behind him in his waist band. The meeting was agreed to and Alan left for Kissey Town.

The bar was like something in the bar scene in the first Star Wars movie on Tatooine. Dark, dreary, and reeking of smoke and cheap beer, Massaquoi sat in the back facing the door. Alan went over to him and sat down. No handshakes, just a stare-down. Massaquoi was wearing a red beret and mirror shades, and the gold in his front teeth glimmered in the dim light. He had a bayonet, which he was rolling around in his hand, sticking it into the top of the table from time to time. Finally Massaquoi and Alan began to chat.

I sat at my desk, nervous, not sure when Alan would be back. Finally, after three hours, Alan returned to Seaview and entered my office. He was smiling as he dropped a book on my desk. "It's a diary. The son of a bitch wrote it all down!" I was floored to be sure. "What does he want for this?" I asked, returning Alan's smile. "Immunity. He said he would work with us completely in return for protection and immunity from prosecution."

After a brief discussion, I agreed to the deal. The diary was our first piece of evidence, and Massaquoi would become a key material witness for us in our trials against the leadership of the RUF and the Armed Forces Revolutionary Council (AFRC).[3] It was a stroke of luck. As we say in my home state of North Carolina, "sometimes you get the bear, sometimes the bear gets you."

. . .

Our staff grew appropriately toward our goal of full operational capacity in November, which we achieved. Our support staff arrived first to set up the office, followed by our investigators, who were centered around three task forces headed by a senior trial lawyer. Our trial counsel arrived next, along with our evidence personnel.

My deputy prosecutor arrived in early September, and I gave him the mandate of heading our appellate division. His team of three, along with an academic consortium I had set up, were to list all of the possible jurisdictional and substantive motions we would likely receive challenging the Court, our charges in the indictment, and other ancillary legal matters, and prepare responses to those challenges. Indeed, we received 10 motions in our first year from defense counsel, and we had prepared responses for each. Within a year and a half, we prevailed on all motions made by defense counsel, setting up some very important jurisprudential points.

Shortly after Desmond arrived, he came into my office with a book written by one of our recently appointed appellate justices, Geoffrey Robinson. He handed me the book and told me that he thought Justice Robinson's comments in a section of the book would come back to haunt him and the court. In that particular chapter, he opined on the guilt of several of the persons we were looking at to indict for war crimes and crimes against humanity.

Sure enough, about a year and a half later, a defense council for one of the accused filed a motion to have Justice Robinson removed from two-thirds of the cases before the Court due to a conflict of interest. I concurred in the motion to have him recused. The appellate chamber for the Court agreed, and Justice Robinson was removed. The legal integrity of the Court was at stake. International courts have to be seen as fair and impartial. Not removing Justice Robinson would have been fatal to that trust.

Speaking of judges, if there was one part of the Special Court for Sierra Leone[4] that was a "weak link," it was the persons who were selected by the United Nations to

[3] *See, e.g., Prosecutor v. Issa Hassan Sesay*, Case No. SCSL–03–05–I–001, Indictment, (Special Court for Sierra Leone Mar. 3, 2003), available at www.rscsl.org/Documents/Decisions/RUF/05–003/SCSL-03–05-I-001-B.pdf.

[4] S.C. Res. 1315, *supra* note 1.

be trial and appellate judges. In large part, they were inexperienced in the courtroom. To a prosecutor, they were dangerous. It is the duty of a prosecutor to protect the trial record, and a judge with little to no trial experience is a legal error waiting to happen. I was so concerned that I assigned a senior counsel to be present in the courtroom at all times when a trial was in session to ensure no prejudicial error was made by the three trial judges sitting in one of our three cases. Getting competent judges at the international level remains a continuing challenge.

During that fall of 2002, we worked seven days a week. The OTP and the registry worked hand in hand setting up the Court, starting the investigations, and developing political and diplomatic relations with various states within the region. We started our outreach program, which had originated with the OTP as part of my strategic plan. This innovative plan was a first for an international tribunal and would last during the entire life of the Court. During my tenure, I walked the entire countryside listening to my client, the people of Sierra Leone tell me about what had happened to them over the past 10 years. I began to understand the agony they experienced, and they got to know their prosecutor and their Court.

I recall particularly my first town hall in the Kono District near the killing fields of Tombutu. This was the heart of the blood diamond area that enslaved West Africans who were worked to death and thrown into a watery grave nearby called Savage Waters. We stood in front of several hundred Sierra Leoneans, listening to them tell us what happened there, and I answered questions about the Court. This session lasted over two hours. After the session, a Sierra Leonean limped up to me. He had a single, crude crutch. He was missing his left leg and his right arm. The gentleman came up to me with tears in his eyes and said, "I want to tell you what happened to me." And he did. The rebels had intentionally cut off his limbs, one opposite of the other, just so he would be off balance the rest of his life. This struck me hard. I knew we had to seek justice for him and the tens of thousands of victims of the civil war. As he limped away, Alan came up to me and asked what that was all about. I told him and said, "We are going to get the bastards that did this to you." And eventually we did.

In September, I established covertly what I called the Security Group, which was made up of the British high commissioner, the US ambassador, the inspector general of the National Police, the chief of staff of the UN forces in Sierra Leone, the general commanding British forces in Sierra Leone, our registrar, and myself. We met on a monthly basis or at my direction, and I would brief them on the activities of the OTP that could affect their organizations or countries. We also discussed offline the support I would need to execute what I was calling "Operation Justice," the takedown of all of the heads of the three warring factions in a simultaneous arrest operation across the region. Each member was given the information they would need to seek approval for their support in Sierra Leone. I promised them they would all know at the appropriate time when I planned to "put the hammer down." I told them that there would be no surprises.

Unbeknownst to all of them, British High Commissioner Alan Jones and I secretly traveled to London for consultation with Her Majesty's government. It was agreed that the British government would provide direct military support for Operation Justice. That support would be in the form of a battalion from the British Parachute Regiment and from the West African Squadron of the Royal Navy. I agreed to give them at least a month's notice of the arrest operation. Only my deputy prosecutor and the chief of investigations were aware of this. Secrecy and timing were key to the success of this operation.

Part of my strategic plan related to the military operation was an information operation to throw off all of the potential indictees, making them think that any action by my office was some time off and to keep them at ease and comfortable that their possible arrest was not imminent. I held regular press conferences telling the world that the trials of any possible indictees was around two years away and that the investigations were complicated and moving forward slowly. All of this was true. The information operation worked perfectly in the end. The eventual indictees never knew what hit them on the day we arrested them.

Of course, there were times to relax, and I ensured, when it made sense, that we would do just that. Every Friday night, I hosted a pizza party at Momba Point for my staff where we could drink beer, have some great pizza, and talk about anything other than our investigations. It was fun, and I got to learn a great deal about cricket and rugby, two sports I knew very little about.

Robin Vincent, our registrar, and I agreed to host a Halloween costume party at Seaview. It was a huge success. We held a contest for the best costume. I was amazed at how clever our staff was in coming up with amazing costumes. One of our Swiss trial counsel dressed as a pumpkin, and the winner was our IT manager, who dressed up as Carmen Miranda. He danced all night and was asked for a date several times. It was held on our patio at Seaview. The entire Court staff was in attendance, including our Sierra Leonean colleagues. The music blared, and the beer and wine flowed well into the night. It was moments like these that created permanent bonds of friendship.

During the month of November, US Ambassador Pete Chavez invited me to a dinner honoring a visiting former US ambassador to Sierra Leone. Invitees included various members of the diplomatic corps; myself; and Hinga Norman, who was the Minister of the Interior and a personal friend of the visiting US Ambassador. There was a reception with gin and tonics all around. Chief Norman, as he was called, was late. Just before dinner, he arrived bedecked in traditional robes. Quite resplendent actually, he apologized for being late. He was quite the gentleman. As head of the Civil Defense Force (CDF), he had fought the RUF for a decade yet had committed terrible atrocities against his own citizens. I was actively investigating him, and he was one of my future indictees.

Ambassador Chavez walked Chief Norman around the living room, introducing him to people. By coincidence, from where I was standing chatting with British High Commissioner Alan Jones, I was the last person to be introduced. I had never met him. Pete came up to me and introduced me to Chief Norman. I looked the Chief directly in the eyes and said, "Chief Norman, it is a pleasure to meet you. I have heard so much about you." I smiled and said that I was sure we would meet again. Both Alan Jones and Pete were wide-eyed as we moved into the dining room, and Alan was trying not to laugh. He told me later, "That was f**king brilliant."

As we approached the holidays, I hosted a dinner on Thanksgiving Day for my staff. I had arranged through our new Lebanese friends at Momba Point for roast turkey with all the dressing, as well as pumpkin and apple pie. It was a first for most of my staff, and we had a very special meal. We had just come to full operational capacity, with most of the staff hired and working. They were focused on the investigations and the drafting of possible indictments. The meal was a nice respite.

My strategic plan was going according to schedule, but it was not perfect. As in any setup of an organization in a very dangerous place with direct threats to the health and safety of that office, the extreme environment caught several people unprepared. That fall, I had to ask two of my original staff to leave due to performance, two senior members of my staff resigned due to inability, and one left for mental health reasons. I would learn later that almost all of these people suffered from the effects of Lariam, a particularly powerful antimalarial drug. It literally changed their attitudes and personalities from the true professionals that I knew to bitter and even psychotic individuals. Once we worked through these issues and brought on new members of the OTP to replace them, we had no further personnel problems.

At the end of November 2002, we had framed in the basic plan for the execution of Operation Justice sometime in March. There were now only five individuals in the Court who were privy to the details of the operation. Part of the plan was to build a temporary detention facility on Bonthe Island 150 miles southeast of Freetown. I flew down with the deputy registrar to look at a dilapidated jail. It had eight cells that could hold the leadership of the warring factions. The plan called for us to announce that we were reconstructing the jail as part of a goodwill gesture by the Court to the people of Sierra Leone. Shortly after our trip, we announced the rebuilding of the jail. The renovations began in December and would be completed a week before the takedown in March 2003.

Our investigators and trial counsel were now hard at work developing cases against 13 persons of interest organized into three task forces: one for the RUF; one for the CDF; and one for the AFRC. Charles Taylor's team was part of the RUF. My prosecution plan was for two joint criminal trials against the RUF/AFRC and the CDF. President Charles Taylor was to be tried with the RUF/AFRC, but in my mind I thought it would be a separate trial. This calculation proved to be true.

Our teams were moving up-country on a weekly basis looking at areas that held crime scenes that we could charge representationally. It is important to point out that, in atrocity crimes, one cannot charge every single crime across the region. I had informed the task forces that we would use a notice pleading format and we would charge in the alternative in the indictments. What we hoped was that this would shorten the length of the indictments and make for a more efficient and shorter trial. This proved to be the case.

I also directed my teams to ensure that they had enough evidence on at least two charges for each indictee beyond a reasonable doubt prior to my signing the indictments. My thinking on this was to ensure that when we arrested them, they would not see the light of a free day again. In the atrocity investigation business, you can't just move forward on probable cause only: your criminal case has to be solidly based before issuing any indictments. Our investigators continued to bring in evidence on the other charges over time so when we went to trial our cases were airtight. At the end of the day, all of the persons I indicted were found guilty as charged.

Our Security Group was meeting regularly, and I was ensuring that these critical individuals were informed as appropriate and comfortable with how events were unfolding from a political point of view. During this timeframe, I became a regular on the diplomatic circuit, becoming friends and colleagues with diplomats, politicians, and heads of all of the UN and nongovernmental organizations in the region. I wanted to be seen as helpful, interested, and someone who would not "disrupt the apple cart." I needed these people to step up and support me when I executed Operation Justice.

It had been my intent that, prior to all of us leaving for the December holiday, I would have visited every province and every major town in Sierra Leone. My last town was Port Locko on the Guinea border. I visited that town in mid-December. A typical visit would entail an advance team leaving a day early to meet with the town and provincial leadership to explain what would happen when the chief prosecutor arrived. They would hand out pamphlets and flyers and visit the venue where I was to speak. The local police would be briefed, and security arranged. If there were UN forces close by, they would provide additional security.

On the day of my visit, I would usually arrive around mid-morning. We would land and be driven to the venue or, if close, I would walk. Many were initially timid as they were frightened of me, a white man landing in a big white helicopter some thought was a real dragon. Mindful of this, I always brought candy for the children who would walk with me to the venue holding my hand. I enjoyed these moments.

When I arrived at the venue, I would be greeted by the village chief, the mayor, the district officers, the local Imam and/or priest, among others. I would be welcomed, and then after the introduction, I would step down into the crowd, standing among them in humility. I wanted to send a signal to them that I was just a person who had the honor to represent them in this international trial. For three to four hours sometimes, we would talk, laugh, and cry, discussing the events that took place locally there at the outreach site. I would come away with a more complete understanding of what happened there. It was very helpful to me as I reviewed the charges in the indictments.

A week prior to our heading home for the holidays, I was sitting at my desk when my chief of investigations, Alan White and his deputy, Gilbert Morrisette, came to see me. During the fall, I had directed that we build a criminal information network throughout West Africa to provide us information on our investigations, security threats, and political intelligence on what was going on within the region. We now had several assets run by case officers in the investigations division who were reporting on activities by governments, informants, witnesses, and possible indictees.

Alan and Gilbert informed me that assets were reporting that President Charles Taylor had sent a hit team to Ghana to take out one of our more critical lead witnesses and his family. The witness, President Charles Taylor's driver, had fled Liberia and moved to Ghana. Our investigators had gotten him to agree to work for us. We decided to launch a rescue operation immediately. I picked up the phone and called a local Lebanese friend who owned a travel business. This is where getting out and getting to know the key players in Freetown and the region paid off. He agreed to help and called back an hour later saying he could have a Learjet in Freetown in a few hours that could fly the rescue team to Ghana. It would cost $24,000. I called the registrar, Robin Vincent, who sent $24,000 in cash over to our office within the hour.

Gilbert would lead the team with two security officers and a trial counsel, Aduwa Wiafah. They flew off a few hours later and rescued the witness and his family. It was a close call, as the hit team hit the house an hour later with no one there. The plane flew back to Freetown, and we placed the witness and his family in a safe house. They would be flown out of the country in January to a third country. The witness provided very important information to our investigative team, particularly related to President Charles Taylor and his activities. This was serious and deadly business.

My first holiday, and the only time I had to mentally step away from our work in West Africa, went by too quickly. It was good to go home. My vacation lasted three very fast weeks. On the way back to Freetown, I stopped off in London for a secret meeting with Her Majesty's government on finalizing the military support to Operation Justice. The plan allowed for a battalion from the Parachute Regiment to do its annual training on or around the first week in March between the battalion and elements of the Sierra Leonean army with a simulated takedown of the international airport. The Royal Navy would send its West African Squadron south from Portsmouth a week prior to the takedown and stand by just over the horizon. A frigate would arrive in Freetown harbor just prior to the takedown and sail visibly off the coast at general quarters. With this settled, I flew down to Sierra Leone and the beginning of what was to be an historic year.

By this time, the task forces were finalizing their initial investigations, and each was preparing the indictments of the leadership of the Civil Defense Forces, the Revolutionary United Front, and the Armed Forces Revolutionary Council. A part of the task force working on the case against the RUF was also drafting the indictment of President Charles Taylor. My direction to them was that I would not sign the indictments until I we had evidence beyond a reasonable doubt on at least two of those charges.

I convened our Security Group and began to go over our general plan on the takedown and told them that work was moving forward and to be prepared to assist toward the end of February and the first two weeks in March. I could not give them more specifics, yet promised each of them that individually and collectively they would be briefed, and coordination would be made on their support to the operation.

While this was going on, the detention facility that was disguised as a legacy project for the Sierra Leone National Police was nearing completion. Keith Biddle, the inspector general of the national police, was assisting with all of this. I was meeting regularly with the press at the press center in downtown Freetown and answering questions about the civil war, my work and efforts, the outreach program, and other matters.

Our outreach program was transferred to the registry under the management of Binta Mansarey, with whom I would work for three years walking the countryside talking to Sierra Leoneans. I was up-country during this timeframe every other week. I was beginning to enjoy these meetings, and came to love and respect the people of Sierra Leone.

One group I especially enjoyed was the students. I always made it a point to visit a school, where possible, at each outreach event. It is a challenge to stand in front of up to 1,000 children and talk about war, their lives, and entertain them for an hour or so. Being a father I knew how to talk to children and to get their interest. One of the ways I would draw them out would be to talk about music and the type of music they liked. They were a musical people, so I would sing a song from my generation and then ask them to sing a song they liked. It usually did not take long to break the ice. I learned a great deal about the war from their point of view.

My favorite school by far was the Milton Margai School for the Blind in Freetown. I would meet with them once a quarter and did so for the entire time I was in Sierra Leone. They enjoyed the treats I would bring along with me, sodas and candy a rare treat indeed. We became so familiar that they started calling me “Uncle Dave.” They enjoyed singing to me. The choir had sung before the queen at Westminster Abbey the year prior to my arrival. I can still hear their voices singing “My Salone Home.”

The Office of the Prosecutor now was at full operating capacity. My plan of bringing on personnel as they were needed for the specific time I needed them was working. Forensic teams, human rights experts, investigators rotated in and out some staying but many leaving as their missions were complete. With proper planning we were able to accomplish our goals with 70 people throughout my tenure. This saved money and made for an efficient and focused office.

We were still working six days a week. I directed that we would not work on Sundays anymore. Though refreshed from the recent holiday, my team was tired from the work up-country, long hours reviewing horrific facts, and the daily grind of trying to stay safe and healthy in what was considered the worse place in the world to live according to the United Nations. Our weekly pizza parties at Momba Point were increasingly popular and needed. The light crisp lager of Star Beer, a local brew, sure tasted good after a long week in the trenches. The team was becoming close. The bonds of friendship and respect became strong forged in the blood of the war, the heat of the place, and the challenges of staying healthy. It was a crucible that only those who have investigated atrocities can understand.

My regular briefings to the press continued. The questions and exchange of information led them to believe correctly that the investigation remained complicated, long reaching, and that any trials would not take place for at least a year or so. The daily papers would publish all this, keeping the targeted indictees content that nothing was going to happen soon. In reality, the takedown called Operation Justice was just a month away.

I began to meet with members of the Security Group offline to finalize their support for Operation Justice, which would need careful coordination. Each of the countries and organizations were on board with their role in the operation. The only unknown to most of them was exactly when it would take place. Because of their large military role in the operation, Great Britain was told to prepare to execute their part of the plan about four weeks out. The other countries were told a bit later.

The support provided for this operation was that the Sierra Leone National Police would execute the arrest of the indictees. They would also provide riot control should that be necessary. The United States was to provide contract helicopters to transport the indictees to the detention facility on Bonthe Island. The United Nations was to provide a standby force of Pakistani Special Forces as a quick reaction force to assist if there was trouble and to provide backup security to the police. Great Britain would provide the naval and ground forces to bolster security in the region and step in should there be large-scale unrest and to assist in evacuating the expatriate community. The stakes were very high. We had to be prepared for the worst while hoping for the best.

Only members of the Security Group were involved. We kept the United Nations largely out of the planning and the eventual execution, as the local UN organizations were not reliable to keep a secret, particularly with the special representative of the secretary general (SRSG) who remained hostile to the Special Court.

In February, as we finalized the operation and were completing the drafting of the indictments, a large contingent of our management committee arrived to have a look at how things were going. They did not know about Operation Justice.

Led by Ralph Zacklin, they were there to find fault, not to assist. It was a week of negatives, questions, and demands. Looking back on it, I think they were trying to find a reason to remove me as chief prosecutor but could not find a reason. They left just a few weeks before Operation Justice. The management committee never again tried to interfere with me again.

To deflect any possible focus on our work, I continued to travel regionally and internationally. I wanted to give anyone watching us closely the idea that the Office of the Prosecutor was busy in a general way trying to set itself up and just beginning its investigations. In reality, we were fast approaching execution day. My outreach plans increased, and I completed my goal of visiting every district in the country by the end of February. I was truly beginning to get a good sense of the conflict and its impact on the population.

This sense of place, time, and people was also proving helpful as I sat and reviewed the various indictments that were being completed and readied for judicial review by the sitting Article 28 judge who had to review any indictments for probable cause prior to execution and to also sign the arrest warrants. Our acting chief of prosecutions, Brenda Hollis, had the lead in drafting the indictments and shaping them into the new format I had directed to be used, notice pleading with representational charges. This new format cut down the size of the indictments to about 20 pages per indictee. The reviewing judge would be looking at this new format soon. As it had never been done at the international level, I was keeping my fingers crossed.

Finally on March 3, the indictments containing all of the charges, many of them groundbreaking, for war crimes and crimes against humanity, were ready to be signed by me. Two of the charges against each indictee were now provable beyond reasonable doubt, as I had required. The remaining charges were well beyond the probable cause standard to be sure, but needed further investigation to lock down prior to trial. It was time to get the indictments approved and the arrest warrants signed.

At 4:30 p.m. on March 3, 2003, we held a signing ceremony in my office with the entire legal staff and investigators. Solemnly, Brenda Hollis handed me each of the indictments, and I signed them. Indictment number one was President Charles Taylor of Liberia. I sealed that immediately. It was unsealed in summer of 2003, which ended his presidency and led to his house arrest in Calabar, Nigeria, pending his handover to the court three years later on March 6, 2006. As we signed the indictments, many of my Sierra Leonean colleagues were weeping. They could not believe that justice had returned to their county. Brenda gathered up the indictments and flew to London that evening to have them reviewed by the reviewing judge.

During this week, the Security Group was working diligently in preparation to execute Operation Justice on Monday, March 10. The battalion of the Parachute

Regiment arrived to start to "train" with the Sierra Leonean army, taking up their positions to seize Lungi Airport if need be to secure a safe zone to evacuate internationals. I received word from the British high commissioner that the West African Squadron of the Royal Navy was sailing south from Portsmouth in the United Kingdom to take up position just over the horizon on execution day, March 10.

To ensure we knew of their exact location we had all of the indictees watched and followed. We had to take everyone down at once, or they would flee into the bush. Timing and surprise were paramount. If this was leaked out in any way, these individuals would be gone – perhaps forever.

On the Friday night prior to the Monday execution of the operation, Brenda called me and told me that the judge had approved all of the indictments and signed the arrest warrants. I was at Momba Point with the team. They knew what the phone call was about, and when I gave the thumbs-up sign, there were smiles and hugs all around. We left the restaurant and began to put the final touches on Operation Justice.

Alan White, my chief of investigations, had the lead. The Security Group was notified that the takedown would happen at noon that Monday. All was ready. I recall the day as if it were yesterday. The weather was perfect, somewhat cool and dry. I stood in the back of the room at 8 a.m. listening to the arrest teams get their final briefing, and I shook their hands as they filed out on this "day of days."

There was little I could do that morning. Mike Pan, my special assistant and political advisor, had drafted a press release that I would read to the world at 4 p.m. that afternoon at UN headquarters should all go well. As soon as we knew that all of the indictees were in our custody, we would announce the press conference for 4 p. m. Again, timing was important.

I sat at my desk at noon knowing that hundreds of personnel were out there executing Operation Justice. I silently prayed for success and hoped that there would be no casualties. We just did not know how this would play out. After months of hard work, planning, and diplomacy it was now out of my hands.

Mike Pan came in and told me that the HMS *Iron Duke* was in the harbor sailing along the coast right on time. She was flying a large Union Jack, and it was obvious that there was a military presence close by.

At 12:55 p.m., Alan White called and told me that everyone was in custody and being flown to the detention facility on Bonthe Island. I thanked him and turned to Mike and told him Operation Justice was a success. Not a shot had been fired. The element of surprise was total to include arresting Chief Hinga Norman, the minister of the mnterior, at his desk. I had Mike Pan call the public relations chief at UN headquarters for the press conference at 4 p.m. I then picked up the phone and informed the UN SRSG that Operation Justice had happened and that I had arrested all of the leadership of the warring factions in an hour.

I had never told him of Operation Justice or any of my plans, as he was so hostile to our court. A Nigerian, in January, he had attempted to take two of the indictees, Issa

Sesay and Morris Kallon, out of the country to Nigeria on agricultural scholarships. His deputy, Alan Doss, warned me of this. I notified the United Nations in New York of his possible obstruction of justice, telling them I would have the SRSG arrested for impeding our investigation if he did not back off. Though no one knew at the time, we were investigating Sesay and Kallon: their obvious involvement in the murder, rape, maiming, and mutilation of tens of thousands of human beings as battlegroup commanders within the RUF made them prime targets.

After I told the SRSG what I had done, I hung up on him. I was told by others later that he almost fell out of his chair and began screaming he was so shocked. It was poetic justice for me after all of the problems he had caused me and the Special Court over these past few months. To me, he was irrelevant now.

At 4 p.m. with Desmond de Silva and Keith Biddle, the Inspector General of Police, at my side, I read a statement to the world that a new dawn for Sierra Leone was at hand, a dawn of peace and the rule of law. I then read out the names of the indictees, individuals that had terrorized West Africa for over 10 years. I intentionally left out President Charles Taylor. We would arrest him later in June 2003.

After I finished my statement there was silence, and the reporters tried to comprehend what we had just told them. Then suddenly there was a break for the door as they ran to file their stories. Within seconds, the press room was empty. I was escorted to my waiting car to be taken back to my office. As we drove through the streets of Freetown people were spilling out of homes and offices shouting, cheering and dancing as the news of the arrests spread out across the city and into the bush. They would celebrate well into the evening. It was the beginning of a beginning for a destroyed peoples – an era of the rule of law for Sierra Leone.

That evening, Alan Jones hosted a quick celebratory dinner at the British high commissioner's residence. I stood and thanked these gentlemen, a few of whom had put their careers on the line to assist me and the Special Court in executing Operation Justice. We had finished phase four of my plan. The next morning we moved onto phase five, pretrial.

All of this happened within seven months of our arrival. The incredible team we had put together had more spring in their step that next week. The reaction by the people of Sierra Leone was overwhelmingly positive. We set up several outreach events to go and talk to the people and to listen to them tell us what they thought of the arrests. It was a special time for the people.

For the next few years, we would prosecute the leaders of the CDF, RUF, and the AFRC in joint criminal trials. They would all be convicted as charged. The Special Court for Sierra Leone was an experiment in international justice, the world's first hybrid international tribunal composed of both international and local personnel located at the scene of the atrocity, just like at Nuremberg. Could an international tribunal be more efficient and effective? Could the hybrid model be a future model for international tribunals? Could international and local personnel work together?

So many questions, yet the Special Court for Sierra Leone, the last of the major tribunals to be created, was the first to finish its work in an efficient and effective way.

A poll was conducted after its work, and over two-thirds of the people Sierra Leone were satisfied with the work of the Court. There were so many "firsts" done by what many commentators called "the little engine that could." The Special Court was the first hybrid international tribunal; it was the first tribunal since Nuremberg in 1945 to be located at the site of the atrocities; it was the first tribunal to expand the jurisprudence of international criminal law through its various court rulings relating to head of state immunity, child soldiers, and crimes against women; it would be the first tribunal to have an extensive outreach program; and it would be the first tribunal to convict a sitting African head of state (and only the second time in history).

President Charles Taylor was finally handed over to the Special Court for trial in March 2006. He would be sentenced to 50 years for aiding and abetting the horror that he helped cause in Sierra Leone in 2012. Since the arrests, trial, and sentencing of the main players in the civil war, Sierra Leone has been at peace.

As the world recoils in horror over the destruction of Syria and the surrounding region, the international community is working with the Syrian National Congress to create a hybrid court similar to the Special Court for Sierra Leone to bring justice to the Syrian people. Through the Chautauqua Blueprint[5] and the work of the Syrian Accountability Project, which I modeled after our prosecution plan and methodologies in West Africa, the legacy of the Special Court will live on as an efficient and effective model to bring justice to victims of atrocity.

I will finish up with a vignette from my last day in Sierra Leone. I was visiting the Milton Margai School for the Blind in Freetown to say goodbye. I had visited this school, kindergarten through high school, many times holding town hall meetings with the students there. I brought along candy bars and soft drinks with me, as was my custom. As we munched away, we would hold our meeting. That day, as we concluded our visit, the school choir wanted to sing me a farewell song. As they gathered, a few children came and sat with me. The song they sang for me that final day was "It's a Small World."

[5] *See "Chautauqua Blueprint" to Prosecute Syrian War Crimes Unveiled*, INSTITUTE FOR NATIONAL SECURITY AND COUNTERTERRORISM (Oct. 3, 2013), http://insct.syr.edu/chautauqua-blueprint-prosecute-syrian-war-crimes-unveiled/; *see also* The Chautauqua Blueprint for a Statute for a Syrian Extraordinary Tribunal to Prosecute Atrocity Crimes, available at http://insct.syr.edu/wp-content/uploads/2013/09/Chautauqua-Blueprint1.pdf.

6

The International Criminal Court

Luis Moreno Ocampo

I had never imagined that I would be the chief prosecutor of the International Criminal Court (ICC). I had neither been involved in the discussions on the Rome Statute nor proposed my candidacy for the position. One morning in November 2002, I was parking my car in downtown Buenos Aires when my phone rang. It was a collaborator of Prince Zeid,[1] Jordan's permanent representative to the United Nations. As the president of the Assembly of States Parties of the Rome Statute, Prince Zeid was leading the candidate search for the chief prosecutor of the International Criminal Court. My experience as prosecutor in Argentina's Junta Trial had placed my name at the top of a list of potential candidates. Prince Zeid wanted to meet me in New York to discuss whether I would be interested in the position.

At the time, I thought that my biggest professional achievement lay well behind me. I could never be involved in a bigger case than the Junta Trial. In 1985, I was deputy prosecutor in the case against three former dictators and six other members of the different military juntas that ruled Argentina between 1976 and 1982. They were charged for the crimes they ordered during the "Dirty War," an Argentine version of the War on Terror.

I was very skeptical about my chances to be appointed, but I was not able to reject the possibility of being involved in Rome Statute implementation. I had witnessed the impact of the Argentina junta trial and I thought that a similar effect could be achieved at a global level. But in April 2003, 78 states parties of the Rome Statute granted me the privilege and the responsibility of being the first chief prosecutor of the ICC.[2] My mission was to build the Office of the Prosecutor from scratch to make the Rome Statute's innovative legal design operational.

[1] Prince Zeid bin Ra'ad is currently the United Nations high commissioner for human rights and formerly Jordan's permanent representative to the UN, Jordanian ambassador to the United States, and the president of the Assembly of State Parties of the ICC.

[2] UN Press Statement, States Parties to Rome Statute elect Luis Moreno Ocampo as Prosecutor of International Criminal Court, L/3035, Apr. 21, 2003, available at www.un.org/press/en/2003/L3035.doc.htm.

The context at the time was not the most favorable. The United States had just adopted a new policy to face international terrorism: the "War on Terror." For decades "the US government had officially viewed terrorism as a law enforcement problem."[3] However, on the morning of 9/11 President Bush "decided that the conflict with Islamist terrorists must be viewed as a war."[4] The United States replaced the criminal justice paradigm, using the legal system to control criminals, with military intervention in various countries, aiming to physically exterminating terrorists considered by the United States to be enemy combatants without any right to challenge this characterization during a trial. In March 2003, a coalition of states led by the United States intervened militarily in Iraq against the express will of the majority of the United Nations Security Council members. The War on Terror, which would be implemented without boundaries or foreseeable conclusion, increased the US opposition to the ICC.

Prince Zeid's call reflected a new global legal design. He was not calling me in the name of Jordan. He was representing a new institution: the Assembly of States Parties, a sovereign body that integrates states parties of the Rome Statute[5] – a new legal architecture, going beyond the political system created by the UN Charter and transforming the legacy of Nuremberg and the ad hoc international tribunal into a truly international criminal justice system.

From my office in The Hague, I witnessed for nine years how the innovative system created by the Rome Statute became operational, how it established a working relation with the UN Security Council system and the connections with the War on Terror. In those days, I was aware of the differences between a multilateral political system led by the UN Security Council, where five permanent members could impose their interests, and the new international criminal justice system created by the Rome Statute, where political and military decisions at the international level should respect a legal framework. But I did not realize the long term impact of the War on Terror adopted unilaterally by the United States.

This chapter presents my preparations to face the challenge of being the ICC's chief prosecutor, including how my background and personal experience helped me, the connections between the Argentine Dirty War and the War on Terror, and how we decided the office's priorities and made the Court operational in its first nine years.

The junta trial changed my life, but most importantly, it was part of a national turnover. Between 1928 and 1983, military coups ousted all the democratically

[3] JACK GOLDSMITH, THE TERROR PRESIDENCY: Law and Judgment inside the Bush Administration 102 Norton & Company, New York London (2009).

[4] *Id.* at 102.

[5] Part XI of the Rome Statute defines the role of the Assembly of the States Parties, including how it can change the rules and structure, and how to appoint and supervise the prosecutor and the judges.

elected governments in Argentina before the end of their constitutional terms.[6] All the previous dictators enjoyed absolute immunity after they left power, but in 1985, for the first time, the commanders in chief of the Armed Forces were in the dock.

Kathryn Sikkink considered that the junta trial contributed to create the "Justice Cascade," "an interrelated, dramatic new trend in world politics towards holding individual state officials, including heads of state, criminally accountable for gross human rights violations."[7] She identified three types of judicial enforcement for the most serious crimes: (1) the international enforcement – starting in 1945 with the Nuremberg trials and following in the 1990s with the International Criminal Tribunal for the Former Yugoslavia (ICTY), the International Criminal Tribunal for Rwanda (ICTR), and the permanent ICC; (2) the domestic ones – starting with the trials in Greece and Portugal during the 1970s and with Argentina as the most influential in the 1980s; and (3) the foreign enforcement – such as the United Kingdom's intervention in 1998 in the Pinochet case at the request of Spanish judge Baltasar Garzon.

It was only in 2003 that I realized that my experience as a national prosecutor dealing with dictators, mass killers, guerrilla leaders, and grand corruption was my training to become the ICC prosecutor.

The junta trial taught me how to collect evidence from the victims without using the police or the state apparatus, a practice that was critical in enabling me to run the Office of the Prosecutor of the ICC, which has no police itself and relies exclusively on state cooperation. In applying the complementarity principle, the ICC intervention would be required when the national police and other national security forces are not able to gather evidence, conduct investigations, or to protect witnesses. The ICC prosecution may also be required to act where such national forces are themselves committing the crimes. In both scenarios, the classic investigations methods used by functioning national states could not be available for the ICC investigations.

I also learned to keep my focus on the evidence and the legal work, ignoring the pressures from those who were against the investigation. Part of the elite of my country had helped to sustain the dictatorship and used the media to attack us. At the ICC, I knew from the beginning that different groups, including supporters of the Court, would have different opinions and could be critical of my decisions, but I was prepared.

6 General Juan Domingo Peron completed his first term in 1952 but was ousted in the middle of his second term in 1955. Maximo Langer *Revolution in Latin American Criminal Procedure: Diffusion of Legal Ideas from the Periphery*, 55 AM. J. COMP. L. 617 (2007).

7 WORLD POLITICS (W.W. NORTON & COMPANY INC., 2011), at 5. She argues that: "Together, these three kinds of prosecutions comprise an interrelated, dramatic new trend in world politics toward holding individual state officials, including heads of state, criminally accountable for gross human rights violations." Sikkink calls this trend "the Justice Cascade meaning that there has been a shift in the legitimacy of the norm of individual criminal responsibility for human rights violations and an increase in criminal prosecutions on behalf of that norm. The term captures how the idea started as a small stream, but later caught on suddenly sweeping along many actors in its wake."

In Argentina, I had to face the anger of my own family. My uncle Buby, a retired colonel who visited General Videla in prison, reluctantly admitted that I was his nephew and recognized that he could not stop me. But he promised that he would not talk to me again. He died 25 years later, fulfilling his promise.

My investigations of grand corruption in Argentina forced me to learn how to be firm in the application of the law against those with political power. I knew that powerful states did not support my decision to request an indictment of President Bashir of the Sudan, but I considered that it was my duty to present it.

Most importantly, I learned the importance of the legal architecture to establish a peaceful coexistence, to replace a "dirty war" model based on an enemy paradigm for a justice paradigm where there are no enemies to exterminate but rather crimes to prevent and control. I found how life changed in Argentina after democracy and the constitutional system were reestablished in 1983 – the same people coexisted in peace on the same land simply as a result of adopting a different legal framework.

The conflict between power and law was part of my DNA. The peculiarities of my family and of my country served to feed my interest.

Argentina is a country of contrasts, and my own family expressed them well. At the beginning of the twentieth century, one of my grandfathers was a senator of the Radical Party who promoted free education and civil rights, and the other was a general who had studied in Prussia before World War I and since then had deeply admired Germany.

My father's family had been involved in the independence war and the struggle to establish the constitution. They were liberal thinkers who considered that women should be educated and aim to have professional careers. At the end of the nineteenth century, Trinidad Moreno, the sister of my grandmother was the principal of the normal school for girls in Cordoba, the second largest Argentine city. She was part of an educational effort led by President Domingo Sarmiento who considered that "schools are the basis for democracy"[8] and was a friend of Horace Mann, the "father of the Common School movement."[9] Trinidad Moreno's story exposes the values of my father's family and Sarmiento's struggle to disseminate ideas to build democracy in Argentina.

8 JOSEPH ORISCENT, SARMIENTO AND HIS ARGENTINA 86 (1983).

9 Mary Mann, Horace's widow, helped Sarmiento to hire 65 American teachers who traveled to Argentina to establish schools. Sometimes these young female Protestant teachers were received with hostility. One of the most difficult experiences happened to Francis Armstrong, who established the girls' normal school in Cordoba, which was, according to the *Winona Daily News*, "a city considered more Catholic than the Vatican." The Papal Nuncio considered that Ms. Armstrong was trying to convert the children to Protestantism, but she remained firm. There was a public discussion; the government was involved and supported Ms. Armstrong. Finally, Argentina's president advised Nuncio to take the next steamer for Rome. After four years, Francis Armstrong selected Trinidad Moreno to replace her. Available at *See* www.winonadailynews.com/news/local/a-new-argentina-wsu-teachers-in-s-lead-country-to/article_1f915dae-7929-11e0-83f4-001cc4c002e0.html.

My mother's family was more conservative. My grandfather was a general, and for him, loyalty to his family, to his friends, and to the institution was the most important value. He accepted without any complaint that the Argentine army had expropriated his own farm without proper compensation to use the land for military purposes. Two of my uncles were army officers. I deeply appreciated their strong sense of honor and commitment.

When I was 14 years old, I witnessed the clash between these two very different sides of my family at teatime in the house of my grandmother. My uncles were involved in the planning of the military coup of 1966, and my father was trying to dissuade them. My father's impassioned defense of democracy and freedom did not change the mind of my mother's brothers, who were convinced that a military regime would be more efficient. They were honest men, sincerely committed to changing their country, and while I loved them, I considered them to be wrong.

That day, I decided to study law. I wanted to learn how to establish a democratic framework in Argentina. Since 1930, the Argentinian elite had obtained political power through coups d'etat, and I wanted to learn how to establish democracy and the rule of law in my country. I suspected that there was a way to blend respect for rules and fairness with feelings of loyalty.

I started my university studies at the University of Buenos Aires in 1970. During law school, I established a small company in order to ensure my professional freedom as a lawyer. That income held me in good stead during the dictatorship and after gave me the liberty to pursue work that I valued.

In those days, Latin America was one of the battlefields of the Cold War, and Argentina developed some of the largest urban guerrilla groups.[10] Many of the guerrilla leaders had been trained in Cuba, learning about how to hide within the population and how to use violence to gain power.[11]

I never participated in public life during the 1970s because I did not agree with violence, and I was busy working and studying. The 1966 military regime supported by my uncles fueled the recruitment of guerrilla members and provided legitimacy for them. In 1973, Argentina returned to democracy, but the democratic government could neither stop the guerrilla activities nor control the economy or the security forces.

I got married in 1975 and a few months later completed my studies at the law school. I became a part-time assistant professor of criminal law at the University of Buenos Aires. I had to study the German and Italian authors who are very influential in Argentine penal studies, as both European and American legal thinking are very pervasive in Argentina. I also studied the philosophy of the law with two professors who wrote a seminal book called *Normative System*.[12]

[10] For background about the People's Revolutionary Army, see DONALD C. HODGES ARGENTINA, 1943–1976: *The National Revolution and Resistance* (1976).

[11] ENRIQUE DÍAZ ARAUJO, LA GUERILLA EN SUS LIBROS (2008).

[12] Carlos Alchourron and Eugenio Bulygin.

In March 1976, a military junta took power by promising to reestablish order. The junta leaders were ready to implement a secret military plan to face Argentina's guerrillas. It had some similarities to the one established in the twenty-first century to face terrorism in Afghanistan and Iraq. In both cases, the suspects were made into enemies to be eliminated, not criminals to be controlled. Argentina's commanders used the war paradigm against Argentina's citizens.

During the dictatorship, I had two kids, I continued my business, I got divorced, and, in my free time, I studied music theory. Nothing serious happened to me. I knew one person who disappeared, but it was not clear whether the security forces had abducted him or whether he had left the country. Like millions of Argentinians, I lived under the dictatorship with no clear idea of what was happening. All the security operations were being kept secret.

The junta created a schizophrenic public opinion, imposing ruthless censorship, all the while denying its criminal acts and labeling whoever denounced their criminal practices as "subversives."[13] General Videla publicly declared that Christian values and freedom were under attack from international terrorism, while his undercover forces attacked Argentine citizens in their homes and on the street. My mother loved General Videla because she felt he protected her and her family. In many other aspects, the private life of Argentinians could continue.

It was only later, when I had to investigate the crimes, that I learned how the system worked. There were no paramilitaries or death squads. It was a plan executed by the Armed Forces. Special Intelligence Units were working under the control of a zone commander, a general, to identify targets – individuals under suspicion of being subversives. They were Argentinians, but they had no rights. They were the enemy.

After the approval of the zone commander, the Special Intelligence Units secretly abducted these Argentine citizens. The zone commander also alerted all the military and security forces of the place and time of abduction in order to create a "free zone" for the special units. The police would not interfere with the abductions and would not inform to the judges or any other authorities of the undercover operations carried out.

In the military and police barracks, intelligence personnel tortured the targets using brutal methods, including enhanced interrogations techniques, in order to evaluate the responsibility of the suspect and identify new targets.[14] Military officers would make a judgment on the information collected and make a decision as to whether the target would be executed, sent to prison through the normal judicial system, or liberated.

13 Nunca Mas. The report of the Argentine National Commission on the disappeared (1986.)

14 Iain Guest, Behind the Disappearances: Argentina's Dirty War Against Human Rights and the United Nations (1990).

This procedure was secret and offered no legal recourse of any kind. The suspects had no right to present exculpatory evidence, to be represented by a lawyer, or to have a judge review the determination. To avoid an international reaction, the junta decided to deny all these remedies, to refuse to provide information to the judges, and to hide the bodies by throwing them into the sea or burying them in anonymous graves. The word *desaparecido* described this criminal practice.

In 1980, the intervention of an international institution, the Inter-American Commission on Human Rights (IACHR), forced the dictatorship to end the illegal repression. In well-organized countries, the security forces protect the citizens and no one seeks international intervention. For Argentinians, the inspection of the IACHR was highly appreciated and played a key role in stopping the crimes.

In 1982, Argentina's dictatorship recovered the Malvinas/Falkland Islands by military actions. But the UK reacted, and the defeat of Argentina in the war marked the end of the dictatorship and the beginning of a new period in Argentine public life.

Elections were called for the following year. Contrary to what had happened in Nuremberg, Portugal, or Greece, the proposal of conducting investigations was discussed publicly and adopted by the majority of the society. I missed this social and political support at the International Criminal Court.

During the 1983 campaign, human rights organizations found a space to expand their demands for the investigations of the fate of the *desaparecidos*.[15] The media started to lose its fear and to publish information about mass graves, individuals buried as "NN" with a bullet in their heads, and the stories of torture.

Raul Alfonsin, the candidate from the minority Radical Party promised to fully reestablish the constitution, including investigating and prosecuting military crimes.[16] He opened his public speeches by quoting the preamble of the Argentinian Constitution and received acclamations from the crowds.

A few months before the elections, the dictatorship tried to stop the attempt to review the past by adopting a "self-amnesty." But such a late reaction had the opposite effect on the population and provoked more demands for justice. Several judges decided that the self-amnesty was unconstitutional, and Alfonsin's proposal for accountability gained even more support. He won the elections with 52 percent of the votes.[17]

15 *Desaparecidos* translates to "those who disappeared." *See* Marysa Navarro las Madres de Plaza de Mayo, "The Personal Is Political: Las Madres de Plaza de Mayo." *Power and Popular Protest: Latin American Social Movements* (University of California press, 1989).

16 Mark R. Amstutz, The Healing of Nations: The Promise and Limits of Political Forgiveness (2004).

17 Dieter Nohlen, Elections in the Americas: A Data Handbook: Volume 2 (2005).

All the Argentinian political parties adjusted to the social demand for justice. President Alfonsin's first decrees called for an investigation of the guerrilla leaders and the members of three different military juntas.[18] The first law that the reestablished Congress enacted, almost by consensus, nullified the self-amnesty adopted by the last junta.[19] A few weeks later, the Congress decided that the military courts would investigate the crimes but included a legal and factual review before the federal justice system.

Alfonsin's administration established the National Commission on the Disappearance of Persons (CONADEP),[20] one of the first truth commissions integrated by civil society personalities to investigate the past.[21]

These political decisions were fairly implemented. As part of Sarmiento's legacy, Argentina had people well educated and trained to investigate fairly the past and to do justice. In just eight months, the CONADEP collected more than 50,000 declarations and identified more than 380 clandestine detention centers located in military barracks or police buildings. The Commission created a list with the names of 1,500 persons to investigate.

In a public meeting, while thousands of demonstrators appeared in the streets, the CONADEP provided to President Alfonsin a chilling report that described the systematic crimes committed during the dictatorship and requested that the judges define the individual responsibilities for such crimes.[22]

While the entire country was calling for justice, the army closed its ranks. Loyalty prevailed. The Supreme Council of the Armed Forces, the top military court that was investigating the members of the junta, decided that the public orders issued by the Junta were in accordance with the law and tried to postpone any decision on the case. The Armed Forces were not ready to investigate themselves.

The Federal Court of Appeals of Buenos Aires circuit, which had the legal mandate to review the military courts decisions, ended the jurisdiction of the

[18] The nine defendants were the members of the different military junta integrated by the top commanders of the Armed Forces that ruled the country in the period between 1976 and 1982. They were three former Argentinian dictators, General Jorge Rafael Videla, General Roberto Viola, and General Alfredo Galtieri; three Navy commanders in chief; and three Air Force commanders in chief. It was considered that the secret plan to abduct, torture, and execute individuals considered "subversives" ended before the last military junta ruled the country (1982–1983) and as a consequence they were not charged. *See* Sebastian Brett, *Argentina: Reluctant Partner: The Argentine Government's Failure to Back Trials of Human Rights Violators*. 13 Hum. Rts. Watch IX (2001).

[19] Rebecca B. Chavez, The Rule of Law in Nascent Democracies: Judicial Politics in Argentina (2004).

[20] National Commission on the Disappearance of Persons or Comisión Nacional sobre la Desaparición de Personas (CONADEP), *See* Lilian A. Barria & Steven D. Roper, The Development of Institutions of Human Rights: A Comparative Study (2010).

[21] Priscilla B. Hayner, Fifteen Truth Commissions – 1974 to 1994: A Comparative Study, 16 Hum. Rts. Q. 597 1994.

[22] Nunca Mas, supra note 13.

Supreme Council of the Armed Forces on the junta case and took up the case itself.[23]

In 1980, I became a prosecutor general's legal advisor, preparing briefings and studying US and Argentine Supreme Court decisions.

I did not participate in any part of the 1983 electoral campaign, and I was not part of any political party activity. After the democratic election, in 1984, I accepted a position as the deputy director of the University of Buenos Aires School of Law research center on a part-time basis. I was trying to promote a new way of studying and teaching law in a lawless country. My partner was managing my company, which complemented my income, and I kept my position as legal advisor of the prosecutor general, preparing submissions for the Supreme Court.

Julio Strassera, the chief federal prosecutor on criminal matters in Buenos Aires, had to prove this landmark junta case and requested support from the prosecutor general's office.[24] There was no big search for the best candidates. I was one of the two prosecutor general's office advisors with expertise in criminal matters, and both of us were summoned to Strassera's office. Although, I had not been looking for it, it was my dream job. I resigned from my university position to be involved in the junta trial.

After a few days, the other deputy prosecutor resigned. For me, it was impossible to reject the possibility of fulfilling my teenage ambition of helping to reestablish the rule of law in Argentina. It was going to be my first case as prosecutor.

Strassera asked me to organize the investigation. He explained that we couldn't rely on the police or intelligence agencies to investigate the case because during the Dirty War, those institutions were also involved in the commission of the crimes. He considered my absolute lack of experience in the field as an advantage: we had to invent something new. He granted me the responsibility of planning and supervising the collection of evidence for the prosecution. I had the daunting and exciting opportunity of using my legal skills to represent the citizens of Argentina in the most important trial of our shared history. It was my time to participate in public life, the opportunity to answer a question I had asked myself years ago.

I had to learn on the job how to conduct investigations of massive crimes without using the police. We had to prove through circumstantial evidence that the top commanders were responsible for a criminal plan, and to that end, we created a different model of investigations: one that relied almost entirely on the victims' statements taken by the CONADEP.

My entrepreneurial skills were useful. I assembled a team of seven young lawyers to focus on the CONADEP's report. We selected the most important incidents and

23 Brett, *supra* note 18.

24 Julio César Strassera, chief prosecutor during the 1985 Trial of the Juntas, was formerly a federal prosecutor. He later represented Argentina at the United Nations Commission on Human Rights.

contacted the surviving victims. We asked them for additional witnesses of their abductions and for the habeas corpus writs and other documents issued at the time of the crimes to corroborate their testimonies. The consistent denials of the military and police authorities provided additional indicia. We also looked for impartial witnesses.

Piece by piece, we made the connections between the individual crimes and the commanders' orders. Those who survived provided testimonies of their own and of others' tortures. All those tortures were inflicted in clandestine detention centers that operated for almost four years in military barracks or police stations around the entire country. The generals recognized that they had inspected these places, although they denied that any crime had been committed there, showing nonetheless the commanders' supervision of the criminal strategy ordered by the junta members.

We found some of the bodies of those abducted to prove that the executions were conducted without trial. In just five months, we transformed the CONADEP information into the evidence needed to charge the junta members.

The experience of developing evidence from the victims without police or intelligence support was crucial for my role at the ICC to investigate when the national police force is unable to investigate the crimes or is committing the crimes.

The public hearings began on April 22, 1985, and 20,000 people stood before the Court building, clamoring for justice.[25] Over the next five months, 800 witnesses provided testimony during extensive public hearings before a panel of six judges. More than 20 defense lawyers cross-examined them.

Rapt and horrified, the entire country followed the witnesses' stories – like the abduction and torture of a 16-year-old boy and the testimony of a university professor forced to give birth in a police car while handcuffed. On December 9, 1985, the judges issued their decision: the five commanders who were members of the first two juntas were convicted. General Videla and Admiral Massera received life prison sentences; General Viola, Admiral Lambruschini, and Air Force General Agosti were sentenced to between 4 and 17 years in prison. The crimes stopped in 1980, and as a consequence those who joined the junta after that date were acquitted. The charges for covering up the past crimes and issuing false documents were dismissed.[26]

The trial established the individual responsibility of some of the junta members, but its impact reverberated around the country and beyond its borders. The public hearings in the courtroom exposed the real military operations and changed Argentina's own sociohistorical perception.

25 Paula K. Speck, *The Trial of the Argentine Junta: Responsibilities and Realities*, 18 Miami Inter-American L. Rev. 491 (1987).

26 Members of the Junta between 1980–1982 were acquitted. The judges considered that the systematic plan ended in 1980. *See* National Criminal Court of Appeals, Judicio a las Juntas Militaires Sentencia y fallo, case number: 13/84, available at www.internationalcrimesdatabase.org/Case/1118/Juicio-a-las-Juntas-Militares/.

While scholars made distinctions between punitive and restorative justice,[27] I perceived that the ritual of the trial played in both ways.

During the period of investigation, I failed to convince my own mother that the junta members should be prosecuted. She loved General Videla: she went to church with him, and he reminded her of my grandfather. She thought that the junta was protecting her from the guerrilla threat. For her, General Videla was innocent, and I was wrong. But two weeks after the trial began, my mother called me. She had read some of the witnesses' testimonies and said to me, "I still love General Videla, but you are right. He has to be in jail." I could not convince her, but the witnesses' testimonies, the impartiality of the proceedings, and the public communication of the court hearings prompted my mother to change her mind.

In 1986 and 1987, I was involved in a second large trial against the chief of the Buenos Aires Police and some lower officers and in an extradition from San Francisco of an Argentine general who had fled the country. We also started other cases against navy and army officers.

There was no clarity on how to prioritize the investigations, and that's why from the beginning of my ICC tenure I adopted the policy to focus on those "most responsible." I knew that without a clear initial policy, it would be impossible to decide who should be investigated.

Massive crimes were committed by a great number of criminals, and there was no valid legal criterion to make a distinction between them. In Argentina, the law put no limits on the scope of the investigations, and people demanded the prosecution of very well-known low-level officers who were still in the Army and who were involved in the crimes. There were political tensions leading to a military rebellion in 1987, demanding the end of the investigations against the lower ranking military officers. In response, the Congress adopted a law ending the investigations of the dictatorship crimes committed by officers below the grade of colonel.

Most of the judges involved in the junta trial resigned, and at the end of 1987, Julio Strassera accepted a position as Argentina's ambassador to the UN Human Rights Commission in Geneva. I replaced him and became the senior criminal federal prosecutor in Buenos Aires. In those days, my small company was in bankruptcy, and my government salary was very small – but I felt that the effort to bring justice should continue.

I had the chance of being involved in other big cases. Some Air Force officers had started a new rebellion in 1988, and I had to conduct the investigations and prosecutions of their crimes against the constitutional order. In 1988, I also led the review of a military case against the top commanders and senior officers of the

27 Elmar Weitekamp & Hans-Jürgen Kerner, Restorative Justice, Theoretical Foundations (2012).

Malvinas-Falkland war.[28] I was also involved in an appeal regarding attacks by the guerrilla forces.[29]

During this second phase, I decided to also confront political corruption, a different type of abuse of power that had been widespread during the dictatorship, and had continued during the democratic government. Since President Menem had taken office in 1989, there had been a lot of reports about corrupt practices. I tried to improve the investigations using some of the techniques we had developed to investigate the dictatorship. I supervised multiple investigations into grand corruption cases involving politicians, businessmen, and judges.

There was a difference between both types of cases: politicians fully supported the investigations of the Dirty War and the military rebellions. They had an interest in avoiding a new coup d'etat, in excluding the use of the military to gain political power. But many political leaders were part of the corruption game and were not enthusiastic about my efforts. I had to learn how to conduct strategic litigation, how to use the law to impose limits to power, and how to overcome the lack of support of political leaders. I had to learn how to sail against the winds. It was a challenging time.

Argentina had survived military rebellions, economic and political crisis. The Argentine society and its political leaders kept supporting democracy and the functioning of democracy prevented the commission of more massive crimes.

In 1990, Argentina had its last military rebellion. For the first time, the Argentine Army reacted very strongly and fought against the rebel soldiers. Two loyal officers were killed. I was in charge of the prosecution of the case against the rebels and we obtained a conviction in 1991.

After that trial, I felt confident that democracy was stable, but I had learned that my judicial efforts were not enough to control corruption. Instead of controlling corruption, President Menem was trying to control the prosecutors and the judges. So I resigned as federal prosecutor in Buenos Aires and started a law firm.

My practice focused on what I considered to be good and honest causes. My firm helped private and public organizations to monitor and curb corruption.[30] We

28 The Malvinas-Falklands War was a 10-week conflict between Argentina and the United Kingdom over a group of islands in the south of the Atlantic. They were part of Argentina but in 1836 were occupied by the British Empire. In April 1982, Argentina's military forces occupied the islands, and Margaret Thatcher reacted, sending British troops. The conflict ended with Argentina' s surrender in June of the same year. A total of 649 Argentine and 255 English soldiers died during the conflict. Legal action was brought against Argentine military leaders for a failure to fulfill professional duty. They were found guilty of failing to plan operations beyond the initial invasion. Former president Lt. Gen. Leopoldo Galtieri was sentenced to 12 years imprisonment. Former Navy chief, Jorge Anaya, and former Air Force head, Basilio Lami Dozo, were sentenced, respectively, to 14 and 8 years in jail.

29 *See supra* note 10.

30 We recruited a group of talented young lawyers, aided by a highly skilled and diverse interdisciplinary team that included the use of hidden cameras, financial investigators, a network theorist, and an anthropologist.

needed to understand management and corporate structures to help large companies to control corruption. Additionally, we defended a few highly selective cases before Argentine courts.[31] We represented former Minister of Economy Domingo Cavallo before the IACHR, arguing for respect for his right to a fair trial.[32] We also managed fascinating conflicts on behalf of women who, as shareholders in Argentina's major companies, had been excluded from decision-making by their male family members. My private legal practice forced me to challenge people with political or economic power. This experience would prove invaluable in the years to come.

During that period, my name was proposed to be the first ICTY prosecutor. In August 1993, the UN secretary general proposed Cherif Bassiouni as the ICTY prosecutor. He was the obvious choice. But an informal vote at the UN Security Council to appoint Bassiouni revealed a division of 7 to 7 and one abstention. The United Kingdom led the opposition to his candidacy, convincing the United States of the need for a consensus candidate. In a conflict between Serbs and Muslims, he was described as too victim-oriented and thus biased because he was a Muslim.[33]

In October 1993, the UN Security Council appointed Venezuela's general prosecutor, Ramon Escobar Salom, as the first chief prosecutor of the ICTY.[34] He had a long career as an academic and a politician[35] but was not interested in the international prosecutor's role. I met him in 1992 when I was invited to advise the Venezuelan prosecutors in their investigations on corruption. In March 1993, Escobar Salom had indicted Venezuela's President Carlos Andres Perez,[36] and when he received the offer to be the ICTY prosecutor, he informed the United Nations that before taking on that role he had to finish the Perez case. He finally went to The Hague on January 1994 for few days, met with an Australian prosecutor named Graham Blewitt,[37] appointed him as deputy prosecutor,[38] and then informed

31 Such as the defense of football star Diego Maradona; the famous journalist Jacobo Timerman; Adriana Gallo, a state judge removed from office for her outspokenness; and Thomas Catan, a journalist from the *Financial Times* who was targeted by a federal judge after exposing corruption in the Argentine senate.

32 Inter-American Commission on Human Rights, Report No. 123/11, Petition 12.123, Domingo Felipe Cavallo (2011).

33 Editor, Introduction to International Criminal Law, Leiden, The Netherland, 2013 (M. Cherif Bassiouni, ed., 2d ed. 2013).

34 Luc Reydams, Jan Wouters & Cedric Ryngaert. International Prosecutors. (2012).

35 Prior to his appointment, he was a professor at the Central University of Venezuela, a fellow at Harvard University, and a visiting professor at Cambridge University (1982–1983). He was a member of the House, a senator, a minister of justice, and minister of foreign relations (1975–1977). Between 1994–1996, he was minister of home affairs. He represented Venezuela at the Rome Conference in 1998.

36 Jody C. Baumgartner & Naoko Kada, Checking Executive Power: Presidential Impeachment in Comparative Perspective. (2003).

37 Reydams L., et. al., *supra* note 34.

38 *Id.*

UN secretary general Boutros-Ghali that he had accepted an invitation to become the minister of home affairs in Venezuela. On February 3, he resigned as prosecutor.[39]

The UN Security Council then started to explore new options and reached an informal agreement to appoint me. The Argentinian government was invited to propose my name, but President Menem's administration refused. Because of the investigations on corruption I had led as a national prosecutor, my government considered me to be a political enemy.

Instead, it proposed a different person.[40] The UN Security Council ignored Argentina's proposal, explored other options, and finally, Richard Goldstone, a prestigious judge from South Africa[41] was appointed.

I did not really regret the lack of support from my government to become the ICTY's prosecutor. In those days, I was focused on building my law firm and on my family. My son and my daughter were teenagers, and I had remarried and had a newborn with my new wife.

In addition to my private practice, I continued to participate in Argentina's public life as a private citizen. I was involved in the development of national and international NGOs focused on civic participation and anticorruption (*Poder Ciudadano* and Transparency International).[42] Education had always been my great passion, and in 1998, I explored how network television could disseminate basic knowledge about law, justice, and the resolution of conflicts. In a democratic society, people have to understand and champion the law,[43] especially in a country like Argentina where its own representatives have undermined the legal system.

My anticorruption consultancy work supporting the World Bank's Institute director, Daniel Kaufman, gave me an insight of international organizations. I traveled to 40 countries analyzing corruption problems and discussing measures to control them.

By 2002, my law firm was consolidated, and I took a sabbatical leave to return to academia. I was teaching courses on anticorruption during the spring semester of 2002 at Stanford University, and I was preparing myself to spend time at Harvard Law School as a visiting professor. I was delighted at the opportunity to reflect on cutting edge legal issues.[44]

39 *Id.*

40 David Scheffer, All the Missing Souls: A Personal History of the War Crimes Tribunals 34 (2012).

41 Sanja K. Ivkovich & John Hagan, Reclaiming Justice: The International Tribunal for the Former Yugoslavia and Local Courts 3 (2011).

42 *Poder Ciudadano* (Citizen Power) was founded in Argentina in 1989. It seeks to protect civil rights and to strengthen democratic institutions by promoting citizen participation, transparency and access to public information. Since 1993, it is the Argentine chapter of Transparency International. Transparency International, founded in Germany in 1993, is a global NGO that monitors, documents and exposes corruption with the aim of its eradication from government, business and civil society.

43 According with a Gallup Argentina survey 10 percent of Argentina's population (4 million people) learned how to solve problems with such shows.

44 Since 1988, I had been taking advantage of the richness of the environment at Harvard. I was giving lectures and participating in seminars, and I spent few months as a fellow of the Latin American

Following the phone call in November, I visited Prince Zeid in his office in Manhattan at the end of 2002. He was in his late thirties, a very charming and skillful diplomat, an Arab prince with blue eyes, whose grandfather fought with Lawrence of Arabia and had a Swedish mother. During the 1990s, he had worked with the UN peacekeeping forces in the Balkans, and since then he had been one of the national leaders working for the establishment of the Court. He was evaluating the possibility of reaching a rapid consensus to appoint the prosecutor before February 2003 when the process to select the 18 judges was going to start. We had a fascinating conversation about the role of the prosecutor in developing countries, and we decided to stay in touch.

In accordance with the Rome Statute, the prosecutor shall be a person of high moral character, be highly competent, and have extensive practical experience in the prosecution or trial of criminal cases and be fluent in at least one of the working languages of the Court. These were the requirements by law, but I had the impression that, in addition, states were looking for a candidate from the South and that was why they were interested in me.

The new Argentinian administration under President Duhalde informed me that it would not oppose my nomination, but it could not promote my name because it had presented a Supreme Court justice as a candidate to be a judge at the International Criminal Court. There was a strong competition between the states to appoint their candidates, and it was difficult to imagine that Argentina would have both a judge and prosecutor at the ICC.

In order to understand the process and the expectations involved, I met Silvia Fernandez de Gurmendi in Buenos Aires for the first time.[45] She was an Argentinian diplomat who had played a critical role before, during, and after the Rome Conference to establish the ICC. Her brilliance and sense of humor impressed me. She had close relations with all the relevant actors, knew everything about the process to adopt the Statute, and explained to me the crucial details of the negotiations.

In January 2003, I left Buenos Aires' summer and moved to Cambridge. I remember walking through 10 inches of snow in Harvard Yard thinking how lucky I was to be there. At the same time, I was unhappy with the informal nature of the

Center in 1998. I was discussing with Rafael Di Tella and Tarun Khana from the business school about how corruption affected economies. Samantha Power, who was finishing her book on genocide, gave me the privilege of commenting on her manuscript. The plan was to co-teach a course on corruption with Phil Heymann, a Harvard professor and US deputy attorney general during the Clinton administration who had been part of the team that investigated Watergate. I was also offering a small seminar with an ambitious title "How to Establish Rule of Law in the World." The seminar was going to explore the international connections of the most serious crimes and the efforts to investigate them including through the International Criminal Court.

45 Silvia Fernandez de Gurmendi is the current President of the International Criminal Court and a visiting professor at the American University Washington College of law.

process to select the ICC prosecutor. It was promoting misunderstandings and gossip about me.

I had detractors, but I also had supporters like Aryeh Neier,[46] an iconic figure in the human rights movement who had known me for some years. Aryeh insisted during the informal meetings that I should be the prosecutor. Samantha Power, a colleague from Harvard and a gifted writer, helped me prepare a letter to Prince Zeid presenting my views and concerns about the process. Prince Zeid informed me that it was not possible to reach an agreement on the name of the prosecutor before the judge selection and urged me to keep considering the possibility.

At The Hague on March 11, 2003, Prince Zeid, the president of the Assembly of States Parties, and Queen Beatrix of the Netherlands, representing the host country, presided over the swearing in of the International Criminal Court's judges, who had been selected from 18 countries around the world. The Assembly elected Judge Philippe Kirsch,[47] a former Canadian ambassador who chaired the Rome Conference, as the president of the Court.[48] A prosecutor had to be selected in April.

The Argentinian candidate proposed as a judge had not been elected, and some countries invited me to visit them. I took advantage of Harvard's spring break, and in one week, I visited London, The Hague, Oslo, Berlin, Paris, and Madrid to be interviewed by members of the ministries of foreign affairs who were deciding on the prosecutor nominations. My trip made me even more skeptical.

I had pleasant conversations about my experience as national prosecutor and other legal issues with the Dutch ambassador at a nice restaurant at The Hague and with Elizabeth Wilmshurst, the deputy legal adviser at the UK Foreign Office. But she resigned two days later when the Iraq conflict started. In Oslo, they offered me a lovely lunch, but I confused them with my explanations about the functioning of international crime and a network analysis that I was using in my anticorruption course at Harvard.

My worst meeting was in Berlin. In 2002, I had been involved in a very controversial case in Argentina. The most important TV network had conducted an investigation and denounced a very well-known priest as a child abuser. One of my clients was making donations to the priest, and she could not believe that the allegations were founded. At her request, my firm investigated how the TV investigation had been conducted, and we found that the investigative journalist had influenced the prosecutor acting in the case to eliminate some evidence beneficial to the priest.

The prosecutor was removed from the case, but as a consequence, the TV channel and other parts of its media group attacked me. In Berlin, the German ambassador

46 Aryeh Neier served as Executive Director of Human Rights Watch, President of the Open Society Institute, and the National Director of the American Civil Liberties Union.

47 Philippe Kirsch is a former judge of the International Criminal Court and its first president. He was also chair of the Rome Diplomatic Conference for the ICC.

48 Marlise Simons, *World Court for Crimes of War Opens in the Hague*, N.Y. TIMES (Mar. 12, 2003).

showed me the covers of two different magazines criticizing my role in that case. He was sincerely worried about the possibility that my appointment could damage the reputation of the Court. He was also concerned about my involvement in Transparency International, as he thought it was an American NGO. I had to explain that Transparency International's headquarter was located in Berlin, 20 minutes from the Foreign Affairs Department.

In a beautiful building on the Quai d'Orsay in Paris, I found that my recently acquired habit of speaking fluently in poor English had an unexpected consequence: it completely erased my previously decent fluency in French. I tried to convince the French legal advisor that I could understand his words even though I could not articulate a decent sentence in his language. Madrid was my last stop, and after a pleasant conversation with Ambassador Yañez-Barnuevo, I flew back to Buenos Aires to spend a few days with my family.

That Sunday, still tired after my intense traveling week, I was having breakfast at my house in Buenos Aires and preparing for my return to Harvard. I told my wife, "I am glad that I did the effort but they will not appoint me. I perceived their concerns about independent prosecutors. Carla del Ponte is a natural choice and they are not even considering her name. Don't worry; our lives will not change."

She was reading the newspaper and did not immediately respond, but a few minutes later she showed me a short article on page six under the headline "Informal consensus reached: an Argentinian lawyer, Luis Moreno Ocampo, will be the Prosecutor of the new International Criminal Court."

In April 2003, 78 states from all over the world granted me the responsibility of building an innovative global institution: the Office of the Prosecutor of the International Criminal Court.

I sold my law firm in Buenos Aires to my partners, quit my position as visiting professor at Harvard Law School and as member of the boards of Transparency International and New Tactics for Human Rights. My family stayed in Buenos Aires, and for nine years I was commuting from The Hague on a regular basis to be close to them. I launched an astonishing journey that exceeded all of my expectations.

At Nuremberg, for the first time, prosecutors and judges represented the international community. But the world was not ready to transform it into a permanent institution. The end of the Cold War created the opportunity to do justice for the victims of international crimes, first in the former Yugoslavia and then in Rwanda. Sierra Leone and Cambodia found their own way to establish a partnership with the international community to seek justice. All these efforts paved the way for the creation of a permanent International Criminal Court. But I understood that the design of the Rome Statute is part of a new legal architecture, an innovation modifying an international legal system based on the exclusive interaction of sovereign states.

The prosecutors of the ad hoc international tribunals received a limited mandate: independence to investigate and to prosecute crimes but into a very specific territorial and temporal jurisdiction defined by states. The Nuremberg charter established the first international ad hoc tribunal "for the just and prompt trial and punishment of the major war criminals of the European Axis."[49] The prosecutors had no authority to investigate crimes committed by members of the principals, a limit that exposed Nuremberg to criticism as an exercise of "victor's justice."

During the 1990s, the creation of ad hoc tribunals provided new tools to the UN Security Council but did not change the UN Charter system based on political relations between sovereign states. The UN Security Council carefully limited the territorial and temporal jurisdictions of the ICTY to address only those violations "committed in the territory of the former Yugoslavia between the 1st of January 1991 and a date to be determined by the Security Council upon the restoration of peace."[50] The ICTY prosecutor Louise Arbour created a huge controversy when she mentioned that the NATO campaign against the Federal Republic of Yugoslavia from March to June 1999 carried out by Western forces could be subject to investigation for war crimes.

Legally, the ICTY prosecutor would have jurisdiction because the Statute adopted by the UN Security Council allowed the investigation of any crimes committed within the territorial and temporal limits, but the NATO spokesman Jamie Shea expressed the real thinking of those states acting as principals: "I am certain that when Prosecutor Arbour returns to Kosovo and sees the facts, she will indict the Yugoslavian nationals, and no other nationalities." He considered that the prosecutor could not act against the states that supported her and advised "Don't bite the hand that feeds you."[51]

The UN Security Council limited the territorial and temporal jurisdictions of the ICTR to crimes committed in Rwanda and by Rwandese in neighboring states between January 1, 1994 and December 31, 1994.[52]

The UN Security Council, controlled by the major powers defined the group of people that would face international criminal justice before the ad hoc tribunals.

The states parties to the Rome Statute established a different system: no privileges and no impunity, even for heads of states. To guarantee this commitment, they established a sort of global confederation limited to the prevention of the most

[49] Article 1, Agreement by the Government of the United Kingdom of Great Britain and Northern Ireland, the Government of the United States of America, the Provisional Government of the French Republic and the Government of the Union of Soviet Socialist Republics for the Prosecution and Punishment of the Major War Criminals of the European Axis (Aug. 8, 1945), 82 UNTS 279. The International Military Tribunal for the Far East (IMTFE) was established for the "trial and punishment of the major war criminals in the Far East" arising from World War II; Article 1, Charter of the International Military Tribunal for the Far East; TIAS No. 1589.

[50] S.C. Res. 808, UN Doc. S/RES/808 (Feb. 22, 1993).

[51] Pierre Hazan, Justice in Time of War: The True Story behind the International Criminal Tribunal for the Former Yugoslavia (2004).

[52] S.C. Res. 955, UN Doc. S/RES/955 (Nov. 8, 1994).

serious crime to the international community as a whole and a permanent court to intervene if they genuinely failed to act. As a consequence, the ICC prosecutor's mandate had no precedent.

Similar to the prosecutors of the ad hoc tribunals, the ICC prosecutor's mandate includes the ability to independently investigate and prosecute crimes; but in addition, it incorporates a first-time component: to trigger the jurisdiction of the Court into a given sovereign territory. It is an authority delegated by the states parties of the Rome Statute and, on ad hoc basis, for those states that accept jurisdiction or by the UN Security Council. In accordance with this mandate, the Office of the Prosecutor's duty to act as an independent agent has two dimensions: it should refrain from opening investigations when national authorities conduct genuine proceedings, but it should trigger the jurisdiction of the Court when states were not conducting genuine proceedings. The prosecutor is the gatekeeper of the Rome Statute system.

In Argentina, the legal system was preexistent, and the novelty was the political and social demand to apply the law and investigate massive crimes. In the case of the Rome Statute, the demands of justice led to the creation of a new transnational criminal justice system, an innovative legal experiment.

When I went back to Harvard to present my resignation, a colleague advised me to reject the offer. "It is a great honor," he said, "but without the USA's involvement, how can you carry out investigations? How can you implement arrest warrants? It will be a shame. You will spend nine years in The Hague receiving a salary for doing nothing."

He had a point; there was a risk that the Court would end up doing nothing, and there were precedents. For example, the International Humanitarian Fact-Finding Commission (IHFFC) was constituted in 1991 to investigate allegations of grave breaches and serious violations of international humanitarian law. Although 76 States from all the Continents had already recognized it, the Commission has not yet been called upon.[53]

I took advantage of my last days at Harvard to ask Fernando Oris de Roa for some advice on how to use the private sector efficiency to build an international organization. I had to organize the Office of the Prosecutor, the goals had to be

[53] The IHFFC was officially constituted in 1991 to investigate allegations of grave breaches and serious violations of international humanitarian law. It represents the implementation of Article 90 of the First Additional Protocol to the Geneva Conventions of 1949, which authorized the creation of an International Fact-Finding Commission. The Commission is composed of 15 individuals who are elected by the States that have recognized its competence. As per the safeguards of state sovereignty built into the text, only a state having agreed by declaration to recognize the competence of the Commission can unilaterally request an inquiry, and only against another state having made the same declaration. Thus far, 76 states have recognized the Commission, but none have requested its intervention.

clear, and every member of the organization had to know what to do. Fernando was a very successful Argentinian businessman who had worked in senior positions at multinational companies in New York, Paris, and Argentina. He was 50 years old when he decided to take a sabbatical year to do a Master's of Public Policy at the Kennedy School. He had the personal maturity and the combination of experience and theoretical knowledge that I needed. I set forth our colloquy as I recall it below:

FERNANDO: I would love to help but I have no experience in legal institutions.

ME: The legal issues are not the problem. I have experience, but I could hire the best international lawyers, and I will be able to consult the best world experts. We could study the previous 50 years of discussions of the International Law Commission and 10 years of jurisprudence produced by the Ad Hoc Tribunals. My priority is how to organize my team. My responsibility is to build the Office of the Prosecutor of the International Criminal Court from scratch and transform it into a permanent institution.

FERNANDO: You are a startup.

ME: Yes but a unique startup. At the national level, the Office of the Prosecutor is part of the state apparatus, but we are different. We have to deal with conflicts that take place in different parts of the world, in different languages and in different settings without a foreign affairs ministry, a justice ministry, or a police force. There is no benchmark for that, and I need to think how to combine the different pieces.

Fernando invited me to his home to discuss my ideas. We sat very formally in his house near Harvard Square; he offered me coffee and asked me:

FERNANDO: Start with the basics. What is your mandate?

ME: In the words of the Statute: to ensure the end of impunity for "the most serious crimes to the international community as a whole" and "to contribute to the prevention of such crimes." The Statute is very clear on the first part, and there is less clarity on how the International Criminal Court could prevent such crimes. This is for me a critical part: how to contribute to the prevention.

FERNANDO: What are "the most serious crimes to the international community as a whole"?

ME: The International Criminal Court is not a human rights court. There are many national crimes and wrongdoings that are outside our jurisdiction. Isolated cases of political prisoners, torture, police brutality or assassinations, restrictions of the right to free speech, unfair trials, media censorship, coups d'etat, grand corruption, drug trafficking, terrorism, serious violations of economic or social human rights, or environmental catastrophes deliberately produced are not our business.[54]

FERNANDO: In this context what is your specific mission?

ME: I have to build an institution: the Office of the Prosecutor. The Office will be the main driver of the Court during the first period, it has to identify situations under the jurisdiction of the Court, trigger the jurisdiction, investigate then and litigate before the judges.

FERNANDO: OK. What are your main problems?

ME: There are conflicting expectations. There are 18 judges from all over the world waiting for a case. They had prominent positions previously – they were Supreme Court judges, ambassadors – and they made a personal decision to leave those positions. Now they want to be involved in judicial proceedings as soon as possible. Additionally, I learned that some of them had the feeling that the entire ICC project could be interrupted at any moment, and starting a trial could be the way to consolidate the institution.

FERNANDO: They are probably right. The operations should drive. Can you present a case in a short time?

ME: I have no chance. Today, the entire office is composed of three persons: a legal advisor, a manager, and an assistant. There is no security system to protect witnesses; there are no investigators and no lawyers with prosecutorial experience. I want to appoint people for their merits and the recruitment process will take at least six months.[55] I don't like to make mistakes. The office should attract the best people from all over the world; it should be the Olympus of all national prosecutors' offices. Professionalism is the only way to ensure respect for our mission.

FERNANDO: How did the other international prosecutors do it?

54 The Rome Statute for the International Criminal Court is a unique diagnosis of what values are common to the entire humanity and what others did not reach such a level of acceptance. Using the language of French professor Mireille Delmas-Marty, the debate at Rome was a moment of "ordering pluralism." MIREILLE DELMAS-MARTY, ORDERING PLURALISM. A CONCEPTUAL FRAMEWORK FOR UNDERSTANDING THE TRANSNATIONAL LEGAL WORLD (2009).

55 Article 44 of the Rome Statute for the International Criminal Court provides:

1. The Prosecutor and the Registrar shall appoint such qualified staff as may be required to their respective offices. In the case of the Prosecutor, this shall include the appointment of investigators.

2. In the employment of staff, the Prosecutor and the Registrar shall ensure the highest standards of efficiency, competency and integrity, and shall have regard, *mutatis mutandis*, to the criteria set forth in article 36, paragraph 8.

3. The Registrar, with the agreement of the Presidency and the Prosecutor, shall propose Staff Regulations that include the terms and conditions upon which the staff of the Court shall be appointed, remunerated and dismissed. The Staff Regulations shall be approved by the Assembly of States Parties.

4. The Court may, in exceptional circumstances, employ the expertise of gratis personnel offered by States Parties, intergovernmental organizations or non- governmental organizations to assist with the work of any of the organs of the Court. The Prosecutor may accept any such offer on behalf of the Office of the Prosecutor. Such gratis personnel shall be employed in accordance with guidelines to be established by the Assembly of States Parties.

ME: At the beginning, the ICTY prosecutor had many resource problems and bureaucratic obstacles to hire staff. The only way to start investigations was to rely on a few friends and to accept gratis personnel from the USA. They had no options, but the ICTY needed years to overcome the lack of diversity of its personnel and the improvisation. We need to learn from these lessons.

FERNANDO: Do you have similar resource problems?

ME: Not at all. States parties appointed an advance team to prepare an entire building to host the Court and to acquire the equipment required. There are six floors fully equipped at my disposal and a budget.

Fernando revolved in his chair. I thought that he wanted to insist on starting immediately with a case, but he was trying to be polite.

FERNANDO: Can you use your resources to explore transitional solutions? Can you appoint a small team to develop a case while you are recruiting the permanent staff?

ME: Even if I had the personnel, and I don't, there is no way to start an investigation immediately. The first decision is not about how to collect evidence but rather where to investigate: I have to identify a situation under the Court's jurisdiction.

FERNANDO: Can you appoint a special team for that? Just to conduct this process? What did you call it? Preliminary examination?

ME: I am focusing on that. But we need some clear policies. This is the most controversial part of the ICC project. Everyone is worried about how the Office of the Prosecutor will trigger the jurisdiction of the Court. We should respect the "principle of complementarity" that is the cornerstone of the system created by the Rome Statute.

FERNANDO: Why is that so controversial?

ME: Because it is changing the idea of absolute sovereignty, which has been prevalent for three centuries. The states parties are concerned because they accepted the independent intervention of the Court for crimes committed in their territory. Their heads of state have no immunity before the Court. The USA is afraid of a prosecutor ready to prosecute American soldiers. People from all over the world are requesting an investigation against the USA for its intervention in Iraq. Whatever I decide, it will be controversial. The Office should have a clear policy before taking any decision, a policy that could be sustained in the long run. I cannot move ahead and then backtrack. I will never do that.

FERNANDO: OK. Let me focus on what I know: management. That is the area where I can be more helpful. Can you decide on your human and financial resources?

ME: I have total independence: the Statute provides me with "full authority over the management and administration of the Office."[56] Additionally, because I am the first prosecutor, I have the unique opportunity to design a structure for the Office to fulfill its mandate and to present it for approval to the Assembly of States parties.

FERNANDO: Do you expect problems with the approval of your budget? Who will pay the costs?

ME: The states parties will pay, and we are now in a "honeymoon" period. All the indications that I have received indicate that states are ready to resolve financial problems. In any case, I should be cost efficient because after the end of the honeymoon, the situation will be different. I have the chance to build the most efficient public office.

FERNANDO: Talking about efficiency: how big will your administrative section be?

ME: Almost nonexistent. The registry is in charge of the administration of the entire Court. They are in charge of the back office. Additionally, they have to provide security, protection to our witnesses, and outreach.

Fernando lost his calm.

FERNANDO: Does the registry report to you?

ME: No, it is a different organ, it provides services to us, but also to the defense, the victims unit, and the judges. The Registrar reports to the presidency of the Court.

FERNANDO: You should change that. You could be paralyzed. It is a basic concept: you should not have the responsibility without the authority. This should be your priority.

ME: I am sorry, I cannot change it. That is the legal design.

FERNANDO: That will be a nightmare. You should really change that situation.

He kept insisting on the point. Then he moved on, though clearly convinced that the structural relationship between the prosecutor and the Registrar was unworkable.

FERNANDO: Is there any other problem that you should take into consideration?

[56] Article 2 of the Rome Statute for the International Criminal Court states: The Office of the Prosecutor.

(1) The Office of the Prosecutor shall act independently as a separate organ of the Court. It shall be responsible for receiving referrals and any substantiated information on crimes within the jurisdiction of the Court, for examining them and for conducting investigations and prosecutions before the Court. A member of the Office shall not seek or act on instructions from any external source.

(2) The Office shall be headed by the Prosecutor. The Prosecutor shall have full authority over the management and administration of the Office, including the staff, facilities and other resources thereof. The Prosecutor shall be assisted by one or more Deputy Prosecutors, who shall be entitled to carry out any of the acts required of the Prosecutor under this Statute.

ME: The most important: how to get cooperation from states parties, nonparties, UN and NGOs? As soon we cross the door of the building, we are in international jurisdiction and we need the states' cooperation. We are a stateless prosecutor's office: we need visas, security and support to carry out our work. I am not sure if states parties will provide the support needed, I am not quite sure how much can they resist the USA's hostility, and I don't know how such hostility will affect the cooperation of the UN.

FERNANDO: Are states willing to cooperate with the Office of the Prosecutor?

ME: There is an entire part of the Statute defining the state parties' legal duties to cooperate with the ICC investigations and prosecutions. But there is nothing about preventing crimes or arresting individuals in a foreign territory. These are two areas without solutions: they should be developed by the practice of other actors.

FERNANDO: I don't like to discourage you, but you are facing a really complicated situation. You don't control the basic functions of your own operations, and you have to rely on the good will of external actors. How can you organize them? You cannot plan a network. Each node makes decisions independently, following their own interest. I am not sure how can I help you.

ME: On the contrary, thank you for this exercise. It helped me to organize my mind. As you just said, I have to plan my office but also create a network. I should take advantage of the high value of our mission to attract the support of the other actors. I could describe my options now. I see three choices:

a) To start immediately with an investigation in order to launch the entire exercise; manage state, NGO, and citizen expectations; and align the Office of the Prosecutor with the interest of the judges. But there is a high probability of failure because the office is not ready and such a failure could be the end of the institution.
b) To consult with states, NGOs, and the different stakeholders to align their interests and to ensure their support. The risk is that of being paralyzed by the search for consensus.
c) To prioritize the internal matters and focus our efforts on the Office's policies and structure and in the selection of the staff. The risk is to lose momentum to create the network.

FERNANDO: And what you will do?

ME: Basically I cannot prioritize. I have to do everything at the same time. I will do options b) and c) in one shot. I will show that the Court is moving fast in the right direction and I hope that the other nodes will follow, and I will work in option a) immediately. Before taking the office, I will focus on the structure of the Office and the policies. Morten Bergsmo, the legal advisor, is working on that, he has been collecting more than 100 expert opinions on how to deal with these issues. I will consolidate them and prepare a first draft describing our policy and structure. I will take advantage of the strategic planning process to consult all our constituencies at the same time. Immediately after my swearing in, I will invite states representatives, experts, NGOs, and national and international prosecutors and judges to receive their comments on our plans in a public hearing.

I was determined to show efficiency, and as a consequence, I had no chance of establishing a single priority for the prosecutor office. I had to define the structure and policies while at the same time setting the Court in motion. I had to lead.

As planned, I spent the two days after my swearing in at a public hearing held in a modern annex of the Peace Palace. I was seated at a front table with Morten Bergsmo, my legal advisor, in front of almost 200 persons, including many ambassadors and legal advisors, listening to 60 of the best experts of the world discussing our draft policies.[57] Whitney Harris, a member of Robert H. Jackson's team during the first Nuremberg trial, was giving me advice on how to use documents to prove the case.

Delegates at the Rome Conference, such as David Scheffer (USA), Elizabeth Wilmshurst (UK), Hakan Friman (Sweden), and Juan Antonio Yañez–Barnuevo (Spain) presented their views about how to implement the Statute. Bertrand Ramcharan, the acting UN high commissioner for human rights, was explaining the synergies between the Commission's work and the Office of the Prosecutor. Antonio Cassese, former president of the ICTY, provided his insights. Staff of the ICTY provided comments based on their experience. Bill Pace, the convener of the Coalition for the International Criminal Court, and the most relevant and active members of the civil society organizations were presenting a variety of comments from victims' participation to prevention of crimes. And distinguished professors such as Otto Triffterer, Goran Sluiter, and Bruce Broomhall presented their contribution.

[57] Commentators included Ahmed Ziauddin; András Vámos-Goldman; Anne Rübesame; Antoine Bernard; Antonio Cassese; Arne W. Dahl; Bernhard Braune; Bernard O'Donnell; Bertrand G. Ramcharan; Billon Ung Boun-Hor; Bruce Broomhall; Carla Ferstman; Christopher Hall; Darryl Mundis; David Donat-Cattin; David Scheffer; David Scheffer; Diane Zeverin-McLean; Elizabeth Wilmshurst; Emmanuelle Duverger; Fabricio Guariglia; Fiona McKay; Francisco Rezek; Göran Sluiter; Håkan Friman; Hans Bevers; Hoc Pheng Chhay; Irune Aguirrezabal; J.J. du Toit; James Hamilton; Jeanne Sulzer; Jennifer Schense; Jonathan O'Donahue; Jose-Pablo Baraybar; Jutta Bertram Nothnagel; Jose Guevara; Juan Antonio Yañez–Barrionuevo; Kim Prost; Laurent Grosse; Marieke Wierda; Mark Ellis; Minna Schrag; Mohamed Kebe; Niccoló Figá-Talamanca; Peter Murphy; Peter Nicholson; Otto Triffterer; Richard Dicker; Sara Schifter-Sharratt; Sonia Robla Ucieda; Thomas Verfuss; Umberto Leanza; Vahida Nainer; Vladimir Tochilovsky; Wanda Hall; William R. Pace and Xabier Agirre. *See* all the transcripts at www.icc-cpi.int/en_menus/icc/structure of the court/office%20of%20the%20prosecutor/network%20with%20partners/public%20hearings/Pages/first%20public%20hearing.aspx.

The room was full of energy. It was the first time after the Rome Conference that all these actors had met to discuss the implementation of the project of international justice. Everyone was very thankful for the transparency of presenting our plans in public and for the openness of listening to their opinions. I received many frank comments, including criticism of the "zero case" approach I had described as the ultimate success benchmark of the Court and the suggestion not to rush to present cases until the office was organized.

It was one of the richest experiences of my work as the prosecutor, not just intellectually, but in feeling that we were representing a community, reflecting a group of individuals from all over the world who cared about international justice.

We produced a written report identifying the suggestions received, the areas of consensus, and discrepancies.[58] Following the advice received, the Office published its first policy paper in September 2003, defining three key policies to implement its mandate: a) complementarity, b) a focus on those bearing the greatest criminal responsibility, and c) maximizing the Office of the Prosecutor's contribution to the prevention of future crimes.

With regard to complementarity, states' genuine proceedings are an indicator of the Court's achievement. "The absence of trials by the ICC, as a consequence of the effective functioning of national systems, would be a major success," and the Office would, "take action only where there is a clear case of failure to take national action."

A second fundamental policy described in the 2003 policy paper is to focus investigations on those who bear the greatest responsibility for the most serious crimes in accordance with the evidence collected.

The third key policy adopted in 2003 and further refined later was to maximize the Office's contribution to the prevention of future crimes and to better protect victims from violence.

On June 19, 2003, for the first time as the prosecutor, I stepped up the stairs of the ICC building on the outskirts of The Hague. It was time to start the operations.

I had an office on the corner of the twelfth floor. Silvia Fernandez and Morten Bergsmo were on the same floor. Klaus Rackwitz was on the seventh floor. We had one assistant and six interns supporting our work. That was the entire office. My priorities were to keep working on the structure and policies of the Office, to integrate the Office with the other organs of the Court, to keep promoting the network of cooperation, to appoint the senior staff, and to select a "situation" to start operations. Every point seemed to be a priority.

In those days, there were serious doubts about the ability of the Office of the Prosecutor to carry out investigations and to present a case in Court, and more generally about the viability of the entire Rome Statute to perform as designed. Only 40 percent of the 193 UN member states were parties to the Statute. Many were

58 *See* www.icc-cpi.int/iccdocs/otp/ph1_conclusions.pdf.

concerned about how American hostility would affect the states parties' cooperation that the Court needed to operate. Against those challenges, step by step, in only nine years, the innovative normative system established by the Rome Statute was set in motion as the result of the interaction of different actors.

The states parties have been financing the operations of the Court, cooperating with investigations, protecting witnesses and executing arrest warrants. Most of them are now successfully preventing the commission of the crimes within their own territory. Colombia conducted hundreds of investigations against politicians, military officers, paramilitaries, and guerrilla members, fulfilling its obligations and avoiding the intervention of the Court. In 2005, for example, Colombia demobilized 31,000 paramilitary members, and more than 2,000 leaders spent eight years in jail. Colombia in 2016 finalized a similar process with the Revolutionary Armed Forces of Colombia (FARC), the oldest Marxist guerrilla group on the continent. The UK, Canada, France, Australia, and Germany reviewed their rules of engagement in Afghanistan to adjust to their obligations under the Rome Statute.

During my tenure, the prosecutor's office conducted preliminary examinations in more than 20 situations around the world including Afghanistan, Korea, Georgia, and Colombia, and decided not to open investigations into Venezuela and the allegations against the British troops operating in Iraq in 2006. It also decided to dismiss a Palestinian request for failing to meet the preconditions for jurisdiction in 2012. I dismissed the hundreds of requests to investigate the US intervention in Iraq because neither the United States nor Iraq were states parties to the Rome Statute, and therefore we had no jurisdiction.

The policy to fully respect complementarity has been applied consistently. There were no genuine national proceedings when the Office triggered the Court's jurisdiction in four States Parties: Uganda, the Democratic Republic of Congo (DRC), the Central African Republic, and Kenya. There were none following the UN Security Council referrals in Darfur and Libya, or the acceptance of jurisdiction by Côte d'Ivoire.

The Office of the Prosecutor decided to start working on the two most serious situations admissible under our jurisdiction: the DRC, with almost 5,000 killings; and Uganda, with 2,500 killings, 2,800 abductions, and 1,100,000 displaced. The situation in Colombia, also characterized by 5,000 killings at the time, was not admissible because the national state was deemed to be conducting genuine proceedings.

To trigger the jurisdiction of the Court, we adopted a policy of inviting the territorial government to refer the situation after we selected the situation and before having recourse to my *proprio motu* powers to open investigations. This is the context in which the Office invited the DRC and Uganda to refer their situations, and they successfully did so. This enabled the Court to select its first situations in full harmony with the will of the territorial state and increase the cooperation received. Motivated by the International Federation of Human Rights (FIDH), the Central

African Republic then referred its own situation.[59] Then Côte d'Ivoire accepted the Court's jurisdiction, and after inviting the government of Kenya to refer the situation in its country to the Court, I requested and obtained the judges' authorization to independently open an investigation in Kenya. In every situation, there were thousands of persons killed and/or raped, and in many cases, millions were displaced. The cases before the Court are indeed the most serious crimes of concern to the international community.

The Office had to investigate in the context of ongoing conflicts in the DRC, Uganda, Darfur, and Libya, and took very seriously its duty to protect the witnesses and investigators. I am very grateful that during my tenure not a single witness or investigator was wounded or killed.

Following its specific duty to focus on gender crimes and crimes against children, the prosecution's first case exposed boys and girls abused as child soldiers and how they were trained to kill, to rape, and to be raped. Each case before the Court has highlighted a further aspect of gender crimes, including the case against Joseph Kony and other Lord Resistance Army (LRA) leaders, and the command responsibility asserted for an organized campaign of rape in the case against Jean-Pierre Bemba.

The Pre-Trial Chamber reviewed the prosecutor's evidence and issued arrest warrants and summonses to appear against 33 individuals, including three heads of state identified as those most responsible for the massive crimes committed across all the situations.

Seven of those individuals were arrested and surrendered to the Court;[60] two surrendered voluntarily to nonstate parties such as Rwanda and the United States, and were delivered to the Court;[61] three were killed while they were fugitives;[62] nine appeared voluntarily before the Court;[63] two were arrested by Libyan authorities that challenged the Court jurisdiction; and three were arrested by Côte d'Ivoire authorities. Nine others remain at large: Joseph Kony and one of his commanders, President Omar al-Bashir, Minister Abdel Raheem Muhammad Hussein, Governor Ahmad Harun, militia leader Ali Kushayb, and FDLR leader Sylvestre Mudacumura.

None of the individuals facing justice before the International Criminal Court are low-level perpetrators; all the cases before the judges have been against the top leaders of the organizations involved in the commission of the crimes, including three heads of state when the evidence collected pointed at their criminal responsibility.

We litigated before an independent court that carefully protected the rights of the defendants, included the voice of the victims, and strictly reviewed the prosecutor's

59 After June 2012, Mali, Comoros, and the Central African Republic also referred situations to the ICC.

60 Thomas Lubanga, Germain Katanga, Mathieu Ngudjolo Chui, Jean-Pierre Bemba, Callixte Mbarushimana, and Laurent Gbagbo.

61 Bosco Ntaganda and Dominic Ongwen.

62 Raska Lukwiya, Vincent Otti, and Muammar Gaddafi.

63 Three in Haskanita and six in Kenya.

decisions. Judges stayed the proceedings of the first case and refused to confirm four of our cases against Abu Garda, Callixte Mbarushimana, Henry Kosgey, and Mohammed Hussein Ali; acquitted one of the defendants, Mathieu Ngudjolo Chui; and terminated the case against William Ruto and Joshua Arap Sang.

Since I took office, 44 additional states have ratified the Rome Statute. After my term ended, Mali, Ukraine, the Comoros, the Central African Republic, and Gabon referred new situations to the ICC, and a suspect surrendered himself to the Court.

When I took office, there was no expectation that the Court would ever achieve a constructive relationship with the UN Security Council, but within a mere two years of the Court's operations, the UN Security Council moved from deep distrust to support for ICC intervention to investigate crimes committed in Darfur.

The conflict in Darfur mobilized many US citizens in 2004 and promoted a change. Colin Powell, then US secretary of state, called it a "genocide." In December 2004, a UN Commission of Inquiry, created with US support, recommended referring the crimes in Darfur to the ICC.[64]

Under the leadership of France, the United Kingdom, and 7 Security Council members, who were also parties to the Rome Statute, as well as with the support of Russia, Japan, and the Philippines, the Council referred the Darfur situation to the ICC. The fact that 9 of the 15 members of the UN Security Council were also members of the Rome Statute changed the dynamic of the Council without changing its rules. As soon as France and the UK presented the proposal to refer the situation in Darfur to the ICC, they had the majority, and the United States and China were forced to adjust or to veto.

There were compromises from all sides: the United States abstained, and most of the states parties of the Rome Statute[65] accepted the inclusion of the safeguards imposed by the United States. American Service-Members' Protection Act (ASPA). That US statute requires that no UN funds be provided to the Court, that the United States negotiate immunity agreements consistent with Article 98 of the ICC Statute, and that UN peacekeeping authorizations provide for immunity from the ICC for non-state party personnel. An isolated China did not exercise its veto.

In 2011, the UN Security Council referred the Libya situation to the ICC just nine days after the beginning of the rebellion against Gaddafi's regime and before the UN Commission of Inquiry started its investigations.[66] The resolution included the same safeguards adopted in the Darfur situation, which the Bush administration had accepted. It was adopted by consensus after only a few days of discussions, including the positive vote of the United States, China, and India.

64 Colum Lynch, *UN Panel Finds No Genocide in Darfur but Urges Tribunals*, Wash. Post (Feb. 1, 2005), available at www.washingtonpost.com/wp-dyn/articles/A31594-2005Jan23.html.

65 Brazil's abstention expressed its disagreement with the US concessions.

66 *See* S.C. Res. 1970, UN Doc. S/RES/1970 (Feb. 26, 2011).

On December 20, 2012, again by consensus, the Security Council called upon the UN peacekeeping force in Mali to support the ICC in its efforts to bring perpetrators to justice.[67]

Since then, the Syrian and Ukrainian conflicts have exacerbated divisions between Russia and the United States, affecting the Security Council's ability to reach agreements between permanent members.

The "transnational criminal justice system" developed by the Rome Statute is a reality and part of international law's landscape. In addition, states parties were promoting international justice within the UN Security Council system. The fear of a frivolous prosecutor abusing the powers granted by the Statute was replaced by the challenges created by a serious institution.

The decision of Burundi's President Pierre Nkurunziza to remain as president for a third term and to withdraw his country from the ICC is a good example of the challenges ahead. It exposes President Nkurunziza's desire to have a free hand to keep committing crimes against humanity, and possibly commit genocide, with the goal of staying in power. The president of the Burundian Senate has been proposing to "pulverize and exterminate" rebels and to spray "cockroaches" – the very same word used to dehumanize the Tutsi during the 1994 Rwanda genocide. The situation in Burundi is showing how difficult it is for international organizations to stop crimes.

The African Union's Constitutive Act, adopted in July 2000, established the connections between such atrocities and the economic prospects of people in Africa. It stated that "the scourge of conflicts in Africa constitutes a major impediment to the socio-economic development of the continent and of the need to promote peace, security and stability as a prerequisite for the implementation of our development and integration agenda."

And on December 2016, the African Union (AU) tried to implement Article 4 (h) of the Constitutive Act in Burundi: "the right of the Union to intervene in a Member State pursuant to a decision of the Assembly in respect of grave circumstances, namely: war crimes, genocide and crimes against humanity." The AU gave President Nkurunziza 96 hours to accept an AU force, but the Burundian government simply rejected the ultimatum.

Challenged by Burundi, the AU leaders reversed the decision and canceled the request. Instead of protecting the victims, the AU decided to protect the perpetrators. The AU's mediation effort led by President Museveni, Uganda's president since 1986, was also dismissed.

African leaders have learned that not only the AU but also the UN Security Council cannot be relied on to act forcefully. A year ago, the British ambassador,

67 S.C. Res. 2085, UN Doc. S/RES/2085 (Dec. 20, 2012).

as the president of the UN Security Council, warned of a "possible genocide" in Burundi as the international body agreed on a resolution paving the way for a peacekeeping deployment. But, in January 2016, the head of the UN Peacekeepers declared that the UN is ill-prepared to control atrocities in the country.

Since April 2016, 210,000 new refugees have escaped from Burundi into neighboring countries, and the world has looked away as the blood flows. But in the same month, the ICC Prosecutor Fatou Bensouda opened a preliminary examination into the crimes committed there. As national leaders there and elsewhere have learned, the ICC is the only institution with a mandate – and a will – to prevent and punish these terrible crimes. That is why Burundi is now leaving the ICC to have free hands to annihilate the "cockroaches."

Who will defend the Tutsi victims in Burundi if the government continues attacking them? Make no mistake – the alternative to legal protection in this context is war.

The Burundian government is now accusing Rwanda of using proxy forces to protect the Tutsi population, and if the crimes continue, the conflict could escalate – as has happened before. The previous Rwandan intervention to protect Tutsis in the Democratic Republic of Congo at the end of the twentieth century triggered two wars on the continent, drew in dozens of African countries, and resulted in the death of millions of people.

On the other hand, Gabon presents a hopeful example of how the ICC is helping African countries to control violence. Opposition figures said that more than 50 people were killed in Gabon on August 31, 2016, after Ali Bongo – the son of Omar Bongo, who had ruled for 41 years until his death in 2009 – was declared the election's winner by a tiny margin. Demonstrators set Parliament ablaze and clashed with the police who arrested over a thousand individuals.

On September 21, 2016, the government referred its own situation to the ICC. The lawyer of Jean Ping, the opposition leader, said that they would cooperate with the ICC to identify the crimes and the criminals. Both sides have accepted the authority of the ICC to handle the situation, and the ICC investigation could serve as a peaceful mechanism to prevent both sides from escalating the violence.

The twenty-first century needs national leaders with global vision. There are opportunities for these leaders to integrate national and international institutions to protect citizens of the world.

In July 1998, on signing the Rome Statute, Nelson Mandela said, "Our own continent has suffered enough horrors emanating from the inhumanity of human beings towards human beings. Who knows, many of these might not have occurred, or at least been minimized, had there been an effectively functioning International Criminal Court."[68]

[68] Statement by the International Criminal Court on the Passing of Nelson Mandela, ICC-CPI-20131206-PR971, Dec. 6, 2013, available at www.icc-cpi.int/Pages/item.aspx?name=pr971.

Over the past few years, nationalism has been growing across all the continents. Brexit was a vivid example. Venezuela withdrew from the Inter-American Court of Human Rights in 2013, and Burundi is walking away from the Rome Statute. Technological evolution without global institutions will send humanity back to tribalism. ISIS is showing that tribalism promoted by social media in a globalized world can destroy national and international human rights.

We should learn from the past. During World War II, Goebbels insisted on the Nazis sovereign right as a state to decide on the fate of its Jewish, "gypsy," and anarchist citizens. During those days, two Polish Jewish lawyers, Raphael Lemkin and Hersch Lauterpach, were able to move beyond the debate about state sovereignty and had the global vision to develop and institutionalize two new concepts: genocide and crimes against humanity.

It is the time to develop a global vision that is both principled and pragmatic, replacing the war paradigm with a global justice system that prevents and punishes the most serious crimes.

7

Extraordinary Chambers in the Courts of Cambodia

Robert Petit

When, in the fall of 2005, I saw the email in my work inbox, the name didn't ring a bell – but the address, @un.org, was very familiar. After all by then I had, over the preceding nine years, been a legal officer with the Office of the Prosecutor of the International Criminal Tribunal for Rwanda[1] (ICTR), the Mitrovica regional legal advisor for the United Nations Mission in Kosovo,[2] and a prosecutor at the Serious Crimes Unit of the United Nations Mission in East Timor.[3] Even my last international assignment, as a senior trial attorney with the Office of the Prosecutor for the Special Court for Sierra Leone[4] (SCSL) was with an institution that had all the trappings of a UN body.

Despite all that, I was not expecting any contact from the UN, given that I had not applied for any position in the almost two years that I had been back in my job as a counsel with the War Crimes Unit of the Department of Justice Canada in Ottawa. Therefore, I was floored when upon opening the attached letter, I learned that I had been shortlisted for the post of international co-prosecutor with the Extraordinary Chambers in the Courts of Cambodia[5] (ECCC). I still remember that the letter was "on behalf of the Secretary-General of the United Nations" and was signed by the then legal advisor to the UN, Nicolas Michel. That was pretty heady correspondence for a guy whose last assignment had been at P5 level. I called my wife and read her the letter over the phone. I then brought a copy to my boss, who was also suitably impressed although, after my various leaves of absence, not exactly thrilled. I assured him that I had no clue how I had ended up on the short list, but he seemed dubious.

The mystery of my selection would later be cleared up. Months before the email, I had seen a web post from an NGO, whose name I forgot, inviting candidates interested in what was then a very theoretical court, to send in their CVs in order to be included into a database. I remember thinking at the time that it sounded

1 S.C. Res. 955 (Nov. 8, 1994). 2 S.C. Res. 1244 (Jun. 10, 1999).
3 S.C. Res. 1246 (Jun. 11, 1999). 4 S.C. Res. 1315 (Aug. 14, 2000).
5 G.A. Res. 56/169 (Feb. 28, 2002).

almost like an internet scam. It did not sound very serious for an NGO to be recruiting candidates off the Web for a United Nations institution that might never see the light of day. Nevertheless, it was only a few clicks to send in my CV, without even a cover letter. Little did I know.

The letter stated that arrangements would be made for my interview in New York, which left me time to start researching the Court in earnest. I was of course familiar with the Khmer Rouge and their bloody reign over Cambodia. The group, espousing a radical Marxists ideology, took power in Cambodia in 1974. For the next four years, eight months, and three days until they were ousted by their arch-enemy, Vietnam, the Khmer Rouge attempted a complete social reengineering of Cambodia. They forcibly emptied out whole cities, abolished all individual rights, forced the population to toil on huge construction or agricultural projects, and ruthlessly exterminated anyone opposing them or deemed unfit for the new Cambodia. Estimates vary, but two million victims is believed to be an accurate count.

Working in the field of international criminal law since 1996, I kept abreast of any significant development in that area. I was therefore indeed aware that, 30 years after their crimes, the remaining leaders of the Khmer Rouge would possibly, finally, answer for their atrocities. The court was to be a hybrid model, with a majority of national judges but with two co-prosecutors and two co-investigative judges, in each case one international, one national, and sitting in Phnom Penh, Cambodia. I quickly searched and got a copy of the statute of the Court and saw that much of it was familiar. It had jurisdiction over the crimes of genocide, crimes against humanity, and war crimes as usually defined in international criminal law. It also had personal jurisdiction over "senior leaders and those most responsible" for the crimes committed during the Khmer Rouge regime.[6] I was comfortable with that type of jurisdiction, as it allowed some discretion to the prosecutor while at the same time providing guidance as to the limits of the mandate. But there were some clear oddities with the statute starting with a conflict resolution mechanism that obviously foresaw fundamental disagreements between the internationals and their national counterparts. The genesis of such mechanism was to be found in the history of the court itself. As I started digging deeper I became aware of the complex issues facing the court starting with the government of Cambodia's avowed opposition to the Court's very existence. That government, led by former Khmer Rouges who had defected to Vietnam before the war's end and had ruled the country ever since, had initially requested the UN's assistance in creating the Court but then had a significant change of heart and put up roadblocks to its creation almost from that initial request. That same government was also on record as dictating that the mandate of

[6] Law on the Establishment of Extraordinary Chambers in the Courts of Cambodia for the Prosecution of Crimes Committed During the Period of Democratic Kampuchea, as amended and promulgated on Oct. 27, 2004, Art. 1 (NS/RKM/1004/006) (Cambodia), available at www.eccc.gov.kh/sites/default/files/legal-documents/KR_Law_as_amended_27_Oct_2004_Eng.pdf [hereinafter ECCC Statute].

the court should not exceed the five senior leaders still currently alive and residing in Cambodia.

Obviously the process of accountability for mass crimes, in any setting, has a political dimension. No court, wherever it may be located, operates in a vacuum, and how to correctly discharge one's mandate while being sensitive to the political ramifications is a reality shared by anyone working in these courts. But this was a whole different dimension, and I would come to find that in Cambodia the level of political interference, perceived or real, was beyond anything I had previously experienced.

Nowhere was this political dimension more accurately reflected than in the statute of the court itself. At all levels where a crucial decision could be made about who could be prosecuted for what, the statute clearly envisioned that nationals would disagree with internationals. The statute called for a convoluted conflict resolution mechanism so that cases could somewhat progress despite such disagreements. For instance the statute provided that if the co-prosecutors disagreed on who to prosecute they could file a notice of disagreement with the Pre-Trial Chamber. The judges of that Chamber could rule by a single majority on the fate of the prosecution, but if they failed to reach such a majority, the case would "proceed," whatever that meant. It was an unprecedented disposition, and it was hard for me to imagine how a court could function efficiently if it had to resort to such a mechanism in the course of its existence.

Another thing that became quite clear from the beginning of my research was that there was an incredible amount of information about the crimes committed by the Khmer Rouge. Over the course of 30 years, hundreds of individuals and organizations had apparently devoted their lives to documenting the era of Democratic Kampuchea (DK), as the Khmer Rouge called Cambodia under their leadership. Some of the names of the most prominent scholars in the field quickly became familiar to me and indeed some of them would come to be an integral part of the Court's process as staff members.

Having such a massive amount of information was a double-edged sword. It flattened the learning curve for anyone wishing to understand the circumstances of the crime, and it provided a massive number of leads to follow in the search for evidence. On the other hand, it created in the general public – and in particular in the Cambodian population – an unreasonable expectation that this information could be quickly transformed into evidence and used to reach a verdict. I had previously encountered a somewhat similar circumstance in which everyone knew what had happened and was asking why it was taking so long and why so much money was being spent to prove the obvious. It leads to one of the most important tasks of any judicial official, that of explaining to all stakeholders, but more importantly to victims and survivors, that for a verdict to have any value, the truth must be established with the best evidence, in strict adherence to the rules. There is a fundamental difference between information and evidence, but it's difficult to accept for those who know what happened to them.

Nevertheless, from that information, I quickly started to get an idea about the scope of the cases and the available evidence. Indeed I laughed out loud when I found, right off Amazon, a book titled *7 Candidates for Prosecution*. It was the first time in my career that somebody had been kind enough to outline, very well it turned out, who I should be going after and what I should use to do so. One of the authors of the book, Dr. Stephen Heder, would end up playing a crucial role in the work of the court as one of its first investigators.

Another thing I realized through my research was that if anyone had wanted to create an institution destined to fail, he or she would have been hard-pressed to find a better model than that envisioned for the ECCC. Through my contacts I obtained an outline of the budget and the proposed structure for the Court. Right away it was apparent to me that these were based on mistaken assumptions about the reality of prosecuting and trying mass crimes. The documents envisioned a court with a three-year lifespan with internationals and nationals sharing responsibilities and a very limited budget to be funded by voluntary contributions. Now, I knew very well that the hundreds of millions of dollars spent on both ad hoc tribunals and the other institutions that preceded the ECCC had led to pronounced donor fatigue. Even so, I thought that the projected budget allocated and the manner with which the court would be funded was unrealistic. After all, the ECCC was to try cases for the highest number of victims of any of the tribunals since Nuremberg, would have to do so 30 years after the fact, and was expected to complete its mandate in barely the time it usually took to bring one war-crimes case to trial.

Worse, however, was how the responsibilities were to be allocated and the number of staff supposed to carry them out. The most glaring issue was that investigations, either by the co-prosecutors or the co-investigative judges were to be carried out by the national police. No investigative posts, national or international, had been envisioned in the staffing or budget. Even with my limited knowledge of Cambodia and the political circumstances of the court, it was readily apparent to me that this was a problem. This was confirmed in conversations I had later with a good friend of mine who had worked in anticorruption initiatives throughout Asia. He warned me about the competency of the national law enforcement, its probity, and the lack of separation between the political and the judicial. He also cautioned me that assassinations were a common means of resolving political or business conflicts, and that the powerful who ordered them often remained above the law.

So, as I set about collecting as much information as I could, I developed serious misgivings, which I carried with me to my interview in New York.

My interview was arranged to coincide with a trip to New Delhi, where I was going to give a speech. It was beautiful crisp fall weather in New York when I arrived and met up with a friend who was also interviewing for the position. We had not seen each other in quite a while, and we had a good time catching up over dinner. His interview was before mine the next day, so in the morning I had time to go for a run in Central Park. It was my first time doing that, and ever since it's been a not-to-be-missed event whenever I'm in town. Just the view along the reservoir with the tall spires of buildings against the beautiful blue sky of that day will forever be etched in my mind.

After a trip back to the hotel I walked over to UN Headquarters, fully confident that I had done what I could to prepare. All the interviews were conducted at the Office of the Legal Advisor (OLA), with a panel consisting of UN legal counsel Nicolas Michel; assistant secretary general for legal affairs Ralph Zacklin; a former judge of the International Criminal Tribunal for the Former Yugoslavia, David Hunt; and the late judge Claude Jorda, then of the International Criminal Court. My most vivid memory of that interview is the very first thing said by any member of the panel. As soon as I was introduced by Ralph Zacklin, Judge Jorda looked at me and said, "With your background why are you not applying to be a judge"? Coming from someone of Judge Jorda's stature, I thought it was a flattering assumption, albeit a weird way to start an interview. I answered truthfully: that I had never wished to be a judge, and that the responsibilities of a prosecutor were enough for me.

I also remember Nicholas Michel toward the end of the interview expressing surprise that I seemed to be, as he said, more "easy-going" than he would've thought a prosecutor usually was. I answered that my profession had taught me that it is the strength of your arguments, not the decibels at which they are uttered, that win the day in court. That got a clear approval from Judge Hunt, no doubt given his Common Law background.

I left the interview feeling that I had done what I needed to do to express what I would bring to the table. However my concerns about the court had not abated. In fact, in our discussions, my friend and I agreed that the weaknesses within the structure of the court, coupled with potential security issues, made it almost impossible for the court to succeed. During the long trip to New Delhi, I pondered my position: if it was fair for me to remain a candidate while having growing doubts about the capacity of the court to deliver any kind of justice to the victims of the Khmer Rouge. By the time I landed in New Delhi, I had made up my mind to withdraw. Thankfully the government of Canada, at least back in those days, could afford to put up its traveling staff in higher-end accommodation, and my room at the aptly named Taj Mahal Hotel had a fax machine. I quickly drafted and printed a letter addressed to the OLA stating that for reasons having to do with security and the structure of the court, I wished to withdraw from consideration for the post. As I pressed the send button, I felt relieved that I was putting an end to an ambiguous situation where I had run the risk of being involved in a process that was so important but at the same time looked ill-fated.

As soon as I returned to Ottawa, however, things became a bit complicated. I started receiving emails from Ralph Zacklin indicating OLA's deep regret at my decision, especially since I was a strong contender. As the exchanges of emails went on, it became clear that I had become the frontrunner and that the United Nations wanted to try to address any concerns that I had in order for me to accept the position. It even got to the point where one night while I was giving a bath to my two kids my wife brought me the phone. She said it was the Canadian ambassador to Cambodia wanting to speak to me. It turned out that OLA had reached out to the Canadian mission in New York, which in turn had asked the ambassador to give me a call so that she could tell me how wonderful Phnom Penh and Cambodia were, and how important it was for Canada to be involved in something as important as the ECCC.

All of this contradictory information was the subject of much discussion between my wife and I. We came to the conclusion that, given the opportunity to contribute to such an important endeavor as that of justice to the victims of the Khmer Rouge, I had to at least give it a chance. I therefore agreed to travel back to New York and meet with officials to see if some of my concerns could be addressed. I met again with Nicholas, and we had a very frank discussion about my concerns. He shared some of them but reinforced the importance of the Court and promised me his full support. I then met with Sir David Veness, who was then the under-secretary general for security and safety. He agreed that following his security review the UN would provide 24/7 close protection by armed internationals. I left those meetings reassured that the UN was taking this issue seriously. That is until my next meeting. Michelle Lee was to be the first UN administrator of the court. She was by then close to retirement, having served in various capacities all over the UN system. She had no previous experience supporting a judicial process and was adamant that the UN involvement with the Court was to only assist what was a Cambodian institution. Although we had a pleasant first contact, our relationship at the Court would be difficult, marred by her ignorance of the judicial process and her narrow focus on the bottom line above all considerations. However, during this first meeting, she agreed to rearrange the budget and the staffing table so as to create investigator posts within the office of international co-prosecutor. As I explained, to me this was a *sine qua non* condition. If I could not conduct adequate preliminary investigations, I would not be involved in a process that could undermine the validity of the cases brought forward. As I explained to her, even though investigative judges would conduct the bulk of the investigation, I knew from experience that these cases and their successful outcome depended on a competent, focused, and sound initial investigation. As that investigation was to be conducted by my office, I needed more than Cambodian national judicial police with no experience or knowledge of these types of cases. So at the end of this trip, with some of my concerns alleviated, I really thought I had a chance to bring an acceptable measure of justice to the people of Cambodia.

The ECCC being a Cambodian court, all judicial officials had to be nominated by the National Council of Magistracy. So the United Nations submitted a list of candidates, and then we all waited for the assent from Cambodia. While the outcome was not certain, I was assured that it was only a question of time and therefore could count on being eventually appointed. That allowed for several months of preparations.

For me, one of the most important aspects of this opportunity was the fact that I was coming in at the inception of the Court. In all my previous postings, most if not all of the major decisions had been made by others, and I had to deal with the consequences of their actions. Here, in Cambodia, I alone would be responsible for the decisions, at least those made by the international side of the Office, and I could shape my side of the organization the way I thought it should be organized. For better or for worse, I alone would be answerable for my decisions and their consequences. When that means deciding who gets held responsible for the deaths and victimization of hundreds of thousands of people and of justice for the survivors, it carries with it a humbling moral weight. To uphold that responsibility, I needed the best team I could put together.

This meant another trip to New York to interview potential deputy candidates, as well as numerous telephone interviews for various staff positions. I knew that the reputation of the Court as a difficult and limited institution led many in the field to not apply, but at the end of the recruitment phase I believed I had a solid team. To my mind the most critical positions, however, were those of the two investigator/analysts that I had wrangled out of the UN. Those two individuals would be responsible for guiding our investigation on the right path. With the sheer volume of information generated by the Khmer Rouge regime and those who sought to document it afterwards, I felt I needed the most competent individuals to cut through that mass and lead us in a timely manner to what we would need to establish the truth. It quickly became apparent that the two most qualified individuals for this were Stephen Heder and Craig Etcheson. Both were Americans who had devoted their life and their considerable intellect to the study of the Khmer Rouge regime, with a particular focus on its ideology and its atrocities. Both were well known, and indeed, Heder had already been tapped to be an investigator in the office of the international co-investigative judge.

The ECCC was to be based on the French penal system, as Cambodia was a former colony of France. Under that system the prosecutor conducts a preliminary investigation before referring the file to an investigative judge. The notion of preliminary investigation, however, was not defined in the statute of the Court. I knew that none of the Cambodian judicial officials nor the other international judges had any previous experience in international criminal law. Given this, I made up my mind at the outset that my preliminary investigation needed to be as fulsome as possible both in law and in fact so that the investigative judges would benefit from being referred as substantive a file as possible. That's why it was important to me to have the most qualified individuals leading our investigation, and I was happy that the international co-investigative judge, Marcel Lemonde, agreed during our conversations to second Heder to my office for the six months of my mandate. Along with Etcheson, who was directly hired to my office, I felt I had the two most qualified individuals in the world working on this investigation.

While my preparations and research continued, things got slightly surreal. Several media outlets, including a national magazine, did pieces on my appointment. I even made the front page of our capital's newspaper when the *Ottawa Citizen* published an article on the date of my departure to Phnom Penh. I was uncomfortable with the attention. As a Crown attorney, you had to exercise a certain reserve. I had learned that you let your case speak for itself, hoping that the press would get it right, which tended to be the exception rather than the rule. I carried that principle and my discomfort with me to Cambodia, and reporters were quick to note it.

At the time my wife, our four-year-old daughter, and our three-year-old son were living in a small house in the western suburbs of Ottawa. Our neighbors two doors down were a Cambodian family. Both parents were in their early 30s with two young boys and had come to Canada as boat people in the late 1970s. The husband, who was Anglophone, was one of the hardest working people I've ever met. He had a full-time job, and when he came home, he worked as a mechanic out of his garage with an apparently endless list of clients. When there were no cars to be fixed, he worked on his house. The only leisure I had ever known the man to have was hunting, a sport to which he was introduced by one of our Canadian neighbors. The wife, a Francophone, also worked full-time, and they shared a house with her mother, an old dignified woman who also spoke cultured French. I would later learn that the ability to speak French indicated that the family in Cambodia had been part of the "bourgeoisie" so despised by the Khmer Rouge, which in part no doubt explained their exile.

We were on good terms with that family, and when it became apparent that I had a shot at the job of prosecutor, I shared the news with them. I was startled by the reaction I got. Whenever I would bring up the subject of the Court with the husband, he would close up, not comment, and change the subject. As the weeks passed and I was confirmed in the post, he finally could not hold it any longer and let me have it. He became visibly angry and agitated and asked me where I was when his family was starving to death under the Khmer Rouge. Where was the international community when he had to step over the body of his sister to flee? What was going to be accomplished by putting on trial old men when his remaining family in Cambodia still had to eke out a living? Would all those millions that were about to be spent bring back any of the dead? I was taken aback; I had never seen that man so emotional, much less under barely controlled anger. But, of course, some of his points were not new to me. Anyone who has ever worked in one of these courts has heard the same legitimate questions. You had to try and explain why, despite all its apparent issues, accountability for mass crimes was necessary for any society to be able to rebuild. But more importantly than the principled position, anyone involved in bringing justice to victims must respect their pain and how they are coping with it. You certainly never question the depth or honesty of their feelings. So I listened, agreed when possible, and most of all tried to convey how much I respected what he felt. His wife on the other hand was cautiously optimistic and positive about my involvement. Although neither ever spoke directly about the victimization of their family or themselves, she did say that whatever justice could be brought would be a good thing. She told me that she knew that I would do my best. And wished me luck. That difference in attitude, that stark contrast, exemplified what I would find once in Cambodia.

I departed for Phnom Penh on Canada Day, July 1, 2006, leaving behind my wife and children. We were used to the drill: she would stay behind with the kids while I went ahead to find us a suitable house, this time for the next three years. Connecting from Bangkok, I was approached by Steve Heder, whom I had never met but had talked to many times over the past few weeks. When I asked him how he recognized me, he said I just looked like a prosecutor; I played it safe and did not ask for clarification.

During the one-hour flight, I told him some of the conclusions I had reached during the last few months of preparations. The overriding one was that the sheer magnitude of the crimes and the amount of time elapsed for their reckoning meant that I had very little room to maneuver. If I was to help in delivering any kind of justice in this long overdue process, I had to get it right from the get-go. It also meant that I could not let anything affect the quality of the justice that was going to be delivered. The victims of the Khmer Rouge deserved a process and a judgment that was above reproach to end their 30-year wait for the truth and for justice. I also had to acknowledge that we had limited resources and limited time to deliver this. I was faced with the prosecution of crimes committed by perpetrators over the longest period of any previous international tribunal, with the highest number of victims and the longest period of elapsed time since the crimes – and yet with the fewest resources of any of those previous tribunals. More than ever, I would have to stick to my principle of not reinventing the wheel, deferring to the best practices I had learned through my experience. I also told Steve that I had no time to learn what he had learnt over the course of the last 30 years and that I counted on him and others to school us on what we needed to understand in order to do the job. Finally, I made it very clear to him that I would be as transparent as I could in my work because that was owed to the people of Cambodia. To me there existed no other pressure than that of my mandate and justice for the victims.

On arrival in Phnom Penh, all the soon-to-be-appointed international judicial officials were housed in the grand dame of hotels, the Raffles. I did not think it boded well for a barebones administration to book half of the most expensive hotel in town, but the UN works in mysterious ways. So all of us internationals spent a week in this beautiful establishment, getting acquainted with each other and with our national counterparts who came for frequent meetings.

It was there that I met my counterpart, the national co-prosecutor, Chea Leang. I knew very little about her other than what I had been told by Heder and Etcheson, as well as some UN sources. She was a lawyer, educated in Germany, spoke almost no

English, and had very limited work experience but one big advantage: she was the niece of the second-most powerful man in Cambodia, Deputy Prime Minister Sok An. Himself an old Khmer Rouge cadre who had fled before being purged, he'd come back on the coattails of the Vietnamese troops and been in power with his ally, Prime Minister Hun Sen, ever since. He had been very active in representing Cambodia in the negotiations with the international community over the Court and was perceived as not totally opposed to it. However, like Hun Sen, he was openly opposed to an expansive prosecution, and it was thought that his niece had been tasked with one primary objective: limiting the number of accused. In fairness, she also knew little of me and how I viewed my mandate. All this probably explains in part why the beginning of our relationship was somewhat guarded, though having to use an interpreter for every exchange (my German being limited to "bier bitte!") certainly did not help. In time we would develop a working relationship that endured our ultimate disagreement over who to prosecute.

At one point early on in the week, I managed to get away to one of the iconic genocide sites in Phnom Penh. Along with the two investigators, I went to Tuol Sleng, better known as S-21. It is a former high school that the Khmer Rouge took over and transformed into Hell's antechamber. In its former classrooms, partitioned into closet-like cells, thousands of prisoners were kept shackled, starved, and abused. They were only dragged from their cells to be relentlessly tortured until they signed full, written confessions admitting to whatever crimes they thought their torturers wanted to hear. They were then executed either on the premises or, when there were just too many to kill, brought to another site, the Killing Field of Choeung Ek, where they were finally dispatched. The prison was administered by one of the surviving Khmer Rouge cadre and anticipated indictee, Kang Kek Lew, also known as Duch. He was a highly organized individual who had set up a system that documented the short miserable life of every prisoner to ever walk into S-21. From the initial log entry, which often included a picture, to the final list of prisoners executed daily, Duch and his staff left behind a treasure trove of evidence documenting their crimes. Those records proved to be an essential part of our cases but at the same time would present a difficult moral and legal challenge.

After the fall of the Khmer Rouge, the Vietnamese troops found the records, as well as seven surviving prisoners. S-21 then became a propaganda tool in the Cold War and eventually morphed into the Tuol Sleng Genocide Museum, with various exhibits trying to convey the horror of what had taken place there. However, like most unimaginable concepts, it was a difficult task, sometimes rendered even more so by the setting itself. Peering into the cells looking at the rusted chains, then walking out into the sunny courtyard with the palm trees swinging slowly in the wind, it was hard to grasp what had happened there. In fact, I was reminded of how I felt when I first looked out onto the hills of Rwanda while flying into Kigali in 1996. It's almost as if the most horrible crimes are purposely set against such idyllic backgrounds to cynically underscore their horror.

As the week wore on, we started working on developing a working relationship with our national colleagues. We held various meetings trying to determine an order of priority for the work. It is during one of those meetings that we were confronted very early on with the intersection of politics and power in Cambodian law. It happened when our national colleagues tried to pressure us into accepting the transfer of the only two Khmer Rouge detainees then in custody. Many years ago, Duch, along with a former Khmer Rouge cadre called Ta Mok, had been arrested and detained by the military. Their arrest and continued detention without charges or trial was obviously fraught with legal issues. The available information made it clear that they were legitimate subjects for investigation; however, to my mind, that investigation could only be done by us and in accordance with our own rules to be legitimate. Some of my national colleagues did not share that opinion, or at least had been instructed otherwise. This led to an extraordinary exchange between the national co-investigative judge and myself in the presence of various other colleagues. Through an interpreter, You Bunleng told us that we needed to take custody of the two detainees and take over the investigative file as created in the military, and basically that would be our first case. One of You's colleagues even blurted out that "it has been ordered; the elder brothers have already signed," which led to a sharp rebuke from You Bunleng!

As the prosecutor whose responsibility it was to conduct a preliminary inquiry into any eventual case, the answer for me was quite simple. I told all the national colleagues that until such time as I had completed my preliminary inquiry, I would have no qualms in ignoring any attempt to force me to take custody of anyone, nor would I defer to any findings or orders from any other authorities than that of the ECCC. The international investigative judge openly agreed with me, and eventually we moved on to other topics. It was to be the first in a long series of tests between our interpretation of our mandate and that of our national colleagues.

In between meetings, we took the field trip to our new home away from home, the site of the future court. As part of its contribution to the budget of the Court the Cambodian government had granted use of a facility that was initially designated to some sort of military college. As we would soon find out, it was an ill-suited facility for our Court.

The buildings, still smelling like fresh concrete, had been dropped in the middle of this huge field on the outskirts of Phnom Penh. Dotted with guard towers and surrounded by a fence topped by barbed wire, it was not exactly a welcoming sight to anyone courageous enough to reach it through Phnom Penh's mind-boggling traffic. With the help of a police escort it was, however, easily done and upon arrival we were given a tour of the facilities. The first order of business was visiting our future courtroom. It was a huge auditorium capable of seating hundreds, with a big open stage that was originally designed for giving lectures. It looked, for all intents and purposes, like a theater. Our hosts seemed genuinely perplexed when we, the internationals, told them that we could not possibly hold trials of mass crimes in such a setting. I believe I said something to the effect of "I don't do Broadway."

We explained that it was not simply a matter of putting furniture upon the stage, but that security, audiovisuals, and the simple decorum of a court meant that major changes would have to be made if this was going to be the public image of the Khmer Rouge tribunal. To its credit, the administration of the Court would quickly see it our way and eventually allocate the necessary resources to turn it into a fully functional, proper court.

We were then treated to a tour of our future office building that we would share with our national colleagues. That was also an eye opener. The building was four floors high, with over 150 offices positioned along four long corridors with shiny marble flooring. What was shocking to me was that someone had thought it would be a good idea to have all the national offices on one side of the building and all the international's on the other side of the corridors. It was as if someone had wanted to physically enshrine one of the main challenges of the Court, with each of us facing the other across a divide. My team and I, along with the other sections of the Court, would spend the next years bridging that gap.

This "us against them" impression was almost comically reinforced when I first walked into the national co-prosecutor's office. As I walked in, accompanied only by an investigator, I was faced with my colleague and her entire staff lined up, 12 deep. Going down the line, shaking hands one after the other, almost like at the end of a hockey game, I could not help but laugh. To this day, I remain convinced that my colleague had wanted to make a point and let me know whose turf this was. It would take a few weeks before the full complement of my staff was on board and I would feel a little bit less outnumbered and outgunned. Yet for all its challenges, the site of the Court would eventually prove to be an acceptable venue for all those working there and for the thousands of Cambodians who would stream through its courtroom to attend the trials.

Eventually all judicial officials convened at the Royal Palace for a swearing-in ceremony. I must confess that it was a humbling moment, full of solemnity and importance. In a courtyard, full of gilded buildings, amidst Buddha and other statues of deities, after prayers and official declarations, I took an oath to serve to the best of my abilities, as the international co-prosecutor. And from that day the real work began.

The statute of the Court established that we would apply international law as well as Cambodian national law. However, at the time, the state of criminal law in Cambodia was somewhat murky. Because of all the upheavals, it had endured in the last 30 years with various forms of government or international administration, it was arguable what Cambodian criminal law actually was. That's why the government had spent years drafting a criminal code and a code of criminal procedure, neither of which, however, had been enacted by the time we took office. Therefore, all the judicial officials agreed that the Court needed to adopt its own internal rules, much like all the previous international courts had done. That process was to be led by the judges, since it would not be appropriate for either of the other parties, the defense or the prosecution, to have decision-making power over the rules of the Court. We, the prosecution, and the defense did, however, avail ourselves of our right to comment and make suggestions, but that process in essence gave my office a full year in which to conduct our work without the pressure of idle judges wanting to have a case.

As my staff trickled in, and the two investigators briefed me on various topics, I set about clarifying with all of them what our prosecution strategy would be.

First and foremost, it was clear to me that it would be supremely important to be transparent about how we would interpret the terms "senior leaders and those most responsible."[7] We would need to make it clear those criteria were guides to our discretion to be interpreted solely in accordance with the evidence and the law. However, I was also aware of the reality that this Court was to operate in a very politically charged context and that I would need to secure a certain degree of cooperation from my national counterparts if we were to forge ahead.

Second, we would need to be able to explain to the people of Cambodia why this Court would be limited in its prosecution and that its proceedings would, at best, deliver only a certain measure of justice for the victims. We would have to select the right targets responsible for the most emblematic crimes and yet accept that we would fall far short of justice writ large. We would need to be able to articulate in our proceedings, as well as in our outreach, that the judicial process of mass crimes litigation set in post-conflict settings constitute only a small, albeit crucial, part of the solution. It cannot be a substitute for the myriad of interventions needed to rebuild a society torn apart by conflict. It does, however, provide a key building block in laying the foundation for the rule of law that must be at the basis of any democratic free and fair society.

Third, given our limited resources and timeframe, we would need to be as efficient and productive as possible while seizing the opportunity to transfer knowledge and build capacity within our shared offices. I was quite conscious that perhaps one of the greatest legacies that this Court could leave to Cambodia would be a group of jurists convinced of the importance of upholding the law to the best of their abilities despite any obstacles and who would be well-versed in the best practices this field could offer.

Finally, it was obvious that we would have to forge working relationships with key stakeholders who either held information that could be turned into evidence or that could help supplement our meager resources. Clearly we would be dependent on the kindness of strangers if we were to reach our goals.

Those principles would guide my actions for the next three years.

7 ECCC Statute, *supra* note 6, Art. 1.

From the beginning, however, I would also have to pull double-duty and play an active role in laying the foundation for the administration of the Court. There was, after all, no one outside of my office who had any experience in mass crimes litigation or international tribunals. The issues faced by these courts are so specific that they challenge even the most experienced national judicial or administrative staff, and I had to do my best to assist. One early issue was particularly illuminating.

Witness protection and outreach are fundamentally important areas for this type of court. If either of those are not set up well from the start and managed efficiently throughout the life of the court, the legitimacy of the whole court process could be adversely affected. If a witness is lost because of her cooperation with the court or if the work of the court is allowed to be distorted by those with different agendas, you are on your way to losing the game. The individuals responsible for creating the structure of the Court and allocating its resources had decided in their infinite wisdom that, in these two crucial areas, the Court would be dependent on the national authorities for witness protection and on whatever stakeholder was ready to provide a soapbox for us to conduct our outreach.

It took a lot of meetings during these first few weeks to convince the administration to look beyond the budget line and the staffing organization chart, and realize that corrections needed to be made to the initial assumptions about this Court. Eventually we went from a conversation about how it was inappropriate to have witnesses ferried to the Court on the back of moped taxis to the creation of a mixed-staffed, full-fledged witness protection unit within the Court and answerable only to the Court.

Outreach, unfortunately, was a different matter. The Court did have a public information office headed by a Cambodian appointee who was herself a notoriously close friend and collaborator of Sok An. There was, therefore, a risk that the official messaging of the Court would be perceived as perhaps being influenced by this situation. But even in the best of cases, the official newsfeed of the Court had a hard time getting a clear message to its target audience. Explaining in lay terms some of the most complex judicial proceedings and having that message filtered by the media for various stakeholders with their own agendas was problematic. On the other hand, being able through outreach to talk directly to those most concerned by the proceedings could provide a key opportunity to engage people and legitimize the work of the Court. I was lucky enough to have seen examples of both of those situations firsthand.

At one end of the learning curve was the ICTR.[8] One of its most glaring failings had been the lack of foresight in its media and outreach approach. It was not prepared for the challenge of having its judicial proceedings take place thousands of kilometers away, leaving it dependent on the Rwandan media and various local NGOs to explain to the people of Rwanda how justice for the victims of the genocide

8 S.C. Res. 955, *supra* note 1.

was being meted out. Needless to say that message ended up being distorted either willfully or by ignorance and thus created a legitimacy problem with the Rwandan people from which the tribunal never fully recovered.

At the other end, I witnessed what would become almost the standard of outreach programs, to be emulated by other international courts. In Freetown, the prosecutor of the Special Court, David Crane, would take a generator, a TV, and VHS player in a helicopter and fly into a village. Along with an interpreter, he would set up his kit, play a video made by the outreach section in the local language explaining the work of the court, and then answer any questions from members of the audience. Eventually the outreach program would include all members of the courts from defense to administration and lead to a real sense of ownership of the tribunal by the people of Sierra Leone.

I therefore had a pretty good idea of what worked in terms of outreach and what didn't. Luckily, Cambodia had an abundance of NGOs whose work centered on the Court and who were ready to provide us with opportunities to speak directly to Cambodians. I took part in as many of those events as I could and cherished the opportunity they provided to speak directly to those who really mattered in this process. They also were humbling events where I learned a great deal and was reminded how lucky I was to be able to play any role in bringing justice to the victims. It was at my very first outreach session that I was confronted with the unique nature of the trauma endured by Cambodian society. The very first question was from a young man in his late teens who asked "Why did Khmer kill Khmer?" I was shocked.

For me it was my first court in which the victims were unsure about why they had been persecuted. A Tutsi in Rwanda in April 1994 knew why he was being pursued. The resident of a village in Sierra Leone knew that the rebels wanted to terrorize them into abandoning their diamond-bearing fields. But how to explain 30 years after the fact that a Khmer Rouge cadre could send a child to his death because by being able to ride a bicycle, that child had proven himself to be a product of the bourgeoisie and therefore could never be a productive member of the agrarian utopia that would be Democratic Kampuchea. This ignorance was compounded by the fact that the whole Khmer Rouge era would not be part of the national curriculum until 2007. The dominant political class, former Khmer Rouge themselves, had a vested interest in obfuscating the whole period. Even sadder, parents who had survived and were willing to talk about their victimization were often confronted with incredulous children who refused to believe that Cambodians could kill fellow Cambodians over such archaic concept as Marxism. It was an incredibly sad state of affairs, and it highlighted even more starkly to me the importance of the role of the Court in establishing a true and comprehensive record of what had happened and in making sure that that record was accessible to all.

While the judges were often at loggerheads in drafting the rules or were facing hostility from various stakeholders, including the Cambodian Bar, our office was chugging along. One of the early challenges was the sheer sum of documentation left behind by the Khmer Rouge. A government of almost four years generates a lot of paper, and a significant quantity of it had survived and had to be sifted through. I knew from past experience that it was crucially important to establish comprehensive and efficient document-handling protocols from the very beginning or run the risk of being overwhelmed and losing evidence. Luckily, my deputy was highly proficient with evidence management software and succeeded in converting, or in some instances coercing, our staff into using it, with great results. And that included our national colleagues who were part of integrated teams focusing on various crime bases or suspects early on. I had made the argument to my national counterpart that integrating our staff into units dedicated to suspects or crime bases would be an efficient way to develop our cases. I was also hoping that when the difficult questions of who to indict arose, our staff would be aware of the legitimacy of the cases, the magnitude of the crimes, and the responsibility of the suspects. Those factors would give us a better chance to reach a consensus.

Within the first few weeks, I already had a pretty good idea of legitimate suspects and the crimes for which they should be held accountable. That list was a bit longer than the five names I was widely expected to limit myself to. It would have been self-defeating and contrary to the essence of the Court to try and hide those names and have my side of the office work on them unbeknownst to the other side. Therefore, I called a meeting between our two offices and gave my national colleague my list of 12 names. She took one look at it and exclaimed "Oh, too many names!" I agreed with her that it seemed like a lot and that nothing was set in stone. I made the argument, however, that we should work on as broad a basis as possible and then, as work progressed, focus on the most likely suspects meeting our criteria as "senior leaders" or those "most responsible." I emphasized that the work of the teams would instruct us and that we would of course try to agree on who to indict. I told her that we could certainly agree to focus first on the senior leaders who were easily identifiable and I thought deemed safe, while working on various crime bases that could later help us identify other, "most responsible" individuals. Without clearly committing to a particular course of action, Chea Leang did agree to work on both types of files and to eventually discuss targets. Having reached an agreement that allowed the work to proceed, I was satisfied for the moment. I knew that not all the names on my list would cause problems and that working on those that were not controversial would allow us to eventually paint a convincing picture of the Khmer Rouge criminal regime. After that, it would only be a matter of establishing the role of additional suspects within that apparatus to be able to make a convincing case for prosecution. Those first senior leadership cases would make it impossible to legitimately deny the responsibilities of others who had significantly helped them in committing their crimes.

Of those senior leaders, only one was in custody: Duch, the head of S-21. He was still in the custody of the military and alone now that his fellow prisoner Ta Mok had died within a few days of my arrival. No one had dropped him off at the gates of the

Court, and the evidence against him was mounting. Not that it was a difficult case to make: the result of his meticulous record keeping at Tuol Sleng included thousands of incriminating documents signed or written by him. Furthermore, surviving inmates as well as former guards, torturers, and executioners had all given numerous accounts of his reign of terror and were ready to testify. Finally, Duch professed himself ready to plead guilty … with an explanation. Having converted to Christianity, he was allegedly ready to admit to some responsibility in the crimes committed at S-21 but would claim that he had no real authority and that the responsibility for his crimes actually lay with his superiors. Since some of those were also likely accused, it promised interesting times in the defendants' dock.

The S-21 archives were a double-edged sword, however. They also contained the "confessions" of hundreds of inmates that offered the best source of evidence on the command structure of the Khmer Rouge regime and therefore the responsibility of its leaders in the crimes. Because the regime had put secrecy as one of its basic tenets, there was relatively little in terms of contemporary documentation describing the roles and responsibilities of those in the hierarchy. Coupled with the effect of relentless purging of the ranks due to real or perceived opposition, it was difficult for us to properly document the evolution of the power structure. The best source of information on the regime was actually some of the confessions of key members who had fallen out of grace and been sent to S-21. Knowing that the longer they talked, the longer they stayed alive, they recounted – sometimes in great detail – the history of the Khmer Rouge and provided detailed information about the implication of key leaders. Those confessions had served academics well, but in a Court, they faced the internationally recognized ban on the use of torture evidence. From the moment I had become aware of this issue back in Canada, I had struggled with it and now had to make a decision. I decided that we had sufficient arguments to put the matter to the judges and let them decide. I knew that decision would be an easy target for the defense, and indeed, there were strong valid arguments against admissibility. However, I felt that the importance of this source of evidence, the fact that these were essentially historical documents by now and would be used to help prove the guilt of those responsible for the torture, justified arguing for admission. In the end we were not successful, and the judgment was not as nuanced as I would have wanted it to be, but I still believe it was the right decision.

As we moved into 2007, the evidence against other suspects was also coming together, and in the end, there was no surprise as to whom the surviving senior leaders of Democratic Kampuchea were: Nuon Chea, Brother Number Two, who was responsible for internal security; Ieng Sary, the deputy prime minister, who was responsible for foreign affairs; his wife, Ieng Thirith, minister of social affairs; and Khieu Samphan, president of the Presidium and therefore nominal head of state. All of them were well known and had, through the years, denied any responsibility for the crimes of the regime or indeed denied that crimes had actually been committed. Interestingly, one more suspect was identified early: Van Rith, who played a key role in organizing financial support as minister of commerce for the regime. He was on my initial list but was not thought to be one of those the government envisioned as a potential indictee. The teams had been collecting evidence of his role for months, and my colleague was aware that there were strong arguments that he fit both criteria for being considered a suspect. I thought at the time that the ongoing cooperation of the national side in investigating Van Rith was an initial breach into the opposition against expanding beyond the five usual suspects. I was wrong.

While we were making progress, the rules-drafting judges were still struggling to reach consensus on their draft code of procedure. From what we could perceive, the national judges seemed illogically obstructionist on some issues, while the international judges could sometimes not contend that, as a national court, the ECCC[9] had to adhere to Cambodian law, such as it was. There were many conspiracy theories floating about, and I was glad to have the workload to distract me from the ambient noise. Sometimes, though, it was hard to ignore. Phnom Penh is a small-minded town, at least when it came to the expat community, and the local English and French press was only too happy to feed the rumor mill. News about potential suspects, allegations of corruption within the administration, and political interference all regularly made the front page, baseless or not. I soon learned to develop an arm's-length relationship with the press in general although some of the more competent reporters were useful in getting the truth out about key matters.

Eventually, with the one-year mark approaching, I felt that we had enough to make some decisions and move forward. One of those decisions involved deciding how many initial submissions would be filed and who would be named in them. The initial submission is akin to an indictment in the Common Law system. It is basically a document that gives jurisdiction over a crime to an investigative judge and if warranted names a person or persons that may be linked to that crime. Once filed, the judge will conduct an investigation and amass all the relevant evidence, both exculpatory and inculpatory, and then decide if the matter should be sent to trial along with accused persons. Given that there was no statutory limit to the co-prosecutors' preliminary investigation, nor to the form and content of the initial submission, I had been intent from the beginning in providing the investigative judges with the most substantive case file possible. We had the evidence on some of the signature crimes of the Khmer Rouge, as well as on the state apparatus that carried them out; we now had to decide who would be held responsible.

I held numerous discussions with Chea Leang, and we finally agreed on one submission for all six suspects, including Duch and Van Rith. Though it was arguable that Duch was a senior leader, his stewardship of S-21, the apex of the DK's security center system, without a doubt made him one of the most responsible. After all, it was to him that the leadership sent other security directors to be tortured to death when they were purged. As to Van Rith, the evidence was clear that his

9 G.A. Res. 56/169, *supra* note 5.

continued role in funding the regime while being aware of its crimes made his inclusion in both categories a compelling argument. All these suspects were individually responsible for some of the crimes and, through their agreement to a common plan and their command authority, were responsible for the crimes of others, including subordinates.

Perhaps not coincidentally, as word spread within the Court that our work was nearing completion, the judges on the rules-drafting committee found it suddenly easier to reach consensus and by June 12, 2007, the rules were finally adopted. With a legal framework in place, we had no reason to delay our filing. By then the case file amounted to over 45,000 pages of supporting documents, all indexed and in both hard copy (147 binders) and an electronic version catalogued in a database. The initial submission was over 150 pages long, provided in both Khmer and English, and provided a succinct but substantive and compelling narrative of the crimes of the Khmer Rouge and the responsibilities of the six named suspects.

It was a monumental achievement by any standards but all the more so given our limited resources and the numerous challenges we had faced.

Once the case file was ready, I went to see my national colleague to sign the submission. She had had the final draft for weeks, and we had agreed upon a date for the official signing. However, when I went to her office, she refused to sign. She suddenly objected to the inclusion of Van Rith, arguing that in his role as minister of commerce, he was neither a senior leader nor most responsible. We had argued this in the past numerous times, and I believed that I had convinced her that the evidence was quite clear, yet here she was raising the issue at this crucial juncture and threatening to derail our efforts.

I had two choices. I could postpone the filing of the Court's first case indefinitely while Leang and I went through the formal disagreement process, thereby causing unknown delays and undermining the credibility of the institution from the start. Or I could find a way to appease my colleague while adhering to the law and the evidence. I chose the latter and instructed my team to scrub the submission of all mention of Van Rith while leaving all the evidence of his responsibility in the case file. I was convinced that Leang's opposition was simply to a name other than "the Five" and that she would be indifferent to the evidence. However, that evidence could be followed up on by the investigative judges, letting them reach their own conclusion on Van Rith.

I would never know if I was right because Van Rith passed away in 2009. However, I had understood my colleague's position well. On July 18, 2007, after almost a year of intensive labor by both national and international prosecution staff, we delivered the introductory submission to the co-investigative judges.

Exactly, 28 years, 6 months, and 8 days after the fall of the Khmer Rouge, it appeared that there would finally be a reckoning for their crimes and a measure of justice for their victims.

PART III

The Takeaways

8

Closing Perspectives

David J. Scheffer

I have known well each of the prosecutors who wrote the chapters of this book. Some entered my professional life in the early 1990s. Others arrived many years later, after I had left government service for academia. Having negotiated the creation of each of the war crimes tribunals of *The Founders*, other than the one Robert Jackson steered, I have long been deeply invested in what these men toiled to accomplish during their tours of duty on the front lines of international criminal justice. Of course, it is notable that no women were among the founders, a fact my former boss, Dr. Madeleine Albright (former US permanent representative to the United Nations and former US secretary of state), recognized in the selection of Louise Arbour and Carla del Ponte as Richard Goldstone's successors for the International Criminal Tribunals for the former Yugoslav (ICTY) and Rwanda (ICTR). In later years, women served as the chief prosecutors of the International Criminal Court (ICC) and the Special Court for Sierra Leone (SCSL), and its successor the Residual Special Court for Sierra Leone. But in the beginning, for each tribunal, it was a male-led venture strongly supported by women in the prosecutorial ranks who skillfully helped guide a multitude of trials to their conclusion.

The stories related in this book shape the historical significance of how the improbable war against impunity for atrocity crimes (genocide, crimes against humanity, and war crimes) actually was waged in its earliest years. There were no advance scripts written for this endeavor. Robert Jackson, Richard Goldstone, Luis Moreno Ocampo, David Crane, and Robert Petit wrote their own strategies for the prosecution of war criminals who needed to be investigated, indicted, captured, tried, and either acquitted or convicted if history were to treat the founding prosecutors kindly. Each man confronted seemingly insurmountable challenges of law, bureaucracy, politics, finances, geography, or indicted fugitives evading capture. They have the right to complain about such obstacles; their frustrations fertilize these pages. It is an imperfect world, and they stepped into some of the greatest imperfections. But they had the courage to surmount these initial barricades to justice and bring the perpetrators of evil on Earth to a reckoning they never imagined.

What can I add to the prosecutors' quest so well recorded in the preceding chapters and the perspectives that such diplomatic and intellectual heavyweights as Kofi Annan, Hans Corell, Michael Scharf, William Schabas, and Leila Sadat contribute? There are three developments that merit more attention.

If one simply looks at the raw data of the work product of the war crimes tribunals of the modern era, such insight might offer a fresh perspective of what actually has been accomplished in the realm of international criminal justice. The news is pretty good.

As of this writing, the ICTY, which will close its doors at the end of 2017, has almost completed the entire mandate of its cases. Still pending are the Trial Chamber judgment in *Prosecutor v. Ratko Mladić*; the Appeals Chamber judgment in *Prosecutor v. Prlić et al.*; and before the ICTY's successor Mechanism for International Tribunals (MICT), an Appeals Chamber judgment in *Prosecutor v. Radovan Karadžić*, a revived Trial Chamber judgment in *Stanišić and Simatović*, and an Appeals Chamber judgment in *Prosecutor v. Šešelj*.[1]

But witness the results so far. While the abovementioned judgments on seven accused remain outstanding, the ICTY over its quarter century of adjudication convicted 83 individuals, acquitted 19 accused, referred 13 accused to national jurisdiction for trial, and withdrew 20 indictments. Ten indicted individuals reportedly died before being transferred to the ICTY, and seven died after such transfer.[2] Given the complexity and breadth of atrocities entailed with each of these cases before the ICTY, such results speak to the integrity and historic importance of the ICTY's record in international jurisprudence. The total budgetary costs of the ICTY from 1993 through 2016 equaled just over $2 billion, paid for with mandatory UN assessments to all UN member states.

The ICTR demonstrated similar results. All of its adjudications were completed following the indictment of 93 individuals. A total of 62 defendants were convicted, while 14 accused were acquitted or released. Two indictees died before judgment. Two indictments were withdrawn. Among the cases transferred to national jurisdictions, five were transferred to Rwanda, and two are slated for prosecution in France. There are eight indicted fugitives, five of whom will be transferred to Rwandan courts if captured, and three will be prosecuted before the MICT once they are in

1 ICTY, *Prosecutor v. Ratko Mladić*, Case No. IT-09–92, available at www.icty.org/en/cases/party/704/4 (Last visited Apr. 16, 2017); ICTY, *Prosecutor v. Jadranko Prlić et al.*, Case No. IT–04–74, available at www.icty.org/en/cases/party/766/4 (Last visited Apr. 16, 2017); MICT, *Prosecutor v. Radovan Karadžić*, Case No. MICT-13–55, available at www.unmict.org/en/cases/mict-13–55 (Last visited Apr. 16, 2017); MICT, *Prosecutor v. Jovica Stanišić and Franko Simatović*, Case No. MICT-15–96, available at www.unmict.org/en/cases/mict-15–96 (Last visited Apr. 16, 2017); MICT, *Prosecutor v. Vojislav Šešelj*, Case No. MICT-16–99, available at www.unmict.org/en/cases/mict-16–99 (Last visited Apr. 16, 2017).

2 ICTY, *Key Figures of the Cases*, available at www.icty.org/en/cases/key-figures-cases (Last visited Apr. 16, 2017).

custody.[3] These results were achieved at a total expenditure of $1.99 billion, again covered by UN assessments to all member states.

At the SCSL, the results, as previewed by David Crane in his chapter, were impressive by any standard. Of the 13 individuals indicted by the SCSL, 9 were convicted, two were acquitted, three died during proceedings, and one fugitive is believed to have died in 2003. Among the convicted was Charles Taylor, the former head of state of Liberia. The SCSL was voluntarily funded by 40 governments and by subventions for three years from the United Nations. The total amount of the SCSL budget through 2016 was $265 million. The Residual Special Court for Sierra Leone continues to adjudicate remaining legal issues and oversee the sentencing of convicted defendants.

The work of the Extraordinary Chambers in the Courts of Cambodia (ECCC) has had a rocky trajectory since its operations began in 2005 and is entitled to its fair share of criticism, as are all of the tribunals. Robert Petit provides insight into both the good and the bad during the early years. During my service as the UN secretary general's special expert on UN Assistance to the Khmer Rouge Trials (2012–2017), I became very familiar with what has transpired in recent years. Much of what is written critically of the ECCC, particularly in the media, often proves to be erroneous, a shade distant from the full truth, or stoked by outlandish conspiracy theories. The independence and necessary secrecy of some of the ECCC's work sometimes has prevented full-throated rebuttals to the criticism.[4] It remains true that the long passage of time since the atrocities of the Pol Pot regime of the late 1970s has taken its toll in that some leading suspects and indicted individuals have died before judgment day.[5] The long time it took to negotiate the creation of the ECCC, launch its operations, and undertake the mandatory investigations of very complex crimes prior to prosecution have all impacted the proceedings.

The raw data of the ECCC nonetheless reveals compelling facts of justice and truth ultimately prevailing in Cambodia and for the cause of international criminal law. By early 2017, three individuals had been convicted through to final judgment in the Supreme Court Chamber for horrendous crimes during the Pol Pot regime, when an estimated 1.7 to 2.3 million Cambodians perished. Two of the defendants, Khieu Samphan and Nuon Chea, also completed their second trial for further crimes allegedly committed during the nearly four years of the regime (1975–1979). As of this writing, they await judgment by the Trial Chamber. Meanwhile, four additional suspects were charged, although the closing order for one of them

[3] ICTR, *Key Figures of Cases*, http://unictr.unmict.org/en/cases/key-figures-cases (Last visited Apr. 16, 2017).

[4] *See* Nicholas Koumjian, *Opinion*, NY Times (Apr. 13, 2017), available at www.nytimes.com/2017/04/13/opinion/khmer-rouge-tribunal-a-un-prosecutors-view.html; and David Scheffer's speech at www.cambodiatribunal.org/2015/02/25/speech-by-un-special-expert-david-scheffer-what-haas-been-extraordinary-about-international-justice-in-cambodia/.

[5] Pol Pot, Son Sen, Ke Pauk, Ta Mok, Ieng Sary, Ieng Thirith, and others.

was dismissed in early 2017.[6] That leaves three charged individuals awaiting final closing orders of either acquittal or indictment by late 2017 or early 2018.[7]

Thus the work is unfinished for the ECCC, but its relatively small cast of targets for indictment for complex atrocity crimes continue to be exposed to the rule of law and to trials that have delivered powerful narratives through evidence of what transpired many decades earlier. The total cost of this voluntarily funded arrangement between the United Nations and the Royal Government of Cambodia, from 2005 through 2016 and attracting contributions from 29 governments, the European Union, various UN funds, and four private sources, was $268 million ($199 million for the ECCC's international [UN] component and $69 million for the tribunal's national [Cambodian] component). Even at the lower estimate of 1.7 million dead during the Pol Pot regime, the ECCC's operations through 2016 cost about $158 per death (compared to $116 for each death among the higher estimate of 2.3 million victims).

The International Criminal Court (ICC) also has been criticized for having little to show after more than 13 years of operations. There are many reasons for what may be perceived as a slow start. Here it is important to note what has been accomplished so far. By early 2017, 23 individual cases had been or were being pursued before the ICC. Nine indicted individuals had been convicted. One had been acquitted. Six individuals were in custody at the time, and 13 suspects under arrest warrant remained fugitives from the ICC. Atrocity crimes in ten situations were under official investigation: the Democratic Republic of Congo, Uganda, Darfur (Sudan), Kenya, Libya, Côte d'Ivoire, Mali, Georgia, and two situations in the Central African Republic. Meanwhile, 10 other situations were under the ICC's preliminary examination with the possibility of eventually being formally investigated: Afghanistan, Burundi, Colombia, Nigeria, Gabon, and Guinea; British military actions in Iraq, Palestine, and Ukraine; and a situations involving registered vessels of Comoros, Greece, and Ukraine.[8] The total cost of the ICC's operations over 13.5 years, from July 2002 through 2016, collected from assessments levied on its 124 states parties, was 1.3 billion Euros.

These statistics do not begin to tell the story of the enormous amount of jurisprudence that has poured forth into the coffers of international criminal justice since the ICTY began its work in 1993. The content and scope of international criminal law as it relates to the investigation, prosecution, and adjudication of atrocity crimes such as genocide, crimes against humanity, and war crimes has been transformed

6 *Co-Investigating Judges Dismiss Case Against Im Chaem*, CAMBODIA TRIBUNAL MONITOR, available at www.cambodiatribunal.org/2017/02/22/co-investigating-judges-dismiss-case-against-im-chaem/.

7 *Meas Muth Charged in Case* 003, CAMBODIA TRIBUNAL MONITOR, available at www.cambodiatribunal.org/2015/12/14/meas-muth-charged-in-case-003/ (Last visited Apr. 16, 2017); *Additional Charges against Ao An*, CAMBODIA TRIBUNAL MONITOR, available at www.cambodiatribunal.org/2016/03/14/additional-charges-against-ao-an/ (Last visited Apr. 16, 2017); *Yim Tith Charged in Case* 004, CAMBODIA TRIBUNAL MONITOR, available at www.cambodiatribunal.org/2015/12/09/yim-tith-charged-in-case-004/ (Last visited Apr. 16, 2017).

8 ICC, available at www.icc-cpi.int/ (Last visited Apr. 16, 2017).

into a potent weapon of justice worthy of sustained commitments to tribunals and of the talents of seasoned judges, prosecutors, defense counsel, and court administrators. If one were to stack the entire published content of all decisions and judgments of the tribunals since their origins, it surely would reach quite high against the skyline. No one should doubt that the adjudication of atrocity crimes now has a firm foundation upon which to evaluate legal principles and reasoning to achieve accountability. The founding prosecutors can claim much credit for building the platforms upon which so much else has transpired since their tenures.

The cost of international criminal justice is a favorite boogeyman for the critics of the tribunals. Granted, justice does cost money to achieve, whether it be domestically or internationally. Any commitment to the rule of law does not come cheaply, but compared to other societal costs it is a bargain. The cost of the Tokyo tribunal (International Military Tribunal for the Far East) after World War II was, in current dollars, about $112.5 million. (The original dollar amount was $9 million.) The total cost of the modern tribunals throughout 23 years of operations (1993–2016) was about $5.9 billion (comparable to what the United States spent in 2015 alone to fight ISIS).

It is usually underappreciated that the budgets of the tribunals entail the entire cost of pursuing justice in any particular year – including the expenses associated with payment of salaries, benefits, and expenses of judges, prosecutors, investigators, administrators, and the fees of defense counsel, as well as the costs of facilities construction and management, utilities, the protection, travel, and lodging expenses of witnesses, security, translation, and interpretation of multiple languages, various outreach programs to the public, and the preservation and management of archives for the future. For example, at the ECCC, the cost of an international judge's salary, benefits, and expenses living in Phnom Penh can easily reach $263,000 per annum. The cost of translating and interpreting for the French language at the ECCC is an annual tab of over $1.6 million.

The fact that many of these categories of expenses are significant and can easily add millions of dollars to each year's budget is unavoidable if international justice for complex atrocity crimes is to be fairly and competently rendered. But they also represent a totality of costs that rarely appear in the budgets of domestic courts. Many of the costs associated with the tribunals do not get accounted for in the budgeting of domestic courts, as they are buried in the budgets of other agencies, or they do not exist at all – such as major translation and interpretation services or even the high degree of security required for international tribunals. Nor are the expenses of most defense counsels in domestic litigation covered by the government; instead, defendants often have the means to cover the costs of their criminal defense lawyers or the underpaid public defender serves the many poor accused. At the international criminal tribunals, defendants typically plead indigence even if they have assets secretly stashed away and unreachable by the tribunals. Their defense lawyers then are paid daily fees by the tribunals to represent their clients vigorously in order to preserve their due process rights. Those defense fees add up very quickly.

Thus, in a comparative sense, the aggregate costs of the tribunals are eminently reasonable compared to other litigation, even prominent cases, in domestic legal systems where the victim base is infinitely smaller and the crimes of far less magnitude than those being adjudicated by the tribunals. For example, the O.J. Simpson trial cost Los Angeles County more than $9 million to acquit him for the deaths of two individuals, and that does not include the estimated fees of $5 million for his highly talented defense team, which Mr. Simpson presumably paid from his own resources.[9] The Lockerbie trial, held in the Netherlands to adjudicate the downing of Pan Am 103 over Lockerbie, Scotland, on December 21, 1988, with a death toll of 259 passengers and crew, cost a total of about £75 million.[10] The trials of the tribunals typically have involved death tolls substantially higher, even in the millions.

It also remains helpful to compare the tribunals' expenses with other costs incurred by the US government, for example, in its fiscal year 2017 budgets for the US Departments Justice and Defense. The Justice Department *added* $443 million for the Office of Justice Programs, Office of Community Oriented Policing Services, and its Office on Violence Against Women, all worthy endeavors, but for a net grant request of $2 billion in fiscal year 2017 alone. At the Pentagon, the total program cost for one B-2 stealth bomber averaged $3 billion per aircraft, with a $135,000 cost per flight hour. Two new Virginia class attack submarines required $5.4 billion in the budget. One new DDG-51 Arleigh Burke-class guided missile destroyer will cost American taxpayers $1.7 billion.[11] In 2017 the United States was spending $3.1 billion per month to wage war in Afghanistan.[12]

Regardless of how one rationalizes the merit of paying for international criminal justice, the reality is that governments and their taxpayers probably will keep balking at spending strained public monies on such ventures. It will become increasingly necessary in future years to create new funding sources from the private and non-governmental sectors. But it remains important to ensure that lawmakers understand the value of achieving accountability for atrocity crimes, not only as an imperative

[9] The O.J. Simpson trial, by the numbers, USA TODAY http://usatoday30.usatoday.com/news/index/nns062.htm (Last visited Apr. 16, 2017); Seth Mydans, *Meter's Ticking for Costly Simpson Defense*, NY TIMES (July 31, 1994), www.nytimes.com/1994/07/31/us/meter-s-ticking-for-costly-simpson-defense.html.

[10] *Lockerbie bill reaches £75m*, BBC (Mar. 13, 2002), available at http://news.bbc.co.uk/2/hi/in_depth/scotland/2002/lockerbie_appeal/1773734.stm.

[11] David Axe, *Why Can't the Air Force Build an Affordable Plane?*, THE ATLANTIC (Mar. 26, 2012), www.theatlantic.com/national/archive/2012/03/why-cant-the-air-force-build-an-affordable-plane/254998/; Ronald O'Rourke, *Navy Virginia (SSN-774) Class Attack Submarine Procurement: Background and Issues for Congress* 3, Apr. 6, 2017, https://fas.org/sgp/crs/weapons/RL32418.pdf; Congressional Budget Office, *An Analysis of the Navy's Fiscal Year 2016 Shipbuilding Plan* 22 www.cbo.gov/sites/default/files/115th-congress-2017–2018/reports/52324-shipbuildingreport.pdf (Feb. 2017).

[12] Mark Lander and Eric Schmitt, *Trump Administration Is Split on Adding Troops to Afghanistan*, NY TIMES, May 23, 2017, available at www.nytimes.com/2017/05/23/world/europe/saudi-arabia-arms-deal-nato.html?_r=0.

requirement in societies built on the rule of law, but also as a primary tool in preventing further atrocities, which are manmade calamities that always cost societies far more to rectify than to prevent.

Every founding prosecutor described aggravating, even incomprehensible, imperfections in the structure of their respective tribunal. In Michael Scharf's chapter about Robert Jackson, we learn that Jackson had to maneuver between the Common Law adversarial system and the Civil Law inquisitorial system, with inevitable clashes erupting between lawyers trained in one but not both disciplines. Richard Goldstone struggled with "the 13 percent rule" at the United Nations that tended to discourage government-funded secondments for his ICTY and ICTR staffs at a time when he desperately needed more skilled personnel. David Crane and his initial skeletal staff of five had to create their headquarters in Freetown in literally "damp and moldy" premises where everything had to be cleaned and rudimentary furniture acquired during unending downpours of rain. And then there was malaria and dismissive UN officials to contend with at all times. At the ECCC, Robert Petit was astonished at how witness protection and outreach had been conceived for the tribunal and he took great pains to correct those flaws.Finally, Luis Moreno Ocampo faced opposition from some African states parties to the Rome Statute, thus impairing several of the ICC's most critical cases.

The negotiation of each of the tribunals described in this book was an arduous exercise involving not only law and criminal procedure but also international and national politics at every turn. As someone well versed through direct experience in the dynamic process of negotiating and building the international criminal tribunals pioneered by these men, I can well understand why the founding prosecutors were frustrated at times with the constitutional structure of their respective tribunals and the institutional obstacles they confronted with the United Nations and with governments.[13]

In a perfect world, we negotiators would have discerned every weakness in the statute and rules for each tribunal, anticipated every legal conundrum, foreseen every political, financial, and even geographic obstruction, and shielded the tribunals from every possible act of corruption. But that obviously was never to be as negotiators waded through swamps of legal, political, and diplomatic issues facing each tribunal.

For example, the creation of the ICTY entailed a bold initiative in the Security Council that never before had been attempted: to use Chapter VII enforcement authority under the United Nations Charter to create a subsidiary body of the Security Council that would be a criminal court with mandatory powers of investigation, arrest, prosecution, and sentencing, in the middle of the very war and

[13] David Scheffer, All the Missing Souls: A Personal History of the War Crimes Tribunals (2012).

atrocities being examined, and without the consent of the nations in conflict. Proposing language for such a tribunal required a keen appreciation for what would and would not be acceptable to the member states of the Security Council, including Russia and China. The ideal formula was unattainable, as Goldstone notes, and several key compromises had to be embraced before the statute of the ICTY was ready for a successful vote in the Council in May 1993.[14]

Nor did the Security Council perform brilliantly in the selection of the first prosecutor of the ICTY, hampered as it was by the de facto rule requiring a unanimous vote of all 15 member states, and no veto, before a prosecutor could be approved. The more than one-year delay in the discovery and selection of Goldstone ultimately resulted in a superb individual for the job. But there should have been a far more efficient means to have selected one of the highly talented candidates (such as Cherif Bassiouni or Charles Ruff) who emerged earlier in the process or at least Goldstone himself within months of the Council resolution establishing the tribunal. Politics interfered and that was the simple reality. There was intense criticism of the Clinton administration for delaying a process that we tried vainly to break through, only to be blocked by geopolitical maneuvering at every turn.[15]

At the ICTR, negotiators would have addressed in the statute itself the potential for corruption at the tribunal if they had thought of its possibility. But we were focused in late 1994 on the fundamental structure and jurisdiction of the tribunal and not its administrative integrity. I personally spent years after the ICTR's creation addressing issues of corruption and maladministration within its ranks – though not involving the chief prosecutor – and thus often pondered, in hindsight, what could have been built into the tribunal's registry to overcome such machinations. We also were dealing with intense political pressure from the victorious Rwandan Patriotic Front government in Rwanda, which had its own ideas about justice for the suspects. While, for example, many would complain in the aftermath that Arusha, Tanzania, was not the best choice for the ICTR's location, negotiators of the statute left selection of the final site open until an exploratory team from New York had reviewed options. We could not possibly establish the tribunal in Kigali, as demanded by the government, given security concerns and the need, frankly, to operate at a relatively neutral site with proper resources following the genocide. Nonetheless, there was great merit in situating the deputy prosecutor's office in Kigali so that investigations could proceed more efficiently.

The creation of the SCSL entailed thorny political issues that intruded regularly on any pure conception for an international criminal tribunal. Months transpired before there was any resolution of whether teenage boys, many high on drugs as they mutilated their victims, would be subject to prosecution by the SCSL. The government insisted on such personal jurisdiction because the public was demanding it, while most of the international players in the negotiations vigorously opposed the

[14] S.C. Res. 827 (May 25, 1993). [15] SCHEFFER, *supra* note 13, at 29–33.

plan. In the end, a compromise was struck for the statute's language and then, in practice, Prosecutor Crane simply excluded all such young individuals because he decided to prosecute only those whom the statute gave him the authority to prosecute, namely those who had the "greatest responsibility for violations of international humanitarian law,"[16] and no youthful offenders fit that profile.

Two other compromises had to be struck in the negotiations, one with the UN Security Council and the other with the UN Secretariat. The Security Council insisted that peacekeepers in Sierra Leone be subject to their respective national judicial systems for any "transgressions" committed in Sierra Leone, while many parties in the negotiations and in civil society insisted that such individuals be subject to the direct jurisdiction of the SCSL. Language addressing both points of view ultimately was crafted by the negotiators, albeit imperfectly in the eyes of all involved.[17]

The second compromise concerned the voluntary funding of the SCSL. The tribunal's operations were delayed by one year following the close of the negotiations and adoption of the SCSL statute because the UN Secretariat insisted that a reserve of three years of funding be pledged (and significantly collected) before beginning a process that must ensure that investigations, trials, and judgments can be accomplished thoroughly. The delay upset the Sierra Leone government, some of the negotiating parties, and civil society, but it was an arrangement that had to be swallowed for the sake of ultimately pursuing justice, and successfully at that. In its final years, however, the SCSL failed to raise sufficient voluntary funds for its operations and had to obtain subventions (lines of credit) from the UN General Assembly in order to survive.

The political compromises required to conclude the constitutional documents for the ECCC were many, and that has stoked continuous criticism of the tribunal for perceived flaws in its structure, undue political influence in its operations, and the efforts required to secure sufficient voluntary contributions. Without most of those compromises in the structure of the ECCC and without its reliance on voluntary funding (rather than the security of UN assessments of member states), the ECCC never would have been created. Such an outcome – of never being created in the first place – may have satisfied the perfectionists, but accountability for the devastation of Cambodian society and of an estimated 1.7 to 2.3 million individuals never would have been achieved. After witnessing the entire judicial process closely since January 2012, I believe the ECCC, always beset with difficulties not uncommon to other tribunals, has been worth the commitment of those governments that have invested in it each year with significant contributions.

The ICC has been at the center of political influences since the earliest days of UN negotiations in 1995. The negotiators all represented governments, not only in

16 Statute of the Special Court for Sierra Leone, Art. 1(1), Jan. 16, 2002, 2178 UNT.S. 145.

17 SCHEFFER, *supra* note 13, at 335.

the talks leading to the Rome Statute in July 1998 but for years thereafter as supplemental documents, like the Rules of Procedure and Evidence and the Elements of Crimes, were negotiated. They each brought the political perspective of their government to the negotiations. There are many political compromises built into the Rome Statute and its supplemental documents. Some may view these provisions as acts of imperfection in the quest of justice, but without them there would be no Rome Statute and no ICC.

For example, the fact that the Security Council has the authority, under Article 16 of the Rome Statute, to prevent the commencement or the continuation of an investigation or prosecution for at least 12 months, was a heavily negotiated provision, which in content would seem to defy the integrity of the entire purpose of the ICC. But it is an exercise of power over the ICC's operations whenever the Security Council believes that matters of international peace and security should prevail over the immediate pursuit of justice. Some would view that provision as grossly undermining the Rome Statute; others would understand it as a reality check when political interests so demand.

Under Rule 73(4) of the ICC's Rules of Procedure and Evidence, one particular type of witness, namely personnel of the International Committee of the Red Cross (ICRC), need never divulge to the ICC what atrocities he or she has seen take place, no matter who is responsible for those crimes.[18] That may be viewed as exceedingly imperfect in the eyes of jurists, but it was negotiated for the benefit of the ICRC, which lobbied hard for the provision because of the exposure of its personnel in the field to risks and the organization's secrecy in what it examines and then communicates to targeted governments.

Despite the master plan of international criminal justice to distribute atrocity crime prosecutions among national courts capable and willing to undertake them and the International Criminal Court when such "complementarity" fails, that will not be the reality for the foreseeable future. National courts in many countries do not have the subject matter jurisdiction, competency, or integrity to undertake atrocity crimes trials. The ICC has not achieved universality in its membership yet, and that is a severe setback when it comes to various atrocity situations erupting across the globe. The United States, Russia, China, most of the Middle East, South Asia, and Southeast Asia, and a good number of African states have not yet joined the Rome Statute of the ICC. At least 70 nations remain essentially outside the ambit of the

[18] ICC, Rules of Procedure and Evidence, Art. 73(4): "The Court shall regard as privileged, and consequently not subject to disclosure, including by way of testimony of any present or past official or employee of the International Committee of the Red Cross (ICRC), any information, documents or other evidence which it came into the possession of in the course, or as a consequence, of the performance by ICRC of its functions under the Statutes of the International Red Cross and Red Crescent Movement, unless: (a) After consultations undertaken pursuant to sub-rule 6, ICRC does not object in writing to such disclosure, or otherwise has waived this privilege; or (b) Such information, documents or other evidence is contained in public statements and documents of ICRC."

ICC unless the Security Council refers a situation concerning any such country to the ICC. Only atrocities occurring in Darfur (in Sudan) and Libya have been referred by the Security Council by early 2017, and those referrals occurred in 2005 and 2011, respectively. More such referrals appear unlikely as long as Russia and China project a negative view of the ICC and of international justice generally. Both countries vetoed a US/British/French-backed referral of Syria to the ICC in May 2014.[19]

Where the ICC lacks jurisdiction to investigate and prosecute atrocity crimes and national courts fail the test, there will be a continuing need to build hybrid tribunals if national courts do not meet the challenge of accountability. The need for hybrid tribunals continues unabated during the early twenty-first century. There remain historical atrocities that occurred prior to the beginning of the temporal jurisdiction of the ICC in 2002 that still generate appeals for accountability. Such atrocities occurred, for example, in Afghanistan, Sri Lanka, Sudan, Indonesia, North Korea, Bangladesh (when it was part of Pakistan), Liberia, and Syria. The ICC cannot examine any of these pre-2002 atrocities and thus, just like the crimes adjudicated by the ICTY, ICTR, SCSL, and ECCC, a hybrid tribunal could be created to exercise temporal jurisdiction over events that precede the start date of the ICC, which only has prospective jurisdiction from July 1, 2002 onward (and even then it can be a complicated jurisdictional formula).

One pathway, of course, would be for the Security Council to approve the establishment of tribunals of the same character as the ICTY and ICTR. But that may prove uncommon, for if the permanent members of the Security Council are willing to create a new hybrid tribunal under Chapter VII of the United Nations Charter, they probably would have the same political will to refer the atrocity situation to the ICC with a Chapter VII resolution in conformity with Article 13(b) of the Rome Statute and thus avoid the significant cost and delay entailed in building an entirely new court. Only if the atrocity crimes occurred prior to July 1, 2002 and the Council knew that the ICC was not an available forum for any situation, and it still wished to create such a Chapter VII tribunal, would the opportunity present itself.

The current list of post-June 2002 atrocities that merit the application of international criminal justice in the absence of ICC jurisdiction and sufficient national court litigation include Syria's atrocious situation from 2011 onward.[20] Sri Lanka's atrocities during its civil war with the Tamil Tigers,[21] North Korea's well-

19 Somini Sengupta, *China and Russia Block Referral of Syria to Court*, NY Times (May 22, 2014), at A3.

20 Ben Hubbard and Hwaida Saad, *Dozens Killed as Blast Strikes Convoy Carrying Evacuated Syrians*, NY Times (Apr. 16, 2017), at A7; David Scheffer, Opinion, *Let justice be served in Syria and Iraq*, L.A. Times (June 5, 2014), available at www.latimes.com/opinion/op-ed/la-oe-scheffer-prosecuting-atrocities-syria-iraq-20140706-story.html.

21 Human Rights Council A/HRC/30/CRP.2 (Report of the OHCHR Investigation on Sri Lanka) (Sept. 16 2015).

documented crimes against humanity,[22] South Sudan's wave of atrocities since 2015,[23] and perhaps the persecution of the Rohingya in Myanmar.[24]

The more likely path, if any is taken, for these atrocity situations will be ad hoc endeavors to create hybrid tribunals through either regional treaty arrangements among interested nations or by treaty between the United Nations and one or more relevant governments. The latter approach was utilized for the SCSL, the ECCC, and the Special Tribunal for Lebanon and is not beyond the realm of possibility for any of the situations listed above.

The UN secretary general can be directed by the General Assembly or the Security Council to enter into negotiations with the government where the crime scenes are located (as occurred with Sierra Leone, Cambodia, and Lebanon) or, if that is not politically feasible (such as is probable regarding Syria and North Korea), with governments that have enough interests at stake in the situation because of the violence driving refugees onto their territories or otherwise destabilizing regional peace. Once the negotiated treaty, which would include the statute of the tribunal or reference to a national statute governing the new tribunal, is completed, the UN General Assembly would need to approve it by majority vote, as well as the ratification required by any government joining the treaty in order to activate it. The tribunal might require staff drawn from international circles as well as from relevant national jurisdictions proximate to the crime scenes. The funding may have to be drawn from voluntary contributors, which is fraught with risk in terms of the stability and longevity of the tribunal. But the negotiations regarding the treaty could attempt to guarantee particular funding sources, including multi-year governmental commitments, UN assessments, or subventions approved by the General Assembly.

If the attempt to build a hybrid tribunal rests solely with a regional group of nations (foregoing UN participation), it in theory could be negotiated and launch operations with simply a multilateral treaty among the participating states. This would require exceptional commitment by the treaty parties to ensure recognition of the jurisdiction of the tribunal, talented staffing of it at all levels, a safe location for its headquarters, and sufficient funding (probably assessed to the treaty parties) to see through to completion the mandate established by the treaty. Since the country where the atrocities are being committed likely will remain outside the treaty regime, the difficulties for investigations, arrests, and availability of witnesses will dominate the efforts. One possible exception is South Sudan, where a peace agreement in August 2015 directs the African Union to set up a regional tribunal, outside of UN auspices, with South Sudan's full participation, including providing judges

22 Human Rights Council A/HRC/25/63 (Report of the commission of inquiry on human rights in the Democratic People's Republic of Korea) (Feb. 7, 2014).

23 Human Rights Council A/HRC/34/63 (Report of the Commission on Human Rights in South Sudan) (Mar. 6, 2017).

24 *UN Report details 'devastating cruelty' against Rohingya population in Myanmar's Rakhine province*, UN News Centre, Feb. 3, 2017, available at www.un.org/apps/news/story.asp?NewsID=56103#.WsigWx21vmo.

who would sit alongside judges drawn from other African nations.[25] As of early 2017, this had not occurred.

The founders whose stories populate this book were champions of international criminal justice when the stakes were very high and many cynics had not yet understood the significance of their mandates or the imperative need to persevere in the pursuit of justice. The pioneering prosecutors set precedents of performance that inspired their successors and educated the rest of us in the origins of the tribunals' historic missions. They had to be top class lawyers, jurists, diplomats, innovators, administrators, media-savvy publicists, and humanists at all times. Those who follow in their footsteps must forge ahead with the same determination to bring the perpetrators of the mass atrocity crimes – past, present, and future – to justice, fairly and with unyielding determination against all odds.

25 Agreement on the Resolution of the Conflict in the Republic of South Sudan, Chapter V, Aug. 17, 2015.

Index